PENGUIN BOOKS

ON THE RISE

Paul Goldberger became architecture critic of *The New York Times* in 1973. A graduate of Yale University, where he studied architecture history, he is also the author of *The City Observed* and *The Skyscraper*. He and his wife and their two sons live in New York City.

ON THE RISE

ARCHITECTURE AND DESIGN IN A POSTMODERN AGE

PAUL GOLDBERGER

PENGUIN BOOKS

PENGUIN BOOKS
Viking Penguin Inc., 40 West 23rd Street,
New York, New York 10010, U.S.A.
Penguin Books Ltd, Harmondsworth,
Middlesex, England
Penguin Books Australia Ltd, Ringwood,
Victoria, Australia
Penguin Books Canada Limited, 2801 John Street,
Markham, Ontario, Canada L3R 1B4
Penguin Books (N.Z.) Ltd, 182–190 Wairau Road,
Auckland 10, New Zealand

First published in the United States of America by
Times Books 1983
Published in Penguin Books 1985

LIBRARY OF CONGRESS CATALOGING IN PUBLICATION DATA
Goldberger, Paul.
  On the rise.
  Includes index.
  1. Architecture—United States—Addresses, essays,
lectures.   2. Architecture, Postmodern—United States—
Addresses, essays, lectures.   I. Title.
NA705.G57   1985   720'.973   84-19055
ISBN 0 14 00.7632 8 (pbk.)

Printed in the United States of America by
R. R. Donnelley & Sons Company, Harrisonburg, Virginia
Set in Caledonia

For Susan

and for Adam and Benjamin

Acknowledgments

Every critic at *The New York Times* owes a debt to A. M. Rosenthal, the executive editor, and Arthur Gelb, the deputy managing editor; in my case, however, the debt is more than perfunctory. These two editors offered me the chance to begin commenting on architecture in the pages of *The Times* a decade ago, in 1973, and at that time they were taking a chance on a writer whose enthusiasm was more notable than his experience. Now that my experience has increased (though not to a point where it will surpass my enthusiasm, I hope) it is pleasing to be able to say that *The Times*'s commitment to the coverage of architecture has never waivered.

The pieces that follow have been selected from ten years' worth of architecture criticism in *The Times;* it says much about the continuity of that institution that most of the editors under whose auspices they were written are still a part of the paper. But my thanks go equally to those editors who have left and those who remain: James Greenfield, Bill Luce, Seymour Peck, Bill Honan, Mike Levitas, Sydney Schanberg, Peter Millones, Dave Jones, Nancy Newhouse, Dona Guimaraes, Edward Klein, Ken Emerson, Gerald Gold, and Marvin Siegel. Also at *The Times*, Jennifer Dunning, Lucy Kraus, and Carol Plum have provided consistent help over the years. Frances Margolick undertook the enormous task of first gathering the pieces of the manuscript, and also assisted in the process of obtaining pictures. Shirley Baig provided further help in picture-gathering. But no listing of those affiliated with *The New York Times* would be complete without the name of the person who is no longer there but who did more than anyone else to assure the stature of architecture criticism as a vital part of daily journalism—my predecessor, Ada Louise Huxtable.

While most of the photographs included in the following pages were used first in *The Times*, a few come from other sources. I am grateful to David Dunlap, William Lansing Plumb, Max Protetch, Frank Gehry, Fred Knubel, and Joe Piniero for providing special material, and a special debt is owed to Peter B. Kaplan for the privilege of re-using his remarkable photographs taken to illustrate the essay "The Limits of Urban Growth."

Jonathan Segal has been a sensitive and supportive editor throughout this project. Ruth Fecych at Times Books has acted as organizer, expediter, and headline-writer, all of which she has done with efficiency and graciousness. Marjorie Anderson's design is a major component of the book, and I am especially grateful to her for going beyond the normal designer's duties and permitting herself to be conscripted into the role of photographer and organizer. Pamela Lyons has overseen the task of copy-editing. A final debt, as important as any to this project, is owed to Amanda Urban, for her patience and goodwill throughout.

P. G.

Contents

ON THE RISE

Introduction

I am often asked what it feels like to have the power of a critic of *The New York Times*, and my reply varies. If I prefer not to extend the conversation, I find that I answer more or less as if I had been asked about my health—I say it is fine, thank you, and go on my way. But to more thoughtful questioners, I give a longer answer, and it is not the same. The fact is that the architecture critic of *The New York Times* has no direct and dramatic power, not in the sense of the very tangible power of the theater critic. If the theater critic does not like a Broadway show the odds are that none of the rest of us will see it after next Saturday night. But if I raise objections to a building, it remains—through this Saturday night and the next and the next, and in all likelihood for the rest of my lifetime.

It is difficult not to fantasize about how different my life, and that of the city, would be if buildings were torn down after bad notices. There is, after all, a certain appeal to the thought that the anti-urban garishness of the General Motors Building could be wished off the face of New York, or that the harsh and scaleless World Trade Center could simply empty out owing to the lack of business caused by poor reviews. But such fantasies will not become real, and it is just as well, for the analogy on which they are based—that architecture is more or less like the theater or film or television or a well-intentioned restaurant—is false. The built environment is different altogether from an entertainment, a diversion, or even a work of art. It is part of the public realm in a way that none of these other things are, and thus it operates according to a very different set of rules.

Architecture is, in a sense, where issues of public policy meet questions of esthetics. I do not mean to say that public policy is the crucial element of architecture—quite the contrary. Debates over zoning laws cannot mean more to history than the struggle to express esthetic ideas in built form. But architecture is a public presence. It frequently comes to take its form because of overt public policy, and even where its intentions seem the most purely artistic, the freest of legal and financial constraints, it still plays a constant public role. If we believe that the quality of our lives is shaped by the quality of the buildings that surround us we are naive, but if we do not believe it at all, there is no reason to stay in business.

It is easy to take from all of this a kind of missionary's certitude—and if there is anything I find to be an occupational weakness of architecture critics, it is a kind of moral stance that suggests that they know what is good for all of us, that if the real-estate developers and city planners would only follow what they have to say then the good life would appear for all. In that sense an architecture critic can often resemble a political columnist more than his fellow cultural commentators—far more architecture critics have striven to be Walter Lippmann than Edmund Wilson.

It is in reaction to this, I suppose, that I remain grateful that architecture critics do not have the tangible power of many of their colleagues—I could not imagine a city shaped entirely in accord with a single person's wishes, with a single set of ideas, however catholic they may be. I prefer to leave the disappearance of the General Motors Building to my fantasies, not because I lack the conviction that its removal or that of any of a hundred other mistakes of the cityscape would be an improvement, but rather because I believe more deeply, in the end, in the importance of a certain degree of randomness and disorder, not to mention heterogeneity, in the making of a vibrant and meaningful city. A city cannot be fully and completely planned, and should not be.

What, then, is the purpose of architecture criticism? Is it simply to throw in the towel, to provide a kind of mildly disapproving background commentary to passing events—to be a kind of Howard Cosell for the built world? A laissez-faire attitude toward the city, or toward the design of any building or place within the city, is hardly what I mean when I speak of valuing randomness and disorder. That is not the real opposite of the missionary's pompous moralizing; it is merely a kind of escape. The real challenge is more subtle: it is to argue critically for a set of values and standards without trying to shape a city or a profession in one's own image. It is to evaluate works of design realistically, harshly, and honestly without coming to them with an overpowering ideological bias.

Ada Louise Huxtable has written of architecture criticism in the daily press as having an educational function, and of course she is right. But one hopes that it is pedagogy of the best sort—not teaching facts but teaching the reader to find his own facts, not seeing for the reader but teaching the reader to see for himself. The critic's comments should not be judgments handed down from Olympus; they should be words that make connections in the reader's mind that have not been there before.

If my basic stance is pluralist, there are nonetheless a number of strong ideas that unify the one long and seventy-nine short essays included in the following pages. It might be helpful to run through them briefly. I believe, as more than a few of these essays and articles will make clear, that the ideology we associate with modernist architecture has failed us and that we are groping, with mixed success, toward an alternative. To say that the ideology of modernism has failed us is not the same as to say that modernist architecture itself has failed us, for much of it has not, and the modernist esthetic remains a powerful and often beautiful one. The disenchantment with its product that is so widely felt today is not the result of a failed esthetic; it is the result of our realization that modernism emerged out of a vision of the world that was excessively utopian, basically revolutionary, and fundamentally anti-urban.

The faith of the early modernists that they could change the world no longer convinces us, and properly so: architecture can never, in and of itself, change society. In the case of the sleek and austere buildings of International Style modernism, however, there was a problem deeper than the hubris of their architects. The vocabulary of modernism does not seem to contain within it the elements of a successful architectural vernacular—the elements that permit the creation of a language out of which we can build entire cities. Georgian architecture, to take but one example, was such a language, capable of yielding masterpieces and everyday buildings alike, and in Georgian London we find a city of brilliant consistency yet infinite variety and visual pleasure. There is no such quality to Third Avenue in New York or the Place de la Défense in Paris— there is only a kind of bleak glitter.

The comfort one feels for the modernist ideology today is not much increased by the fact that this style, which evolved with such socialist certainties in the 1920's, became, after World War II, the very embodiment of capitalism, the architectural expression of the corporate state. Could one tolerate this inversion if the buildings themselves were better, and if they fit together to make more civilized cities? Perhaps so—I admit to no despair over such corporate masterworks as Mies van der Rohe and Philip Johnson's Seagram Building or Eero Saarinen's Deere & Company headquarters, and have lately found myself rushing to the defense of these and other great modernist works when the current mood of antimodernist sentiment threatens to sweep them aside. (In the case of one important modern building, Lever House, there was at this writing a possibility that the building might literally be swept aside; a real-estate developer has called it too old and too small, and has proposed a twice-as-tall replacement.)

For the issue, once again, is not ideology—not the moral rightness or wrongness of modernist buildings or any other kind of buildings—but the appropriateness of a particular design for a particular place and circumstance. Here, I hold out the hope that the work of the so-called postmodern architects will help shift our concerns more in that direction and away from architecture as dogma first and problem-solving second. For the postmodernists, though passionately concerned with esthetic issues, seem to me to approach design as a matter of composition first. Their impulses are primarily picturesque, which is a nondogmatic attitude if it is anything. And beyond this, postmodernism indicates sympathy for the idea of a building fitting into an urban context, with respect for the street and acceptability of ornament and elements drawn from the architecture of the past—all of which I find encouraging. If there is less emphasis on the shaping of space than in modernist architecture, and too much concern with the making of facades, this is the price we pay for reaction—it is a pendulum that is sure to right itself.

It is not, after all, as if modernism did not occur or were not still powerfully with us. Indeed, what has been termed late modernism—the tendency to merge the sleek and cool materials of modernism with the picturesque impulses of postmodernism—is as vital a part of American, not to say international, architecture as the 1980's unfold as anything more purely postmodern. In late modernism and postmodernism alike, we see a desire to make the building a sensuous object, to make it stimulate our emotions as well as our intellect. It is not easy to do this well, for a building that is aimed only at our emotions cannot help but be destroyed by its own sentimentality and fails as completely as the building that has no emotional message at all.

Where we are going is not perfectly clear. It never has been at any moment in architectural history, and such a time as this, when pluralism seems to dominate, is less easy than most to predict the future from. What *is* certain right now is that there is not merely a wider sense of what constitutes good design, but also a growing constituency for it in every form. There is more public dialogue on the subject of architecture than there has been in at least a generation, and that has to be to the good. Curiously, and ironically, both Lewis Mumford and Ada Louise Huxtable have noted that same phenomenon of increased public awareness, Mumford as long ago as the publication of his book, *The Highway and the City,* in 1964. Is it just the critic's wishful thinking, then? I think not. There *are* more books, more publications, more lectures, more exhibitions on architecture than ever before in New York and elsewhere in the United States, from small cities to large; there is more public debate over the quality of built works, and more of an attempt by architects to present works in a way that will earn the public's interest. All of this has yet to yield us the built environment we aspire to—but there is more real concern about how to achieve that than there has been in a long time, and the purpose of the writing that follows is to help nurture that concern.

Paul Goldberger

New York City
April, 1983

Architects on the Future of Architecture

The American Institute of Architects did something radical at its convention here the other day—it talked about architecture. And not only did it talk about architecture, but it also assembled eight of the nation's most respected designers—Peter Eisenman, Frank Gehry, Michael Graves, Charles Gwathmey, Charles Moore, Cesar Pelli, Robert Stern, and Stanley Tigerman—to show their most advanced works and engage in a discussion, led by Philip Johnson, about where the art of architecture is going.

This was all significant because the art of architecture is usually the last subject the American Institute of Architects, the nationwide architects' professional society, tends to care about. Most institute conventions are filled largely by discussions about liability insurance and marketing and licensing and professional ethics, and there is little way for a visitor to know that he has not stumbled into a meeting of accountants or insurance salespeople.

This year's convention had its share of that, of course—business sessions were occupied by major debates over the institute's code of ethics, which was changed to permit architects to advertise and engage in contracting. And the president of the institute, a San Francisco architect named Elmer Botsai, didn't show up at the first part of the two-day design workshop—he was leading a session of his own on problems of water infiltration in buildings that had somehow been scheduled for precisely the same time.

But while 100 architects wanted to hear Mr. Botsai talk about water seepage, more than 800 showed up at the design sessions—as clear a sign as one might ask for that, as Mr. Johnson said as he concluded the workshop, "Yes, architects really do care about the art of architecture, whatever the A.I.A. might think."

The architects on the design panel, like many in the audience, had come in part to honor Mr. Johnson himself. He has been one of the nation's most outspoken proponents of architecture as an art as well as a business for all of his career, and this year he received the gold medal of the institute, the highest award the organization gives to any architect in the world. He used the occasion to prod the institute into more concern about design by organizing the panel of eight younger architects—"the kids," he kept calling them, even though many were over fifty years old—and when he received the medal at the formal banquet last Wednesday night, he spoke about his own current concerns.

"We are at a watershed, at the end of modernism as we have known it," he said. "We have new attitudes today, a new pluralism, a new belief in many streams flowing at once. There are no certitudes today. And we have a new willingness to use history, to use symbols—we don't want everything to look like a glass box anymore." If Mr. Johnson seemed to be building up to a defense of his controversial design for the new American Telephone & Telegraph Company headquarters in New York, he was. He argued that the granite tower, which is to be topped by a broken pediment, would be an appropriate "symbol of our time."

The first day's design sessions consisted of separate presentations by each of the eight architects who showed their works; the next day they joined Mr. Johnson in a panel discussion. It was clear that he saw himself as a sort of godfather to the younger architects and that they liked seeing him in that role, too. He alternated between beaming like a proud father and talking like a master of ceremonies, a sort of architectural Johnny Carson.

Most of the architects on the panel, different as their own works are from one another's or from Mr. Johnson's, agreed with Mr. Johnson's belief that orthodox modern architecture, the glass boxes of the international style, was no longer the advanced style of the age. But two of them, Mr. Pelli and Mr. Gwathmey, offered sharp disagreement, and the discussion was as lively a debate over the state of architecture as has been heard anywhere in some time.

Mr. Pelli, a designer of sleek glass structures, agreed with the notion of postmodernists, as the younger architects are often called, that the modern movement's belief in romanticizing technology was no longer valid. But he did not see conventional, old-fashioned materials and the use of historical styles as an answer. "If the myth of technology is gone, that doesn't make the reality of it disappear," he said. "We must learn to use whatever appropriate technology exists. I feel as if you are sometimes walking east on a plane that is flying west— and the plane is the new technology."

Mr. Gwathmey, for his part, spoke of the importance of the creation of abstract, ideal spaces, and eventually the discussion came down to a division between those architects who saw their mission as the creation of pure space and form and those who saw themselves as making buildings filled with symbolism and historical illusion.

Nothing was decided, of course; it never is at such sessions. One clear observation was the difference in style between the architects on the design panel and those in the audience. There was a bit of a culture clash: The design architects tended to be better dressed, for one thing, and they were more willing to spice their conversation with subjects other than architecture. Mr. Eisenman, for example, quoted Proust. Several questioners asked why the architects were not talking about the energy crisis or about the need to build more housing; Mr. Johnson said they recognized those needs, but felt they couldn't do much about them by themselves.

As to how worthwhile it would be if architects like these were permitted to design everything, here is Peter Eisenman: "If we had Bach coming out of every Muzak, we'd go out of our minds. If you had buildings by all of us on every block all over Dallas, it would be the same."

There was a long standing ovation for Philip Johnson when he received his gold medal, but not everyone came to applaud the New York architect, who for years had attacked the institute as antidesign. The New York City chapter of the institute came to Dallas with a box of buttons bearing Mr. Johnson's picture, and while hundreds found their way onto architects' lapels, "about one out of three members refused to wear a Johnson picture," Emily Samton, who was handing out the buttons, reported. "One architect asked me, 'Who is Philip Johnson?' "

Convention-goers are always loaded down with literature, and some of it is especially characteristic of the region in which the convention is being held. One brochure seen around the architects' convention this year was a pamphlet entitled "The Architect and Master Builder." Architects, their eyes caught by the title, grabbed it up eagerly, and it was only after they opened it that they learned it was not about architecture at all: it was an evangelical brochure, full of biblical quotations, put out by a pair of architects from Georgia and Florida.

—*May 29, 1978*
Dallas

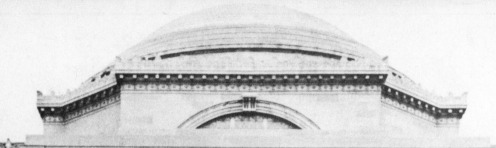

Architecture at Columbia:
Legacies of a Radical Era

"We oppose stylistic and empty form-making. We oppose architecture that is whimsical, or for fun. We do not believe that the goal of architecture is to produce buildings as works of art."

Thus read a portion of a manifesto produced by a group of students at Columbia University's School of Architecture in 1967, just a few months before their entire university was to become enveloped in massive radical upheaval. The manifesto, which was published in a now defunct Columbia publication called *Touchstone*, summarizes an attitude toward the making of architecture that seems completely at odds with the philosophy prevalent in architectural schools today. In the radical 1960's students rejected esthetics and sought to shift their profession's focus toward social concerns; now they seem more inclined to do the reverse, to celebrate the making of pure form that has no justification save for its abstract beauty.

The dramatic change in attitude was the subject of a symposium last Saturday at Columbia's School of Architecture entitled "Legacies of a Radical Era: Architecture at Columbia, 1968–80." The session's subject was far more than Columbia University and far more than architectural education: it provided a keen focus for the dramatic shift in priority that has occurred throughout much of the architectural profession. It is a shift from broader, societal concerns to more personal ones, and it parallels changes in other professions, such as law, where alternatives from traditional methods of practice that had been sought by young lawyers in the 1960's seem now to be replaced by a willingness to join conventional law firms.

What was perhaps most remarkable about the symposium at Columbia was how few of the participants, facul-

Columbia
in 1968

13

ty members and students alike, seemed inclined to praise the status quo. The radical upheaval of the late 1960's—which affected Columbia's architecture school dramatically, leading to a sharply revised curriculum intended to better reflect social concerns—seemed to be viewed with an almost nostalgic air by many of the speakers, who bemoaned the attitudes prevalent today.

"The sixties are thought of as a special moment, but the issues raised then go on today," said Max Bond, the New York architect who has taught at Columbia since 1968 and has just been named chairman of the architecture faculty. "Inequality goes on, urban decay goes on, architectural schemes unrelated to human need go on. What has changed is our attitude—we feel that these things are less critical now."

"I find myself now more conservative than my students," said Tony Schuman, who received his architecture degree from Columbia in 1970 and now teaches architecture at the New Jersey Institute of Technology. Mr. Schuman worked actively with community groups in East Harlem when he was a student, offering not design skills but technical assistance in such areas as housing-rehabilitation projects and landlord-tenant relations. "I am a housing activist, a social activist," he said.

Romaldo Giurgola, the distinguished architect who was chairman of the faculty at the time of the 1968 upheaval, recalled that the architecture faculty had registered an official protest at Columbia's decision to erect a gymnasium in Morningside Park, one of the events that sparked the disturbances. "The whole question of 1968 was the emergence of an urban consciousness," he said. "The legacy of 1968 calls us as architects to become aware of different cultures, of different ways of life. The idea of pluralism is very important to it, but today that word has been translated into something totally insignificant, something that means no more than esthetics."

The participants in the symposium included faculty members, former students who, like Mr. Schuman, were actively involved in the radical movement, former students who were less active, and also recent graduates to whom the entire event is no more than ancient history. The latter group seemed almost lost at times; one of them spoke of the difficulty of getting a job in today's employment market, and another talked of the need to create an elegant portfolio of drawings to enhance employment possibilities, concerns that seemed a world apart from those of the radical era.

The conference's unspoken theme, if there was such a thing, seemed to be a sense that the pendulum had swung too far—that the architects who are influencing students today, designers such as Michael Graves and Robert Stern, to cite two whose influence is apparent at Columbia, are excessively predisposed toward esthetic concerns. These two architects' work tends to be more directed toward the solving of esthetic problems than social ones, and where it comes to esthetics, they reject the austere, formal tradition of modern architecture in favor of a more decorated style that makes frequent reuse of historical, even classical, forms.

Postmodernism, the label frequently applied to this style of historical allusionism that has lately become fashionable, was seen by Mr. Schuman as diametrically opposed to the architectural approach favored in the 1960's. He recalled that the modern movement in architecture in the early decades of the twentieth century had put great emphasis on social concerns, and he juxtaposed its utopian attitude with what he considered the somewhat more self-indulgent approach of many current practitioners.

It is an age-old struggle, of course—architects have always battled over whether their mission was to create art first and serve social needs second, or the other way around, and the prevailing judgment seems usually to reflect the overall temper of the times. But the irony of Mr. Schuman's admiring references to modernism is considerable, for it was in rejection of the very sterility and indifference to human need of much modern architecture that many radicals argued back in the 1960's. The cold towers of a red-brick public-housing project were a central target of the revolution among young architects, a symbol of how the architecture profession had, in their eyes, failed in its social responsibility.

But these same austere modern towers have also been the target of postmodernists, who complain not only of the modern buildings' poor social workings but of their stark esthetic, which they feel inadequately satisfies another kind of human need. The young architects of the 1960's looked at the modern tower and saw a social failure; those of the 1980's seem to look at the same thing and see an esthetic failure.

Both are right, of course, and both reactions emerge out of larger currents of their times. What we tend to notice today is what the red-brick tower looks like, not how poorly it serves its occupants. For now, in all fields of culture as well as architecture, the temper is romantic and conservative; form is what seems to matter most, not content, whereas a decade ago content seemed to be everything. It is a mood that is at best introspective and at worst self-indulgent.

It is not likely that such yearning for the values of the 1960's as was seen at Columbia could have been expressed even a couple of years ago, and if there is anything to be learned from it, it may be an indication that the pendulum has indeed gone too far, and that we may well see a reaction in the coming years, a move against the set of values that holds that a work of architecture is no more than an esthetic object. Perhaps the message last week at Columbia is that the romanticism of the last few years, itself a reaction against the ardor of revolution of the 1960's, may be beginning to ebb.

—*April 29, 1980*

Postmodern Architecture and Its Origins

There are a lot of lessons about architecture and design in this small village, and they are not the ones you expect to learn. Woodstock, Vermont, is one of those New England villages that is often described with words such as perfect, and picture book, and picture postcard.

Happily, it is not perfect—if it were it would be intolerable—but it does indeed resemble a classic view of a little New England town of the sort we expect to see in books of color photographs. There are a central green lined with white, Federal-style houses from the nineteenth century, some white-steepled churches, other fine old houses on nearby streets, and a main street of two-story brick commercial blocks.

It is no surprise, then, that such places are fabled not only by tourists in general, but increasingly by architects as well. The old buildings of a town like this—and the way those various buildings come together to make a coherent and civilized environment—are, in a sense, the true models for the work of so many architects active today. Not in the sense of any kind of colonial revival or any revival style at all—rather, the architecture of rural New England has provided the inspiration for a vast number of the houses and other domestic structures that have shaped the architecture of the past decade.

It is not for nothing, for example, that Charles Moore's Sea Ranch condominiums on the California coast are often compared to New England sheds and barns. The buildings of Sea Ranch set the tone for literally hundreds of slant-roofed multi-unit residential projects around the country. But beyond the stark forms of the barns and the sheds, there are houses and churches here that are truly archetypes.

The Federal houses of Elm Street in Woodstock, and

those along the Green, are as good as any to be found in the eastern United States: to eyes tired of the dozens of earnest, but banal, imitations of such buildings that fill the suburbs, these originals are refreshing indeed. There is something important about seeing originals, especially at a time like this, when the idea of an imitative architecture, of an architecture that relies heavily on historical style, is again in fashion.

A decade ago, when the notion of creating a house that was called colonial could bring forth only laughter and derision among serious architects and designers, the meaning of houses such as those to be found in Woodstock was simpler. They were masterpieces of their time, to be admired as such—they were not expected to have any real meaning for our own time.

Now, things are not so easy. Houses such as these are looked at as models, not merely as historical relics, and that makes a great difference. Suddenly one notices the quality of their details, the neatness of their proportions, and also—surprisingly enough—their eccentricity.

Not a single house on Elm Street here is dull, and not a single one looks as if it could have come out of some sort of textbook. Each one has some sort of unusual element. One otherwise fairly normal Federal house has a dormer window that might best be called Flemish baroque. Another has an Ionic portico that is more elaborately detailed than almost anything else in the main structure itself.

Such idiosyncrasies are not limited to the grand and formal architecture of Federal townhouses. The Vermont farmhouses lining the roads just outside town are similarly unusual; they, too, seem not to have come out of books at all. For example, a detail that one sees frequently throughout the back roads of Vermont, in houses in which a smaller shedlike section abuts a larger wing, is a double-hung window set into the side facade on the diagonal so that it fills the slanting space where the little roof joins into the side of the larger structure.

It is these eccentric details, of course, that have so influenced the so-called postmodern architects who are active today, designers like Robert Venturi, Robert Stern, and Mr. Moore. The presence of such things is a crucial reminder that nineteenth-century architecture was not something done "by the book"—there is no right way to do it, there are no rules.

The most gifted architects of the nineteenth century, as well as the makers of the vernacular style of farmhouses, created within a framework of guidelines, and that, of course, is all style is—a set of guidelines and a set of directions. It is not a set of rules by any means.

But there are significant differences between this work and the work of the postmodernists. One senses among the Federal houses in Woodstock and the farmhouses just outside town a certain serenity, a relaxed assurance, that is so often missing in most postmodern houses. Even Mr. Venturi's best houses, as well as those of Mr. Stern, Mr. Moore, and others, have a certain awkwardness to them. The eccentricities of their forms can be fascinating and provocative, often quite powerful, but they are rarely comfortable in the way that a great Federal or colonial house is.

Today's architects seem to wear their eccentricity on their sleeves. It is as if, when looking at their colonial models, they saw only the eccentricity and transmitted that into their own work, but did not see the overall order. That is a reasonable assumption, since the postmodernists are reacting not only against modern architecture but also against architects who imitated colonial designs generations back and saw only the order, not the eccentricity.

The reaction is understandable: most imitative, by-the-book colonial architecture is banal and dull, lacking in the kind of life and imagination that makes all the houses of Woodstock so fine. But there are occasionally times when it can still be best, and one of them is right here in this village. It is the Woodstock Inn, the large hotel opened in 1969 on the Green, on the site occupied by a wonderful, rambling old Victorian inn that was demolished to make way for this new hostelry.

When plans for the new Woodstock Inn were announced, there was an outcry from architectural purists—what could be worse than a fake colonial building in the late twentieth century? Some honesty was needed—if the fine old Victorian building absolutely had to be torn down, why not erect a good modern building in its stead?

Eleven years later one can only be grateful that this advice was not taken. While it is true that the town of Woodstock does indeed contain a mix of architectural periods and styles—including a first-rate Romanesque library—nothing could have been more intrusive than a large modern hotel.

And while the "1960's colonial" style of the inn is hardly a work of creative genius, it is in fact comfortable, serene, and reasonably dignified. It is respectful of what is around it, and it is easy and relaxed as a composition. Of how much modern architecture can that be said?

—*February 19, 1981*
Woodstock, Vt.

The Backward Flying Wedge

There was a time—and it was not so very long ago—
when the architectural profession was led by people
whose work was at once popular and profound, at once of
interest to the public at large and to their most serious
colleagues. The work of a few crucial practitioners
seemed to provide the key to understanding an entire
time. In the 1950's, for example, Eero Saarinen's buildings seemed to sum up everything that decade was
about—a sense of technological daring, a sense of bold
geometric forms, and yet also an underlying respect for
the status quo. Buildings like Saarinen's TWA terminal
at John F. Kennedy International Airport or his Dulles
International Airport outside Washington, D.C., both
completed after the architect's death in 1961, were of
interest to architectural cognoscenti and laypeople alike.
Their swooping forms and sense of adventure excited
everyone, and though the buildings challenged no fundamental notions of what architecture was about, they
seemed to herald a new age.

So, too, with the work in that decade of a far greater
architect, Le Corbusier. Buildings like his monastery at
La Tourette, France, of 1955–61, a bold and tough and
utterly unsentimental structure of raw concrete, excited
the imagination of the public and the architectural profession alike. La Tourette has been the model for everything from the Boston City Hall to countless suburban
office buildings, and while none of the imitations has
anywhere near the subtlety of the original, the point is
still clear—a work by a brilliant architect had great popular impact.

It was no accident that when *Time* magazine and the
American Federation of Arts decided to sponsor an exhibition of important new architecture in 1959, they called

it "Form-Givers at Mid-Century," an acknowledgment that major architects created shapes that others followed. Their work had an impact of almost equal measure on the minds of both the public and their fellow architects.

Now things seem very different. Architecture has forms galore, but no formgivers, at least not in the sense we were once accustomed to. No one is producing a kind of architecture that is able to seem new and bold, as Saarinen's or Le Corbusier's did, and yet is also able to set serious design directions.

It seems as if we have two kinds of professional leadership right now. There are the esthetic leaders—architects like Michael Graves, Robert Venturi and Denise Scott Brown, Frank Gehry, Charles Moore, John Hedjuk, and Peter Eisenman, to name just a few. These architects are doing deeply serious, often beautiful work that is almost certainly the most inventive architecture being made today, at least from the standpoint of pure form.

But none of them is at what even their most ardent boosters might call the pinnacle of their profession. Influential as they are—and Charles Moore and Michael Graves are among the most important figures to architectural students, according to a recent survey by *Architectural Record* magazine—they do not have anywhere close to the impact that their predecessors did. Eager and willing as they all might be to design skyscrapers and convention centers, most of them do relatively little work beyond the scale of houses and small academic buildings. And some are as well known for their exquisite, highly priced drawings as for any real buildings.

But if this design-oriented group constitutes one part of the leadership of the architectural profession right now, there is another group that makes up the other side. These are the corporate architects—firms like CRS in Houston; Haines, Lundberg, Waehler in New York; Kohn, Pederson, Fox in New York; and Hellmuth, Obata & Kassabaum, which is based in St. Louis but, like an architectural version of H. & R. Block, has offices just about everywhere.

None of these firms design buildings that could be considered at the cutting edge of architecture, though some of them on occasion do turn out rather good buildings. But where they make their mark is elsewhere—in terms of redefining what the business of practicing architecture today is all about. Kohn, Pederson, Fox, for example, takes great pride in its ability to work with real-estate developers on the creation of cost feasibility studies for its skyscrapers. Other firms in this category emphasize their ability to produce buildings quickly and efficiently, with special attention to concerns such as energy.

CRS, formerly Caudill, Rowlett, Scott, is by now an immense operation with its own holding company, the shares of stock of which are traded on the American Stock Exchange; its chief architect, Paul Kennon, is given the title of president. CRS is proud that it was an innovator in the team approach to architecture, in which no single designer does a building entirely by himself, and it pioneered as well in computer drafting techniques, in which computer-controlled drafting machines produce working drawings by zipping at lightning speed across huge sheets of paper, rendering obsolete the old T-square and triangle, symbols of the architect's office.

In terms of design, firms like this are often followers. They are rarely innovators, even when they are doing their better work, and they are rarely at their best when it comes to the making of form. They tend to pick up ideas from elsewhere, simplify them to the needs of their clients, and then move on. What they have done is become modern corporations for the production of buildings—their innovation has been in terms of technique, not design.

Now, history has always shown us a range of different types of architectural practice; and particularly given the immensely complex economic and technological changes that have come into the business of making buildings in the last few years, it would be absurd to expect that architects not change their way of operation. But we seem to have a curious situation right now, a profession that has design brilliance and corporate skill—but doesn't have too much of a middle ground in which these things are combined.

Is there anyone who joins the concern for design, for really innovative design, of the first group with the commitment to advanced and solidly professional practice of the second group? There are a few, but they tend to be at the rear, not at the front, of the march of architectural progress. I. M. Pei, architect of the National Gallery's East Building in Washington and the upcoming convention center in New York, is a good example, an architect whose firm mixes a concern for design with a commitment to corporate practice. The same might be said of Edward Larrabee Barnes, whose I.B.M. and Asia Society buildings are both nearing completion in New York. But both architects, though they produce thoughtful and often even distinguished buildings, are at bottom conservative. Their drawing boards are not spawning grounds for new ideas: they do not teach us new ways of looking at things in the way that, say, Saarinen did in the 1950's.

So we have the curious case of the architectural profession working like a kind of backward flying wedge—the front ends, where new ideas are being developed, consist of esthetic leadership on one side and what we might call professional practice leadership on the other. The middle of the wedge, where both sides meet, is at the rear.

How different this is not only from the 1950's but from much of history! In the early 1950's Gordon Bunshaft's work at Skidmore, Owings & Merrill, as represented in buildings like Lever House, was an architecture that seemed to define an era and not merely to follow it. The same might be said for the great skyscraper architects Ralph Walker and Raymond Hood in the 1920's and early 1930's, or, to reach a bit further back into American architectural history, of architects like Bertram Goodhue, Cass Gilbert, Charles McKim and Stanford White, and H. H. Richardson. In each case these were men whose work not merely summed up a time but pushed it forward, drove it on to being something else—yet they were all sufficiently in step with their colleagues to be considered professional leaders as well and not pure designers.

There are some architects who do come close to this middle ground, who have made some sort of point of intersection between invention in design and the advanced, large-scale corporate practice. It is hard not to think here of Philip Johnson, who since his partnership with John Burgee has been producing a series of skyscrapers that can surely be called influential—buildings like the IDS Center in Minneapolis of 1972, Pennzoil Place in Houston of 1976, and the as-yet-incomplete PPG Industries building for Pittsburgh and A.T.&T. headquarters for New York.

A.T.&T., the granite skyscraper with the much-debated "Chippendale top" and overpoweringly monumental, arcaded base, may well have been the most talked-about unbuilt structure of the 1970's. Its design, which was made public in 1978, is an attempt to reinterpret classical forms into a building that would seem more a comrade to the lively, eclectic skyscrapers of the 1920's than the stark boxes of the 1960's. Both the public and the architectural profession reacted with a mixture of fascination and outrage, a sure sign that Mr. Johnson and Mr. Burgee had struck a nerve. What is important here is not the specific design of this building itself, but the notion that here, for the first time in many years, a large-scale, corporate skyscraper seemed to be pointing the way toward a different direction.

Mr. Johnson and Mr. Burgee were highly influenced by the so-called postmoderns, the younger architects who have been trying to shift architecture away from the austerity of orthodox modernism toward something more picturesque and reliant on historical forms. Until A.T.&T., most postmodern work had been small and largely private, not public, architecture; with A.T.&T. these ideas suddenly made the leap into the public realm.

Since A.T.&T. there has been a small amount of other work that seems equally committed to bringing these ideas to large-scale, public architecture. Michael Graves's Portland Public Services Building for Portland, Oregon, is that architect's attempt to establish himself as a major practitioner and not as a largely theoretical designer; it has attracted almost as much attention as A.T.&T. There are other Johnson and Burgee skyscrapers, of course, and then there are the recent corporate buildings by such architects as Ulrich Franzen in New York, Helmut Jahn of C. F. Murphy Associates in Chicago, Cesar Pelli in New Haven, and the partnership of Saarinen's successors, Kevin Roche and John Dinkeloo, in Hamden, Connecticut.

A great deal of the work of these architects is innovative. Mr. Jahn's slick skyscrapers, for example, have an immense finesse that seems at once to express the historicizing impulses of one strain of our time and the technological impulse of another. The same might be said of Cesar Pelli or Kevin Roche— Mr. Pelli's addition and tower at the Museum of Modern Art and Mr. Roche's headquarters for General Foods, both now under construction, could never have been conceived in the 1960's. They are too full of the eclectic impulse of the present.

So it is unfair to say that there is absolutely no innovative middle. There is one, if a small one. And it does seem, slowly, to be growing—architects like Der Scutt of Swanke, Hayden, Connell & Partners, designer of the Trump Tower in New York, or Eli Attia, designer of 101 Park Avenue in New York, are clearly trying themselves to innovate.

But despite these signs of an emerging middle, it is hard to be too optimistic. The split between the designers and the practitioners—between the architects who are committed to design and the architects who are committed to getting things built—arose for a number of understandable reasons. Buildings became vastly more complex and expensive in the past two decades; suddenly all sorts of factors apart from pure design, aspects of technology and construction, and energy and sociology, became important. It was no surprise that architects began to advertise their expertise in these other areas, and in some cases began to think of them as secondary to design.

At the same time, the slowdown in building brought on by the recession in the early 1970's led to a lot of quiet time for many architects, and it was easy for them to turn inward, toward drawings and theories. To many of the serious architects coming into active practice a decade ago, there was only a limited chance of landing large-scale building projects—why not, then, think and teach and draw?

And thus the profession drifted, rather unsuspectingly, into the present situation, as one flank of younger architects wanted to build and edged gradually away from any real interest in design innovation, and the other flank edged away from real building. The intersection, the point where both concerns met, was left to older architects.

The conditions that brought the profession to its present point have not really changed: there is, if anything, a greater need than ever for the sort of technological expertise that some architectural firms provide. And yet there is a growing desire, on the other side, for an architecture that would be art. The boom in sales of architectural drawing attests to that, as does the vast increase in architectural exhibitions and publications.

Perhaps from that last impulse, an interest in architecture on the part of society at large, some larger and more secure middle ground will emerge. The public has certainly made its desire felt in one way, in that virtually every new skyscraper going up in an American downtown is now "interesting," even if it is not good, and that shows that priorities have certainly changed in terms of the kind of architecture the public wants right now. It is demanding something that looks to have been designed, even if it is not the best.

But we are still far from a time in which the most interesting and advanced work is part of the public realm. No one knows at this point what the architectural historians of the future will select from our time as the most significant buildings to record—but it is hard not to think that relatively few of them will be the biggest and most conspicuous structures on the skyline.

—March, 22, 1981

The International Style After Half a Century

If any fact can be said to underscore how quickly revolutions age, it is that half a century has passed since the day the Museum of Modern Art put a few photographs and models into its galleries under the title "International Exhibition of Modern Architecture." Behind that bland and unassuming label was one of the most determined efforts at design proselytizing this or any other museum has ever engaged in. For this exhibition was the celebrated International Style show, in which the museum presented the stark, white buildings of stucco and glass and metal by Le Corbusier, Walter Gropius, Mies van der Rohe, and others who it wanted us to think would pull us out of the stultifying classicism of the nineteenth century and pave the way to a glorious new world.

How old all of this now seems, and how far away from what has happened to architecture since. The freshness, the daring, the triumphant sense of newness that was the International Style's stock in trade is today neither fresh nor daring, and least of all is it new. If anything, the works of architecture that appeared in the exhibition by now seem quaint; the sense of revolution they represented comes across now not as powerful but more as prim, puritanical, and not a little innocent.

Architecture has gone in different directions altogether since the day, fifty years ago this month, that the International Style exhibition opened. It is not that modernism did not turn out to amount to anything—it amounted to very much indeed, since buildings in some way influenced by the International Style dominated the American downtown for decades. Without the International Style, there would have been no Third Avenue—or at least a very different Third Avenue.

But the stark boxes of modernism are now, clearly, the

buildings of the past. We still build in glass, and we still build sleek, crisp forms, but we have almost completely given up the International Style's cold, rigorous austerity. And what we have wisely given up on altogether is the International Style's firm moral posture—the sense its architects had that they knew what was right for us, the belief that the precise and hard-edged lines of modernism were a positive force liberating us from the harsh stranglehold of history.

This was precisely the stance taken by the museum's International Style exhibition. The show, which was organized by Philip Johnson, who began his career as the museum's first curator of architecture, was seen by 33,000 people at the museum and by thousands more as it traveled around the country. Several times this many people, of course, have read and continue to read the book *The International Style* by Henry-Russell Hitchcock and Mr. Johnson, which appeared at the same time. Together the exhibition and the book are generally thought of as comprising a watershed event in the history of modern architecture. The exhibition was a sort of debutante cotillion at which the style was dressed up and given its formal presentation to a waiting world; the book recorded the happy debut for posterity.

The importance of this event has always been more symbolic than real, fifty years ago as much as today. In February 1932, the International Style was not really brand new—its great monuments, buildings like the Villa Savoie in Poissy, France, by Le Corbusier; the Bauhaus in Dessau, Germany, by Walter Gropius; or the Tugendhat House in Brno, Czechoslovakia, by Mies van der Rohe, had all been complete for at least two years and were fairly well known. And by then the style had already begun to cross the Atlantic, too. The exhibition contained such American buildings as the Starrett Lehigh Building in New York of 1931, by Russel G. and Walter M. Cory; Raymond Hood's McGraw-Hill Building, also in New York, of 1932; and Richard Neutra's Lovell House, in Los Angeles, of 1929.

What this famous exhibition and the long-lived book that accompanied it did was to grant a certain legitimacy to a style that was coming, by virtue of forces far more powerful than those controlled by anyone at the Museum of Modern Art, to play a larger and larger role in shaping the cityscape. The Museum of Modern Art's stamp of approval made the International Style's growth somewhat smoother and easier, but it did not, of course, bring all this modern architecture into being in the first place. Popular writers such as Tom Wolfe have lately made great sport of the myth that the International Style was some sort of foreign plot foisted upon an unwilling America by a group of European intellectuals led by the Museum of Modern Art; in fact, Frank Lloyd Wright's American architecture was an important International Style antecedent. And acceptance of modernism in its various forms had been growing slowly for years; the museum show merely confirmed that fact.

The real point of the show was to argue what, back then, was a relatively new notion: that these buildings collectively constituted as important a style as anything in architectural history. To make this point all the stronger, the organizers were ruthlessly selective. Only those modern buildings whose clean lines seemed intended to exemplify the esthetic of sleek, light form were welcome. Not only was anything that even hinted at ornament banished, so were modern buildings of what might be called a merely functionalist bent. Plain old factories, in other words, need not apply; industrial buildings with the right lines, however, were the heroes of the day.

Modernism continued to spread through this country for at least four decades after the exhibition, but not quite in the way the museum's proselytizers had hoped it would. Its acceptance was fueled less by esthetics than by the economics of the postwar years, as glass curtain walls finally became cheaper than masonry and as the decline in craftsmanship made it seem financially prudent to join the parade against ornament. By 1950 modern architecture had become the American corporate style, its clean, sparse lines ideally suited to the cool and anonymous world of American business in the postwar years.

As the style grew, however, it became harder and harder to tell what was the International Style and what was not. By the late 1950's we were seeing not only more and more weak imitations of International Style masters—the kind of bargain-basement Mies van der Rohe that fills Third Avenue—but also the flamboyant shapes of Eero Saarinen, whose picturesque architecture at its best has an appealing stage-set quality; the decorative modernism of Minoru Yamasaki and Edward Durell Stone, who tried to break away from the International Style toward a delicate, rather prissy kind of architecture; and the powerful imagery of Kevin Roche, whose buildings back then had a strong, almost brutal sculptural quality to them.

So there was considerable diversity in modernism—modern buildings were more than just the products of the single-minded, narrow dogma of the International Style itself. But there was a kind of hubris to all of this architecture, a certainty that it represented the right way, the one true way to the making of right buildings. And if the International Style did not encompass all that modern architecture was about, it certainly exemplified modernism's hubris. Nowhere but here did there seem to be such narrow dictates, nowhere but with the gurus of the International Style was there so much concern with pronouncing buildings acceptable or unacceptable.

And this is where the Museum of Modern Art exhibition played a major role—it presented what amounted to a set of rules for the making of modern architecture. There was a right way, which was to create buildings that fit into a particular esthetic, and a wrong way, which was to do anything else. The International Style was never really about much of anything except esthetics anyway, in the end. There was much talk about social responsibility, and about using new technology and modern materials, but these factors could never hold a candle to the question of how a building looked.

It is the very notion that there could be such simple rights and wrongs that dates the International Style to us today, far more, even, than the specifics of its esthetic. The European architects who brought the style into being in the 1920's and 1930's deeply believed that the new architecture would bring about the good life for everyone; it was not for nothing that Richard Neutra called his Lovell House the Health House. In so doing he was expressing the feelings of many of his colleagues, who were certain that the clean lines of modernism would in themselves improve society.

That esthetics alone could do this is something almost no one, not even our most zealous architects, believes anymore. We ask of our architecture today something much more particular, something much less moralistic. We expect it to shelter us and, quite frequently, we expect it also to please and even entertain us. At its best—when its aspirations to art are the most serious—we hope that it will uplift us. But we still do not look to it for a cleansing of the soul; neither do we look to it for a sense of absolutes.

And thus there is, at this moment in architectural history, no clear sense of style at all. Our best architects are divided between those who seem to be taking some modernist themes—a sense of sleekness and abstraction—and using them in a far more decorative and playful way than the International Style architects did, and those who are trying to reject all that modernism has been about and bring into their work the very aspects of historical architectural style that the International Style rejected. (Philip Johnson, of course, has kept his career on the cutting edge by leapfrogging over the heads of his younger colleagues to begin designing such eclectic buildings himself.)

It is perhaps no accident that fifty years after the International Style's great exhibition the work of those architects with whom the International Style's practitioners felt in deepest competition, the eclectic architects of the 1920's, is riding a crest of popularity. The picturesque, relaxed, and easy Georgian mansions of Delano & Aldrich, the sumptuous Renaissance buildings of McKim, Mead & White, the lush Gothic of James Gamble Rogers are all very much in fashion now. They are admired by historians and, more significantly, they are imitated by younger, postmodern architects.

The best eclecticism of the 1920's and 1930's was an architecture of a certain ease, a certain self-indulgent but not unsophisticated pleasure. It displays far more knowledge of what makes buildings physically and emotionally comfortable than the International Style was ever able to do. But what makes eclecticism most appealing right now is that it is an architecture without dogma—an architecture without a rigid ideology to foist upon the world. The International Style was a kind of missionary architecture, and it is that, more than anything else, that sets it apart from the sensitivities of our age today.

—*February 28, 1982*

SAVE OUR HERITAGE
SAVE PENN STATION
ACTION NOT APATHY
AGBANY

Twenty Years After the Penn Station Catastrophe Classicism Is Back

There are not a lot of people who remember what A.G.B.A.N.Y. stands for, but twenty years ago next week these initials were on the front page of *The New York Times*. They signified the Action Group for Better Architecture in New York, and the reason they made page 1 is that on August 2, 1962, such members of A.G.B.A.N.Y. as Philip Johnson, Aline Saarinen, Ulrich Franzen, and Peter Samton put aside the dignity that architects normally affect, picked up picket signs, and marched back and forth in front of the old Pennsylvania Station on Seventh Avenue to protest its demolition.

There is no mystery as to the outcome of this unusual protest. It failed entirely, and not too many months later the somber Doric columns of McKim, Mead & White's great station began to disappear, the victim of the Pennsylvania Railroad's belief that it could do better treating the station as a piece of exploitable real estate than as a symbolic gateway to a city.

In exchange for one of the greatest monumental public buildings in the history of this nation, New York got a new train station that combined the spatial expansiveness of a subway station with the warmth of an airport. On top, on the land that Charles McKim had so foolishly wasted with grand concourses and expansive waiting rooms, the architect Charles Luckman produced a Madison Square Garden shaped like a drum and an office tower that made any Third Avenue box look welcoming.

It was surely the cruelest loss of a landmark in a city beset by cruel illnesses of the built environment. But this anniversary—which I am grateful to Peter Freiberg for pointing out in *Skyline* magazine—is worth reflecting on, for a lot has happened in the two decades since the architects tried to man the barricades. In 1962 the idea

Picketing at
Pennsylvania
Station, 1962

29

of fighting to save a landmark was strange enough to merit front-page coverage. Today, however, such things happen all the time, and they are successful far more than they seemed likely to be twenty years ago. Now, thanks in part to the catastrophe of Penn Station, we have a Landmarks Preservation Commission, which is a way of saying that the city sees the saving of certain older buildings as a matter of legitimate concern for the public realm.

But more intriguing than the general growth of landmarks preservation has been a change of attitude toward new architecture as well as old, and here is where we can really see how much has happened in the last twenty years. When the architects' protest against Penn Station's demolition occurred, the press reports began with phrases like, "A band of architects, including the designers of some of New York's most modern buildings, paraded on Seventh Avenue yesterday to protest the razing of one of the city's more venerable neoclassic structures." The irony was intended—wasn't it hypocritical for anyone who designed modern buildings to march around trying to save an old one?

Now, the picketers back in 1962 probably respected McKim's great interior space more than anything, and many of them tended to see the classical style of the station as a trifle embarrassing, worth saving mainly because it was big and grand and its replacement cramped and ugly; in their heart of hearts, many of the architects were not all that comfortable with the idea of parading around to save a building that had been constructed in an architectural style that they themselves found so wrong for twentieth-century New York.

But in 1982 we find Mr. Johnson overseeing the completion of the American Telephone & Telegraph Building on Madison Avenue, a 37-story skyscraper of granite with overt classical details, Mr. Franzen, another picketer, designing towers with less literal classical references, and just about everybody talking about the resurgence of an interest in classical architecture. If anything has changed since 1962, it is not our desire to see landmarks saved, though that has surely grown in intensity; it is our renewed ability to endorse the eclectic impulse that motivated Charles McKim.

What seems altogether out of tune with today is an attitude like the one expressed by Lewis Mumford in the mid-1950's, when he praised the station as a brilliant work of organization and planning and as a strong and handsome symbol for the city, but seemed almost ashamed and embarrassed that such success should be sheathed in classical garb.

Today we realize that that very system of reasoning may have been in itself a part of the problem—that perhaps Penn Station was so good not in spite of its being classical, as Mr. Mumford thought, but because it was classical. For the classical architectural vocabulary carries within it a set of values that make both clear organization and monumental civic grandeur absolutely natural. Of course McKim's design genius gave this building its extraordinary presence—but he was working within an architectural language that could not help but communicate clearly.

But how about the old argument about the basic inappropriateness of Penn Station? Wasn't it faintly ridiculous to have a train station in twentieth-century America modeled after a Roman bath, as Penn Station was? Well, it was no more ridiculous, surely, than the earlier use of those same architectural forms for a monumental public bath; all of those columns and arches and grandiose space were not a little overblown as a means of fulfilling that architectural program, too.

But the reason this building type made sense in Rome is why it also made sense on Seventh Avenue—certain kinds of buildings fulfill symbolic roles that go far beyond their simple functional tasks, and the monumentality of Roman classicism lends itself naturally to the kind of symbol that was sought both in Rome and in early twentieth-century New York. It was a means of expressing the nobility of the city, and hence of the people within it, a kind of shared grandeur.

The eloquence with which this architectural vocabulary can still speak to us was made clear to me the other day when I had occasion to spend some time in the State Supreme Court at Foley Square, the building by Guy Lowell that is entered from a flight of steps that seems to tumble out gently through the huge Corinthian portico. This building *looks* like a courthouse; it feels like a courthouse with every stone of its being.

The building was designed in 1912 and finished in 1927, and the fifty-six years since its completion have done nothing to dim the eloquence with which it expresses authority—authority, that is, as opposed to power. A harsh building like the Criminal Courts up the street or the recently completed Family Court across the square speaks of raw power; the Supreme Court has a refinement that suggests authority, the shared commitment of a society to follow certain ideals herein expressed.

Why this happens—why this building communicates so convincingly after so many years and looks not the slightest bit trite—gets us, I think, to the very essence of classicism. It is not large scale, although that surely helps, and it is not ornament and decoration, though these, too, play a role. It is a question of a certain order and dignity that comes from the classical spirit; it is why a courthouse building like Mies van der Rohe's Federal Center in Chicago, an international style slab of glass nearly as fine as the Seagram Building, has a kind of authority despite its lack of decoration, and why the pretentious and glitzy Manhattan federal office building at 26 Federal Plaza, just across the street from the Supreme Court, has no authority at all.

The interior of the courthouse is no less distinguished. The floor plan is unusual—the building's overall shape is hexagonal, and inside the front door there is a vestibule with a vaulted ceiling and then a long, nave-like corridor leading to a central rotunda. The rotunda is a serene and dignified space, pleasantly lighted with natural light and decorated with a set of murals that attempt to represent the great traditions of the law from Western cultures; they are, sadly, in poor shape, urgently in need of restoration.

Indeed, most of this fine building is in need of help. The state has taken relatively good care of it—there are few thoughtless renovations, save for tacky, fake-wood elevator cabs—but there is plenty of peeling paint and leaky plaster. No one doubts that we are no longer a society that can afford to build a courthouse of this caliber, but it is startling to realize that we may have also become a society not even capable of maintaining one.

County clerk Norman Goodman, who tends to this splendid building with the care of a loving parent, laments the lack of funds and has tried to seek private support from the city's prosperous bar. But the community of lawyers that so depends on the courthouse has thus far been unwilling to see to its physical restoration.

There is one happy chapter in this, however, and that is in the jury room, a high, formal paneled space quite similar to the courtrooms throughout the building. During the Depression a Works Progress Administration project filled this room with two remarkable sets of murals, one of which shows New York in the eighteenth century and the other in the 1930's. The set from the 1930's is as fine a period piece as exists anywhere in New York, a document of the look of the city at that time as clear and precise as the photographs of Berenice Abbott. Long darkened by age and the cigarette smoke of waiting jurors, they were recently restored, and they look splendid—a reminder of how noble and how pleasing the entire Supreme Court Building could again some day be.

—July 29, 1982

A Postmodern "Stage Set"

Architectural exhibitions tend to be vicarious experiences—they cannot put us in the presence of a real building as art exhibitions put us in the presence of real art, and so they fall back on such representations as drawings, photographs, and models. "The Presence of the Past," the immense exhibition which recently arrived here from Venice, would be of note if only for the fact that it pays no heed to this convention and endeavors instead to show us something of real buildings. Its main section consists of twenty-two facades, each roughly three stories high and each designed by a prominent architect as a representation of his work.

Not quite real buildings, of course: stage sets is more like it, since these facades are made of inexpensive materials, have no backs, and give entry to relatively anonymous spaces behind. But they are still an overwhelming, and surprisingly exhilarating, presence. They are so big that they could fit into no conventional museum space, and they have thus been lined up as a mock street inside a pier at Fort Mason Center beside San Francisco Bay. To see this exhibit, then, is to walk into a warehouse-like space and watch it turn into a kind of academic version of Disneyland.

"The Presence of the Past" was originally created for the Venice Biennale in 1980 and exhibited in an old rope factory in Venice. It was seen there by Virginia Westover and her husband, Joseph Weiner, who decided that it would be just the thing to enliven the somewhat staid architectural community of their hometown of San Francisco. They managed to raise more than $300,000 from a number of corporate sponsors, and the show—with several local additions—was reassembled at Fort Mason Center last month. It will run until July 29, but its future after that is uncertain, and at this point it would seem as though the only chance to see the exhibition in the United States will be over the next few weeks in San Francisco.

The exhibition is not by any means a general catalogue of contemporary architecture. It is quite selective, and not a little polemical as the title, cleverly chosen to be at once direct and vague, suggests. The architects who were invited to design the facades for the "Strada Novissima," as the street of facades was called in Venice, are all among the group that has become known as postmodernists—architects who reject the austerity and abstraction of orthodox modernism and seek instead a return to ornament, picturesqueness, and the use of elements from the architecture of the past.

The exhibition aims to be for postmodernism what the Museum of Modern Art's celebrated International Style exhibition of 1932 was for modernism—a way of conferring legitimacy on a style that has been of gradually increasing importance in the architectural scene over the past few years, and of trying to move that style from the avant-garde to the mainstream.

Postmodernism is not the International Style, of course. It is by its very nature more diverse, less concerned about rules and rights and wrongs. Last week I overheard a man who was obviously making a repeat visit to the Biennale tell his guest that "the first thing you have to do here is forget all of your inhibitions," and it was not bad advice. Postmodernism as shown here is extravagant, self-indulgent, and wildly eclectic. Much of it is also exciting, and some of it is good.

Each facade is a kind of logo for its creator. Few of the architects chose to offer what might be called a true facade; most are symbols, intensely packed summaries of style that are far more active than a normal townhouse facade would be. And significantly, given postmodernism's avowed interest in working within existing architectural context and in not creating monuments that stand aloof from their surroundings, these facades clash terribly with each other. Only one architect, Leon Krier, seems to have paid any attention to the context of Venice, for which the facades were originally created. His strong and stark facade is an eloquent homage to the Venetian palazzo, and one of the only things in the exhibition that makes a true statement of urbanity.

For these are not, one must say again, real buildings. They are sets, and they will do little to discourage the frequent criticism that postmodern architects are interested only in facade decoration and not in the solving of "real" architectural problems. But such a view, if common, is unfortunate and unfair. First, there is nothing wrong with stage sets in the first place—much great architecture of the past has been as concerned with the shaping of a facade as with anything else, and history hardly shows that paying heed to this concern gets in the way of other architectural needs. Postmodern architects can rightly point out that they are trying, through the device of these facades, to shift our attention back to issues of composition and decoration, and that hardly means indifference to other things.

But if the facades are too studied to stand as true, off-the-rack examples of these architects' work, most of them are not without considerable visual interest, and all of them manage to tell us a great deal about the preoccupation of their creators. We can see instantly, for example, how the talented Allan Greenberg is in his own way as much a dogmatist as any of the modernist theorists whose work he seeks to supplant. Thomas Gordon Smith, younger than Mr. Greenberg, comes off as a kind of naive or folk classicist; his facade has none of the sternness of Mr. Greenberg's pure pristine white classical composition, but is instead a rather zestful, splashy, and slightly vulgar parade of images, classicism filtered through the lens of California.

Michael Graves's facade shows his continued concern with a kind of abstract composition that, despite his interest in classicism, still retains much of the cubist esthetic; revealing as this project is, it lacks, unfortunately, a sense of surprise and celebration that Mr. Graves's real buildings often have. On the other hand, Stanley Tigerman's customary playfulness could not yield a better result than the facade as a literal stage set that he has created here, with proscenium and all. Of the four San Francisco architects included, the most pleasing facade is that of Andrew Batey and Mark Mack, who have created a structure of corrugated metal atop a base of stone—tying, in effect, the formality of classicism to the California style of Frank Gehry. The townhouse facade rendered in fabric by a group from Skidmore, Owings & Merrill is pleasing as well, not the least for the extent to which it shows that firm's new eagerness to be counted among the postmodernists.

The exhibition includes more than the facades themselves. Behind most of these stage sets is a small section of buildings designed by each architect, so that the facades act as gateways to the mini-exhibits. A classical pavilion designed by Thomas Gordon Smith functions as a kind of commercial interlude, showing work by the corporate sponsors, and another section includes the works of numerous postmodern architects from around the world who were not invited to design full facades.

The layout, unfortunately, is not as good as it was in Venice—the street here is too wide, and angled rather than straight. And outdoors in front of the pier there is a rather ungainly entry portal, chosen, surprisingly, as the winner in a competition to erect a special ceremonial gateway to the building for the Biennale. Designed by Crosby Thornton Marshall Architects, it consists of a truss atop columns, awkwardly mixing classicism and high-tech—a trite entrance to an exhibition that, whatever its extravagances and eccentricities, is clearly dedicated to provoking architectural thought on a much more subtle level. "The Presence of the Past" is an experience like none other available at this moment in architectural history—a piece of showmanship that captures precisely this instant in our architectural development when architects have plunged into history, to wallow in it as much as to build on it.

—June 20, 1982
San Francisco

Now the Religion Is Antimodernism

It is common to speak of this as a time of pluralism, as a moment in architecture when the eclectic impulse is paramount—as a time, even, when we yearn to expand our esthetic to take in all of history. After all, if there are any buildings that seem to sum up the concerns of the moment they would have to be the Portland (Oregon) Building by Michael Graves, which is a brightly colored pile of reinterpreted classical decoration, and Philip Johnson and John Burgee's A.T.&T. Building in New York, which twists and turns Renaissance and Chippendale forms into a sumptuous skyscraper.

These two buildings—and dozens more that represent a similar impulse—emerge out of the belief that the austere, cool forms of modern architecture are no longer a valid expression. This is not, of course, in itself much news: the reaction against the glass box has been with us for more than a decade now, and the term "postmodernism," which is often used to describe this reaction, has already become part of the architectural lexicon.

Now, postmodernism is a term that is either comfortably or irritatingly vague, depending upon what you expect of it, and it means very different things to different people. At its best it suggests a movement away from the rigid, almost puritanical orthodoxy of modernist architecture and an openness to the values of pure composition, decoration, and historical style. It seeks not to turn these things into a new orthodoxy but to avoid the notion of any rigid orthodoxy at all—to be pluralistic in the best sense, which is to say to embrace the idea of quality more than the dogma of any individual style.

But as this reaction against modernism becomes more and more of an established thing, it has shown signs of turning into something much more than a movement toward pluralism. It has become, in certain circles, as utter a dogma as anything modernism ever represented. We are increasingly seeing an attitude that is summed up less by the term postmodern than by the word "antimodern"—a tendency to reject modernism in all its forms and aspects, to declare it wrong in every fashion. It is a view that argues that modernism is not just an inappropriate style at this moment in history, but something more akin to an immoral one.

Antimodernism exists both in theory and in actual buildings. Its most prominent spokesperson among practicing architects is probably Allan Greenberg, the Connecticut architect who has designed Georgian and classical buildings as precise in their historical recall as anything created in the 1920's. Now, Mr. Greenberg is a gifted designer, and his own buildings manage to have the pleasing and civilized, if rather stiff and dry, air that much revivalist work of the 1920's had. If such architecture were all we were getting right now, this would be a less exhilarating time, but a less disturbing one, too.

Far more troubling than a classical building by Allan Greenberg is the antimodernist rhetoric that we are increasingly hearing from nonarchitects. For years the writer and critic Henry Hope Reed has been arguing vehemently against modernism, calling it "a cancer destroying visual America," a view that has led him to dismiss such a masterwork as Frank Lloyd Wright's famous house, Fallingwater, as "a large split-level."

Years ago this kind of view tended to be considered eccentric—even by those who harbored serious doubts about modernism themselves. But now it is more difficult to consider Mr. Reed's attitude entirely outside the mainstream. His extreme attack on modernism has been joined by numerous other commentators, the best known of whom is surely the writer Tom Wolfe, who has raised the cry of modernism's dangers to a fever pitch.

Mr. Wolfe first began to sound the alarm about the evils of modernist thinking in *From Bauhaus to Our House*, a book suggesting that modern architecture was a plot foisted on an unwilling world by a sly group of European intellectuals. He returned to the subject recently in an essay in *The Washington Post* that tries to make the point that the primary goal of modern art and architecture is to perplex and annoy the public, and separate the artist or architect from the "bourgeois" taste of the general public. The people really hate all modern things, Mr. Wolfe tells us, and it is the refusal of the artistic community to recognize this that is the source of all our problems. If architects and artists would stop trying to jam this awful stuff down people's throats and give them what Mr. Wolfe knows is the truly right kind of art, serene joy would descend upon all of us.

This antimodern attitude is more than a little frightening, for it sounds so much like the kind of arguments of moral superiority that the modernists themselves made early in this century—when they claimed their way was the only true one. Architecture that relies on historical style, buildings that have decoration, were somehow unclean, decadent—even immoral, the modernists argued back then, their polemics reaching a climax, surely, in Adolf Loos's famous essay equating ornament with crime.

The issue is not the moral rightness or wrongness of a particular style, and it never was. The modernists' dogma was as foolish as the antimodernists'; each makes claims to a moral superiority that neither history nor common sense can support. It is simply not true, as the antimodernists now tell us, that people have always preferred classicism, that modernism was a perverse break from a great historical continuum, and that the only priority for us today is to get back on that simple, single track. If only the history of art and the history of culture were so simple.

What is the case today, certainly, is that we have lost faith in the rhetoric of the early modernists, and properly so. The Bauhaus promised a kind of social redemption that no architecture, modernist or otherwise, can truly provide. A world of modern buildings will not assure the good life for all of us, any more than a world of classical buildings will.

There are, however, certain failings that distinguish the modern movement, and it is important at this moment in architectural history to keep them in mind. Modern architecture—and modern art, for that matter—has created great masterpieces; only a determined Philistine could be blind to the greatness of Fallingwater or Le Corbusier's Villa Savoie, or Mies van der Rohe's Seagram Building, to name but three. The problem is not in the inability of the modernist vocabulary to create meaningful works of art.

What modernism has failed to do, however, is to create a workable, sound vernacular—a language that can be comfortable not just for unique works of art, but for the broader needs which buildings must serve. Modernism *can* create great buildings as much as it can create great paintings; what it cannot do as successfully is create great cities. The exquisite, self-assured presence of the Seagram Building is deadening when multiplied by ten, twenty, or a hundred buildings all across a city—its abstraction, so remarkable when seen in contrast to classicizing stone buildings around it, becomes merely emptiness when it takes over all of Park Avenue.

Mies van der Rohe's buildings were once described as "the ideal background architecture of our time." Nothing could be farther from the truth; modernist buildings, by Mies or any other great modern architect, are foreground buildings through and through. They demand our complete attention; they deal in subtleties of spatial manipulation, movement, materials, and proportion, and they are, at bottom, abstract. It is these subtleties that can make them so powerful as works of art, and that disappear so completely when modernist ideas are crudely reproduced in building after building across the cityscape.

But to complain about the wretched effect the modern movement has had on cities, and to assert that modernism could never function as, say, Georgian architecture did—to take but one example of a style that yielded both great masterworks and a viable vernacular out of which an entire city could be beautifully molded—is not to reject its continued value to us. To pretend, as the antimodernists do, that modern architecture never existed is as foolish as pretending that Stravinsky never wrote music or Joyce a novel. The works of modernism exist, and inevitably shape our own experience. And, after all, even if you believe that modernism *was* sinful, who could ever claim complete innocence after tasting sin?

There continue to be times and places in which the modernist esthetic speaks appropriately to us, and to reject it is to approach architecture with an attitude that can only be called Philistine. The best, and surely the most poignant, example of this is the controversy surrounding Maya Yang Lin's design for the Vietnam Veterans Memorial in Washington, D.C., on the Mall near the Lincoln Memorial. When the design was undergoing public review, it received considerable criticism on the grounds that it was too abstract—too much a modernist work that would not relate sufficiently to the artistic tastes of the surviving Vietnam veterans who would see it.

The design certainly is abstract—it consists of two walls of granite, set to form a V, with the land between the walls sloping downward and the names of the 57,000 Americans who died in Vietnam carved into the granite. It is also hauntingly moving and eloquent in a way that no conventional—which is to say classical—monument could be. Abstraction here fulfills a special function; it creates a somber, pensive place that honors the dead and yet permits each of us some leeway in making our own interpretation of the nature of the space.

A group of Vietnam veterans who were unhappy with Miss Lin's design, which was chosen by a distinguished panel of artists and architects, ended up successfully persuading the committee sponsoring the memorial and the Fine Arts Commission of Washington to agree to the addition of a flagpole and a statue of three soldiers to the design. They were encouraged by Mr. Wolfe, who in his *Washington Post* essay argued that Miss Lin's design, because it was modernist, was a deliberate insult to those who died in Vietnam.

The controversy was a sad episode, and only partly because of such foolish points as that last one. It was sadder still because it was so close to being right. The arguments against modern architecture are not entirely wrong—they are half right, which is much tougher. Modernism is no insult to veterans or anyone else, but it is true that the insistent abstraction of modernism has served us badly in too many places that cry out for a degree of warmth and familiar symbol. But a monument is a different thing altogether; what we seek from it is different from what we seek from, say, a house, and applying the general case against modernism here missed completely.

The movement of the last few years away from modernist orthodoxy is the most important esthetic event of the last fifty years, and it is to be welcomed. It is only when it takes such simplistic, antimodernist form—and attempts to deny the value of an appropriate and important modern design when it *is* created— that it is cause for sadness.

—*December 5, 1982*

CITIES: URBANISM AND THE SKYLINE

The Limits of Urban Growth

For most of its history, New York has carried on a romantic, not to say intimate, involvement with congestion. To be New York *was* to be crowded—out of crowding came energy, ideas, excitement, power. If traffic was a bit slower here than elsewhere, if the tall buildings gave you less sun and less sky than there was in Des Moines or Dallas—well, who really cared about moving fast once you were already here? And who came to New York in search of sun and sky, anyway?

All of that is still true—at least in terms of the city's image of itself. But if there is anything that the city's current building boom, one of the largest in its history, has proved, it is that there are limits to density, and that midtown Manhattan has now almost certainly reached them. There is such a thing as being too crowded, and midtown Manhattan has become just that—a place in which enormous buildings block out not just sun and sky, but one another; a place in which traffic moves not just slowly, but almost not at all; a place in which walking is not necessarily more practical than riding, because the sidewalks are as jammed as the streets.

New Yorkers can adjust to anything, but their intense adaptability often leads them to overlook exactly how dramatic are the changes that have come to their city. Since 1979, 30 high-rise buildings containing more than 14 million square feet of space have been completed or begun in midtown Manhattan, the area bounded roughly by 34th and 60th streets and Third and Eighth avenues. These 30 new buildings are in addition to an astonishing 142 new buildings completed in midtown between 1960 and 1979, containing a total of 77 million square feet of space—an amount that is alone more than the total amount of downtown office space in Houston and Dallas

43

together. The streets of midtown, laid out in the nineteenth century with the expectation that they would be lined with townhouses and the like, for years contained a mix of small buildings and large, with an average density that remained reasonable, if hardly light. But now the streets feel as if they contain only tall buildings jammed together.

The city has fallen prey to an attitude that can be called urban Darwinism— the survival of only the most lucrative use of any given plot of land. It gives us not a city of brownstones and larger buildings in balance with each other, but a city of huge towers crowded one upon another, filling block after block. It is a different kind of midtown altogether—one with vastly greater numbers of more people crammed into what feels like less and less space, a city of blocked sunlight and cutoff views, of choking traffic. It is, in short, a place in which the quality of life—which is presumably the reason anyone who has a choice in the matter settles in cities in the first place—inevitably must decline.

The ways in which life changes for the inhabitants of this overbuilt city seem small at first—a few minutes longer to get crosstown, a few more people to dodge on the sidewalk—but they mount. It is now no surprise to see traffic backed up not just on cross streets during rush hours, but at noon on Fifth Avenue from the mid-Fifties all the way up to 65th Street, and for most of the afternoon on Madison Avenue. It can take half an hour at midday to go by taxi from the Queens-Midtown Tunnel to Times Square, a mere dozen blocks, and longer still to go by bus across 57th Street.

This has always been a city in which minor courtesies were expected to fall victim to the press of business, but now it often seems as if the social contract has collapsed altogether. The sense is of constant dodging, constant noise, constant pressure. On a recent fall afternoon, as the sounds of traffic and construction merged into a din, the corner of 55th Street and Madison Avenue was an urban horror. As crowds of pedestrians surged along, two dowagers grabbed for each other in desperation when the force of the crowd pushed one of them into the metal pipe supporting a construction scaffold. Moments later, a more nimble man jumped out of the way of a taxi whose driver chose not to observe a red light; a pair of women following him had to walk all the way into the middle of Madison Avenue to cross 55th Street, since the entire intersection was filled with cars that had stopped far beyond the crosswalk line.

But it is not traffic and crowding alone that change the quality of life. The scaffolds and construction vehicles that block sidewalks and roadways may be temporary; the effects of the buildings themselves are permanent. The north side of 57th Street between Fifth and Madison avenues is a good example. It is a block of low commercial buildings long considered one of the city's most prized, and while it is still intact and as elegant as ever, it is nonetheless changed forever, for now it sits imprisoned in shadow for much of the day, the huge towers nearby guaranteeing it will never again see much afternoon sun.

New York is not alone in suffering from excessive growth—the recent building boom has increased crowding and tension in Chicago, San Francisco, Boston, Houston, and Denver, to name just a few cities whose central business districts have grown rapidly in recent years. But there are real and quantitative differences between New York's overbuilding and that of other cities, and they must begin with the fact that New York was more heavily built up to start with. Houston's freeway traffic may be even more maddening than New York's, but its downtown has wide streets and available land at its edges, and in any event much of that city's growth has taken place in outlying areas. San Francisco's skyscrapers may have altered its profile for the worse, but the bay and the low buildings on the hills still provide a sense of breathing space.

Downtown Boston is troubled by traffic as difficult as New York's but it is a much smaller city, and its new construction, while dramatic, lacks the impact of Manhattan's. Cities like Atlanta, Dallas, and Denver have never been built up to New York's density, and even though their downtowns have undergone wrenching change, the effects of new skyscrapers there are more visual than anything else—there remains room to grow in the core of all these cities.

Ironically, Manhattan, too, has room to grow—but real-estate developers in the last few years have taken little advantage of it. They have chosen, instead, to squeeze more into a tight space that was pressing the limits of density to begin with. For much of Manhattan's history, the borough did pursue its relentless growth by expanding—by pushing one neighborhood into another, by growing northward, by stretching the borders of the midtown business district. So it was even as recently as the building boom of the 1960's, when most new office buildings were constructed at the edges of midtown's central core—expanding that core to the west across the Avenue of the Americas, for example, and east across Third Avenue.

But the current boom has brought us no new neighborhoods—it has been, instead, a case of forcing more and more into what was already there. Real-estate developers, made cautious by the overbuilding in "marginal" areas to the south and west that led to a slump in the city's office market in the early 1970's, and yet emboldened by the insistence upon only the poshest of addresses by the foreign tenants who make up so much of the Manhattan real-estate market, chose to build almost exclusively in the already crowded heart of east midtown.

Instead of spreading out, then, they have squeezed in—putting more buildings on Third Avenue, shoehorning skyscrapers into tiny sites on side streets off Park and Lexington that would have been unthinkable a few years ago, tearing down medium-sized buildings on Fifth and Madison avenues to put up blockbusters instead. Such change is encouraged by a system of land economics that prices land with the assumption that it will be used for maximum development—and that sets into motion a troubling cycle. For if a developer pays top price for land, he then feels compelled to build the biggest possible building to get a fair return on his investment.

All of this has produced a city with the superficial signs of vitality—a city that in one sense certainly is booming, for there have been tenants lining up to sign leases in almost all of the new structures. But can a place like Madison Avenue in the Fifties truly be called healthy? Here is an area that was heavily built up before this boom even started, but now is a street where two of the city's largest new towers—the 645-foot-high American Telephone & Telegraph Building and the 635-foot-high I.B.M. Building—sit side by side at 56th Street, blocking light and sky from each other as well as from street and sidewalk. Around the corner at Fifth Avenue and 56th Street, the Trump Tower climbs higher still, replacing the gracious limestone building of the old Bonwit Teller store with sixty-eight stories of reflective glass. And it is not as if these three towers, clustered so close they could read as one from afar, were alone on the skyline—within a couple of blocks are a half dozen other new skyscrapers.

There is a peculiar irony to this surge of development, since almost all of it is of architectural interest, and some of it—A.T.&T. in particular, but also 535 Madison Avenue—deserves to be called distinguished. And even structures that are not of A.T.&T.'s unusual quality are far more lively and urbane than the average buildings of the last Manhattan boom, combining visually interesting forms with such valued amenities as interior public spaces. But even if all of the architecture were vastly better than it was a decade or two ago, how much can it matter if the buildings themselves are too big and too close together?

Lewis Mumford, the urban historian and critic, foresaw this state of affairs as far back as 1955, when he wrote of his fear that if midtown Manhattan "ceases to be a milieu in which people can exist in reasonable contentment instead of as prisoners plotting to escape a concentration camp, it will be unprofitable to discuss architectural achievements—buildings that occasionally cause people to hold their breath for a stabbing moment or that restore them to equilibrium by offering them a prospect of space and form joyfully mastered."

Mumford's ideal was more a garden city of low density and excessive order than the high-rise Manhattan, but this bias does not destroy his basic prophetic point—that we may have reached a time when architecture is ceasing to matter. We have certainly reached a time when it seems as if no site, no part of midtown Manhattan, is safe.

Not all of the new towers that have been proposed are certain to be built, and, indeed, now that the economy has slowed down, many will not go up for years, if at all. The buildings already under construction were all planned months or years ago, when the outlook was stronger. But the ups and downs of the economy are not the point. Even if not a single other tower is added to those existing or rising in midtown Manhattan, it is impossible not to look around and ask the questions, what kind of city do we have, and what kind of city are we getting?

Manhattan has never been typical of New York City, but in the last five years the section of the borough south of 96th Street has become even more different

The overbuilt corner of 57th and Madison

from the rest of the city. It has become, in the words of the Regional Plan Association, the private planning group, "far advanced into the postindustrial economy," which is a way of saying that it has prospered by switching from a manufacturing-based economy to a service-oriented one. Banks, law firms, financial institutions, advertising agencies, communications corporations—white-collar industries all—are the controlling presence in the borough's economy, and they have grown as other types of employment have declined. This kind of economy requires offices, not factories or warehouses, and the corporations that prosper in it tend to prefer Manhattan locations—hence the enormous demand for more midtown office space.

Indeed, Manhattan has increasingly come to employ not just white-collar workers, but white-collar workers who have nothing whatsoever to do with the making of goods; in the last decade the borough lost the headquarters of industrial companies like Texaco and Union Carbide, even as it has gained white-collar jobs overall. Symbolically, Texaco's space in the Chrysler Building was taken over by an advertising agency, and Union Carbide's building on Park Avenue was purchased by a bank.

The kind of people who work in the sort of service economy that Manhattan has become tend, frequently, to be young professionals—people who prefer city life and are willing to put up with substantial expense and difficulty to live in Manhattan. Thus we have a shortage of Manhattan apartments, the conversion into housing of loft buildings that once contained manufacturing operations, the erection of white-brick apartment towers on what seems like every corner of the Upper East Side, the replacement of old bars and hardware stores by boutiques and gourmet take-out shops to serve the city's new professional class. It is all part of the same phenomenon, and it would seem, if this were all there was to it, to be a healthy state of affairs.

But there is a difference between a loft building that has been turned into housing in SoHo and a block of 5-story buildings that have been turned into a 50-story skyscraper on Madison Avenue. The first involves a change of use and affects the city's economy, but does relatively little to change its physical appearance and ability to function smoothly. The second can play havoc with the way the city looks, feels, and works. A huge skyscraper brings not only an awesome change of scale, but forcibly injects thousands of people into a small space. Multiplied by five, ten, or a dozen huge towers, the dimensions of the problem become clear.

Consider some statistics from the Department of City Planning:

Right now, the average speed of automobile traffic from 4 to 6 P.M. on East Side streets between 40th and 57th streets is five miles an hour. That is not just a rush-hour problem; the speed is only 6.6 miles an hour at noon. But on top of this near-gridlock, the planning commission estimates, there will be 39,000 more trips by private car and taxi and 3,000 extra trips by truck every day in midtown as a result of the new construction under way or planned through the 1980's. It is an increase of 9.8 percent in the total number of vehicles entering the midtown core.

So if traffic is impossible, one can always walk, right? Well, yes—if there is room. The same City Planning Department study estimated there would be 169,500 additional trips a day on foot (including to and from lunch, shopping, and business appointments) on those same Manhattan blocks when all the new construction is completed. And that does not count the sidewalk space taken up by the people walking to work from subway and bus stops. The department estimates there will be 301,500 more such trips.

Of course, even without the crowds, there are a few other impediments to relaxed strolling. The Planning Department has predicted "substantial air-quality loss" for certain sites in midtown should maximum development occur. And the streets are not exactly tranquil—monitoring at six major midtown intersections by the city's Department of Environmental Protection in August 1981 revealed noise levels that were "unacceptable" by federal standards. No one suspects that noise levels have grown anything but worse in the months since.

The wretched condition of the subway system has, of course, been well documented, and it does nothing to make the overall picture any brighter. The Metropolitan Transportation Authority is undertaking a $7.2-billion capital improvement program, but whether even a refurbished subway will be able to handle midtown's growing population remains in considerable doubt. At the moment the subways are dirty, broken down, and overcrowded; the best one can hope for in midtown would seem to be a system that is cleaner, mechanically smoother, but just as overcrowded.

The extent to which this kind of crowding is psychologically damaging to the people who endure it every day has never been quantified, and it is only fair to say that the recent trend in psychology and urban sociology has been to praise congestion, not to damn it. William H. Whyte, whose studies of Manhattan street life remain the definitive examination of the subject, condemns the absence of adequate public seating and sidewalk space, but underscores the positive, energizing effect a certain basic level of crowding can bring. So does Jonathan L. Freedman, the University of Toronto psychologist whose 1975 book *Crowding and Behavior* rejected the dogma that congestion is inherently harmful.

But the value of a moderate level of congestion is not the issue—today almost every urbanist endorses it and rejects the view, identified most closely with Lewis Mumford, that a densely built-up city is itself a mistake. Indeed, it is density that makes every successful downtown—it is what makes downtown Pittsburgh a more lively place than downtown St. Louis, for example, or Georgetown a more appealing part of Washington than that city's southwest urban-renewal area. And of course it is density that makes New York—when it is working right—still among the most attractive urban places on earth.

How far can we push this concept, though, without destroying the city altogether? Would even the most congestion-happy psychologist be able to study traffic and pedestrian patterns in Manhattan's East Fifties today and still conclude that all was well?

More troubling, perhaps, than even the problems of physical crowding are those of scale—the different "feel" of the city. New York has always grown large, but never has so much of it been so large as it is now. Despite the city's pride in being home to the skyscraper, the fact is that most Manhattan buildings, except for a few blocks around Wall Street, used to be small to medium in size—old brownstones, 6-story commercial buildings, 15-story apartment houses of the sort that give Park and West End avenues a densely woven and exceedingly pleasing urban fabric. That mix is increasingly in danger—it was saved on the Upper East Side only through the device of establishing a historic-landmark district, and no such solution is available to most of midtown. In midtown, until recently, most towers stood relatively free—there were views to them and from them, and the occupant of a 40th-floor office was likely to see more from his window than someone else's 40th-floor office across the street.

Now, the 40th-floor occupant is lucky to see as far as two or three blocks away, and if he has direct sun for more than a short period each day he is luckier still. The squeezing seems to go on and on—as if the city were some vast Monopoly board, on which no block is deemed worth owning unless it is developed to the maximum.

Architectural plans have already been drawn up for a tower to sit in the middle of the block between 55th and 56th streets and Madison and Park avenues—even though there are already sizable buildings on the Madison and Park blockfronts, and the A.T.&T. and I.B.M. towers loom just across the street. The notion is that this new building, as tall as A.T.&T., will be squeezed into the middle of the block, as if with a shoehorn.

More troubling still, Lever House, Skidmore, Owings & Merrill's master-work of 1952, and one of the great monuments of twentieth-century architecture, fills only a portion of its site between 53rd and 54th streets and Park Avenue. Legally, a much bigger building could fit there, and now the Lever Brothers Company has begun, quietly, to negotiate for its sale to a real-estate developer, while architects have drawn plans for a possible building to replace Lever House. No deal has yet been completed, but several prominent New York real-estate developers are known to be involved in discussions regarding the property.

Right down the street, St. Bartholomew's Church has been less private—it has trumpeted proudly its agreement to lease part of its land to the developer Howard P. Ronson, who would tear down the church's community house and erect a 59-story glass tower almost on top of the Byzantine dome. The church here is acting as any urban Darwinist would—it has an asset, the air above its distinguished building designed by Bertram G. Goodhue, and it wants to turn that asset into cash. If that means raising the already intolerable level of density on Park Avenue and crowding one of the city's great landmarks to the point of making it look ridiculous, no matter—progress, or at least the freedom to do as one pleases with a piece of property, is more important.

It is already too late, in a sense, for two other great landmarks—500 Park Avenue and 375 Park Avenue, the Seagram Building. Neither modern tower is in danger of demolition, like Lever House, but 500 Park Avenue, designed by Skidmore, Owings & Merrill for Pepsico, was saved only by a creative real-estate transaction leading to the erection, now in progress, of a 42-story tower just behind it that looms over the building's delicate glass facade. Although the architecture here, by James Stewart Polshek & Partners, is more sensitive, the effect is bound to be like that of the Helmsley Palace Hotel bearing down upon the Villard Houses, the Madison Avenue landmark that was truncated and turned into a fancy entrance to a strikingly ugly midblock hotel tower. Much attention was paid to that as a great project of landmark preservation, but it is preservation at a drastically high price.

The Seagram Building, on the other hand, is threatened by a garish tower that is soon to rise just east of it, on the site now occupied by the solid limestone Beaux-Arts building of the Y.W.C.A. That is being demolished, and a new skyscraper will abut Seagram, putting an end forever to the days when Mies van der Rohe's masterpiece appeared to rise alone into the sky, as its architect intended it to.

Was it ever the intention of our city planners to have a midtown in which every block seems to be developed to its utmost financial potential? Did they expect, when they drafted the city's zoning laws in 1916, revised them in 1961, and revised them again last year, that we would reach a point where every owner of every midtown block would want to turn his property into a sky-scraper?

Quite the contrary. The city's zoning laws are intended to provide a kind of maximum "envelope" within which a building can fit. They were created in 1916 as a response to the enormous bulk of the Equitable Building at 120 Broadway, not so much to protect the public's interest as to protect the owners of commercial buildings, who feared that if every block were developed like the Equitable, every building would be in shadow and they would all drop in value. Thus the first zoning laws encouraged setbacks as a means of preserving light, and they gave us the slender towers of the 1920's that are so much a part of the city's romantic image.

In 1961, following the immensely popular success of the Seagram Building, which rises straight up without setbacks behind a large, open plaza, the laws were changed to encourage more sheer towers. It was the 1961 ordinance that yielded the glass boxes that now fill so much of midtown—but the law did not create them all by itself, and here the plot thickens considerably. Concerned that there was not enough active building going on, and also that the city was not receiving the kind of amenities in its buildings that it deserved, planners began to amend the 1961 ordinance to emphasize what became known as "incentive zoning"—granting bonuses of extra floor space on top of buildings in exchange for plazas, theaters, arcades, and other amenities at their bottoms. Soon it became almost common practice for builders to ignore the regular law and negotiate with the City Planning Commission for more stories or a special amount of extra floor area in exchange for including some sort of so-called amenity.

As time went on, however, the deals the city was striking began to look less favorable—even though the city itself was setting the terms, it seemed willing to give away the store. The plaza bonus gave us 8 million *extra* square feet of office space from 1963 to 1975, or the equivalent of three and a half Pan Am Buildings; the arcade bonus gave builders another half million square feet of extra rentable space, this time in exchange for putting public walk-throughs on the ground floor. Builders were winning the right to make enormous profits in perpetuity from this extra space in exchange for the one-time cost of an amenity—and in hindsight it has turned out that many of the amenities were not so desirable in the first place. Many plazas, for instance, have been poorly designed, executed, and maintained, and it is not difficult to question now whether we would not have been far better off without the amenities and therefore without the bigger buildings that came along with them. Smaller buildings, in other words, might have been the best amenity of all.

Edwin Friedman, former assistant district director for metropolitan New York of the New York State Office of Planning Services, summed up the situation superbly in 1972 when he wrote of the 1961 zoning ordinance and its alteration through incentive zoning that "the one philosophical point implicit in the 1961 resolution is that the attainment of zoned capacity is undesirable, unnecessary and unwarranted. . . . The idea of every parcel being developed to its maximum is essentially a perversion of all that planning has traditionally stood for. The major thrust behind much of the new incentive zoning is growth, albeit related to economics. Growth, too, is the major characteristic of cancer."

City officials have always favored growth—it has never been politically healthy not to. New buildings, after all, mean much more than profits for the real-estate industry; they mean jobs for office workers and tax collections for the city. But the city has rarely planned its future with any real vigor or determination—it has tended to react to situations, not to control them. Incentive zoning, for example, was based on the assumption that real-estate developers could not simply be required to build in a certain way—that they had to be given a carrot if they were to submit to the stick of serving the public. The carrot, of course, turned out to be so enormous as to constitute a problem in itself—and the stick a mere twig.

Even now, when the incentive zoning gimmicks of the 1960's and 1970's have been privately, if not publicly, disavowed by many planners, the city is timid. It has tried to encourage staggered working hours and nighttime truck deliveries, but with only limited success, for to mandate such things is difficult, and they do not appear likely to happen out of goodwill.

Where the city does have the power to mandate, in matters such as zoning, it has been slow. The new zoning law for midtown Manhattan, enacted last year under City Planning Commission Chairman Herbert Sturz, makes an earnest and thoughtful attempt to "stabilize" growth in overcrowded east midtown and to shift it to west midtown blocks instead. But the city studied and debated the issue for so long (as builders continued to build) that the new ordinance, when finally passed, came far too late to make much difference.

The law tries to limit growth mainly by increasing the maximum permitted building bulk on the West Side and lowering it on the East Side. To a certain extent, development is shifting to the West Side anyway, if only because so little space is now left on the East Side for very large buildings. There is nowhere on the East Side that the complex of office towers being planned as part of the city and state's redevelopment of Times Square could have fit, and there is no question that this sort of large-scale project can do far more good for the city at Times Square than across town. But the new East Side limits are just enough to irritate real-estate developers, and not enough to make any really major differences in the cityscape. If the economy justifies it, still more buildings will be squeezed into every corner and niche that can be found on the East Side; the only difference is that they will be a tad smaller.

What can be done? It is difficult to argue against density and active new building in New York, since these are the city's lifeblood. New York is supposed to be a crowded city, it is supposed to be a city constantly renewing itself, and it is a city that thrives on a certain degree of disorder. There is no question that the somewhat irrational, helter-skelter New York of Jane Jacobs is vastly preferable to the all-too-rational, perfectly planned city of Lewis Mumford.

Indeed, it is because of a new generation of urbanists, inspired in part by Mrs. Jacobs, that we tend to feel as we do now about congestion—that we realize it can often be an enlivening force rather than a destructive one. So there is no longer a serious belief, as there was during the heyday of wholesale urban renewal in the 1950's and early 1960's, that the way to improve a city is to tear it down and place neat modern buildings in ordered rows amid empty space. But to approve of dense, congested cities in principle is hardly to applaud a city in which land has such inflated value that virtually any building that makes the mistake of being less than a monolith is under threat of extinction.

The frantic rush of development puts special pressure on landmark buildings, since they are almost by definition not monoliths, and smaller than what is legally permitted on their sites—as well as less profitable. The way in which landmarks may be saved—or at least the means that seems to be currently fashionable among planners—is through a complex process known as transfer of development rights, or air rights. The idea is simply that since landmark buildings tend to be smaller than the buildings the zoning law permits on their sites, the unused air over them constitutes a financial asset that can be sold and transferred to another site, thus preserving the landmark and permitting its owners some financial gain.

The city now permits the transfer of air rights from landmarks to adjacent properties, but does not allow it to take place in any other circumstance. It is a concept full of potential—one prominent New York developer, for example, has indicated his interest in saving Lever House if the city would permit him to "jump" air rights several blocks away—but it is also fraught with problems.

For instance, if a landmark is to be saved by the sale of its air rights, who is to set a value on those rights? Can they be sold on the open market to the highest bidder? And then, where can the air rights be transferred? The reason St. Bartholomew's is so eager to build its glass tower is because its land on Park Avenue is so valuable—if the city were to permit those development rights to be transferred to another neighborhood, it would almost certainly be to a site of lesser value, and St. Bartholomew's would not profit as much.

Even if such problems could be solved, how would the city be able to keep the "market" of air rights from overflowing and govern fair use of them? If St. Bartholomew's, which has actually agreed to lease part of its land for a skyscraper, were permitted to transfer these development rights elsewhere, would not St. Patrick's Cathedral have the right to demand the same treatment, whether or not it were in fact really considering a similar transaction of its own? The city government is itself considering a plan to sell off air rights over city-owned properties as a means of increasing city income. The plan, if enacted, could make the city government more of a contributor to this problem than a solution to it.

Even if transferable rights were restricted to landmark buildings, the Landmarks Preservation Commission estimates this would release an extra 9 million square feet of potentially transferable building space, enough to depress the market so sharply that the rights would no longer have enough value to subsidize the very landmarks their sale was intended to save. And worse still, letting another 9 million square feet of potential development—the equivalent of another World Trade Center—float around Manhattan would only make the problem of too much building all the worse.

What the city has never attempted is a drastic change of the principles governing its planning—a complete rethinking of the way midtown Manhattan's building rules are written in the first place. The revised zoning laws adopted last year to push development westward are only a tentative beginning; cynics might liken them to a rearrangement of deck chairs on the *Titanic*, and while this is a bit of an exaggeration—sheer and total disaster will never come to mid-Manhattan, no matter how dangerously we flirt with it—it is only fair to note that the Department of City Planning's environmental-impact statement for the new zoning states that "the first goal of the proposed action is to encourage, not discourage, midtown development. . . . It is not in the city's interest to halt or even slow new midtown development."

While the new law is intelligent and thoughtful, it is in effect a piece of tinkering, not a new way of looking at the city. There is still no answer to the underlying problem of zoning, which is: what happens when everyone wants to build to the utmost? It is a kind of paradox, in fact—to be legal, constitutional, and fair, a zoning law must treat all properties within a certain area equally. But it is precisely this equal treatment that causes the problem. One 50-story tower

Atop the A.T.&T. building

every six or eight blocks, with medium and smaller buildings filling in the streetscape between them, would be a workable, even pleasing, density. But who is to determine which block gets the tower, and which are kept smaller? Who is to prevent a windfall for the lucky owner of the site on which the city permits the one big building?

The most appealing sort of plan is, unfortunately, the most radical—and the sort that would be likely to be challenged in court as an excessive exercise of the city's zoning power. But here is a proposal: it is tempting to wonder what would happen if the city were to decide on a drastic "downzoning," or reduction of the normal allowable bulk, throughout midtown, and then declare that it owns the air rights for all larger development. It would sell to developers the right to build more than the small amount to which they are automatically entitled— with the understanding that the city would sell only so many square feet of extra development rights within any area of a few square blocks, thus preventing huge towers from rising up one beside the other. For example, one might imagine every block on Seventh Avenue in the Forties being legally entitled to a building that, if it filled the blockfront, would be only 10 stories high. Within that area the city would offer for sale (perhaps to the highest bidder) a limited amount of extra development rights, which could be purchased by each owner to permit his site to contain a somewhat larger building, or could be purchased by one or two owners to permit their sites to contain substantially larger structures. All of Seventh Avenue might be developed to a height of 20 stories, for example, or there could be several buildings at the automatic 10-story height and one rising to 50 stories—but the prospect of several towers of 50-plus stories, one after the other, would be precluded.

It is, of course, far too late for such a system to be enacted on overbuilt Madison and Park avenues, and there is reason to question whether it could work in a city in which an altogether different philosophy of zoning—a philosophy that implicity encourages maximum development—has been in practice for years. Moreover, the value of land would probably decline, since the only thing keeping land prices as high as they are is the potential for building enormous structures on almost any site—which of course sets in motion the vicious cycle of high land costs then requiring huge buildings to make those initial costs justifiable.

Such a new kind of zoning is a radical notion, one not likely to win friends in the real-estate industry or among city officials, who would have to redesign their existing system entirely. But it is at least as equitable, and at least as responsive to the free market, as the present system—indeed, it is in some ways more laissez-faire, for it reserves the privilege of building large for the highest bidder. It would mean only that everyone could not build to the maximum everywhere—that once the development rights in a six- or eight-block area were used up, no more large development could occur unless a big building was removed to make way for it.

No city has yet attempted such a total shift of its view on zoning—but there is considerable rethinking going on in several major cities as they struggle, admittedly with less urgency than New York, to address the problems of overbuilt downtowns.

For the first time there is serious talk about the possibility of some zoning restrictions in Houston, a city that has prided itself on being the ultimate example of laissez-faire urban growth, but which is coming to realize that unfettered growth can threaten the very vitality it is supposed to encourage. Indeed, concern over the congestion caused by Houston's immense growth was a major factor in the election last year of Kathryn Whitmire, the current mayor, who argued during the campaign that the city's expansion would require more stringent management and planning.

In San Francisco, opposition to the large amount of skyscraper construction that has taken place in the last decade—San Franciscans, with little respect, refer to it as the "Manhattanization" of their city—was substantial enough to lead to a referendum in 1979 to consider virtually banning high-rise construction downtown. The proposal was defeated—but since then the city government has begun to study the standards it sets for skyscraper construction, with an eye to a different set of restrictions.

Pittsburgh has tried to guide its downtown development with urban-design controls that are among the nation's most sophisticated and to pay particular attention to maintaining light, views, and well-defined open space.

Perhaps the most innovative zoning right now, however, is Denver's. Some years ago that city initiated a system of incentive zoning based on New York's, but, disturbed by its failure to guide development sufficiently, Denver recently cut back sharply the plaza bonus it granted to developers, increased urban design controls to limit the scale of new construction, and put into effect an experimental program permitting the transfer of air rights to more than adjacent sites around the downtown area—the nation's first major city to enact such legislation.

For New York, it is impossible—though tempting—to say that without a complete rethinking of our way of planning only chaos is ahead. The city is not likely to collapse, this year or this decade if ten new skyscrapers are built or a hundred. New York is remarkably resilient, and its total strangulation is not the issue. What is likely to happen is not collapse, but something far less dramatic—a slow, steady increase in the noise and the tension and the crowding and the shadows. Such changes are impossible to quantify, impossible to measure in absolute terms. But they are certain to come—if they are not already here.

—November 14, 1982

The Narrow Parisian Vista

When skyscrapers began to edge their way into Paris a few years ago, there was a predictable outcry. Paris is being destroyed, said the preservationists, and they predicted that the City of Light would be indistinguishable from Manhattan in no time. Enough has gone up in Paris to make the city ripe for reevaluation, and the outcome is not quite what one might have expected. On the one hand, a small victory: most construction has been restricted to the city's periphery, keeping the central sector relatively intact. On the other hand, the new buildings in and around Paris have been designed to an extraordinarily low standard—so low that the modern architecture of the city may, arguably, be called the worst in the world.

Building anything new in Paris is bound to be difficult, of course—the consistent size and materials of older structures have created a unified urban texture that has prevailed for decades, and anything that disturbs this is going to be greeted with skepticism if not hostility. But there are ways to build sensitively in the twentieth century without either disturbing what is there or making a mockery of modern architecture. Unfortunately, few architects here seem to have found them, and the result is a city that has been doubly insulted—once by simply being torn asunder, and again by being torn asunder by such bad design.

The partly successful attempt to restrict development to the periphery is to the city's credit. Nonetheless, projects such as Maine-Montparnasse, a 56-story tower near the Montparnasse railway station, and the development called Front de Seine, along the river near the Eiffel Tower, do cut sharply into the city's heart. (One local art critic calls Front de Seine "Affront to Seine.")

Front de Seine,
Paris

59

Other projects away from the center seem to make up in poor design for the damage they are unable to inflict by location. Among these is La Défense which, at more than thirty buildings and still growing, is one of the most ambitious office and housing developments anywhere. The complex occupies a crucial site: it is in Nanterre, a suburb, right on axis with the Champs-Elysées and the Arc de Triomphe, one of the most powerful of urban vistas. Once the vista was clear; now distant skyscrapers loom behind the arch.

It might be forgivable if it was better. But the towers of La Défense are an incoherent jumble, looking like the worst of American urban renewal of the early 1960's, blown up to huge scale. There is an enormous and desolate central open space, designed to offer at least some protection to the vista from the Arc de Triomphe. The towers that surround it are grouped without rhyme or reason and are all different in design. Yet somehow the total impression is not one of variety or vitality but of utter dullness, as if the architects, lacking ideas, had simply tried every silly facade design they could think of.

There are, incidentally, some buildings by such American architects as Skidmore, Owings & Merrill and Harrison & Abramovitz. Although virtually identical to the firms' dull New York work, they are the essence of dignity here.

The compulsion to decorate surfaces seems quintessentially French. It runs through the history of the national architecture, which has generally been more concerned with surface than with either form or space; now the French seem to have decided to let it solve the problems of modern construction as well. As a result La Défense is full of buildings with fussy window designs, stamped-out panels like those on the Tishman Building on Fifth Avenue, divided metal strips that have nothing to do with structure but are merely set in an abstract pattern.

This, too, is wrong not so much in principle as in execution: decoration done well is becoming increasingly common as we move away from the early modern movement's hatred of ornament. However, the bulk of the new French architecture seems to be able to use decoration only as a means of cheapening itself. The buildings of Front de Seine that now crowd the view of the Eiffel Tower from the south look gimmicky; those around the Place d'Italie, another development area, look tinny; and the Maine-Montparnasse tower—the symbol, to foreigners at least, of Paris gone wrong—looks like the building that starred in *The Towering Inferno*.

Unfortunately, the situation is not much better with regard to housing. Mediocre apartments are springing up, particularly in the increasingly fashionable Fifteenth Arrondissement, and they are being marketed with an aggressiveness that resembles American buildings; as in New York, the style is added by the public-relations man, not the architect.

More interesting are the new towns being built in the environs. Like the guidelines restricting skyscrapers to the city's edges, they are good in principle. Most important, they are a device to prevent urban sprawl by concentrating development in the rapidly growing region into five small areas. The problem, again, is in execution.

The new towns are in varying stages of completion, and none are more than a few years old, so it is far too early for a final evaluation. Architecturally at least the outlook is not promising. The same tendencies that apply in large-scale commercial architecture—silly gimmicks of surface decoration instead of any real understanding of materials, spaces, or architectural form—seem to apply.

At Evry, sixteen miles south of Paris, most of the housing is a densely packed series of blocks, massed in an imitation of Moshe Safdie's superb Habitat housing in Montreal. But the imitation is crude: prefab panels of different materials are used on different sides, creating a jarring effect. One side is an odd pinkish color; another is green with a leaf design stamped, fossil-like, on all the panels; and another side is false brick with mock-Tudor detailing. The idea of architecture as stage set has been carried to the grotesque.

Much of the housing makes lavish use of color, so the French preoccupation with surfaces begins to pay off. Color is being used as a crutch; since the architects seem to have no better ideas, one is grateful for at least this injection of life. Brash color is particularly evident at Cergy Pontoise, a new town northwest of Paris where the police station is a bright royal blue; a school has yellow, red, green, and purple wings; and an apartment tower is in several shades of blue, growing lighter toward the sky.

Much of the color architecture is the work of younger Frenchmen, who are applying color to casual angular forms like those used by such architects as Charles Moore in the United States, deliberately rejecting the formality of much French design.

This group takes its cue from Emile Aillaud, seventy-three years old, the leading "enfant terrible" of postwar French architecture. His buildings are the only ones going up in this country these days that even approach real wit, and it is a positive sign that his influence is gaining.

Among his best-known works is La Grande Borne, an enormous low-rise housing project decorated with mosaic murals and huge pop sculptures of concrete, including one of a pair of ten-foot pigeons; a series of amoeba-shaped apartment towers with round windows; and a plan to terminate the vista at La Défense with a great mirror-glass building, reflecting the Arc de Triomphe. Although the Aillaud work is not profound, it is at least irreverent, something that little in French architecture since Le Corbusier has dared to be.

Why is the situation so bad? In part architecture, like that in New York, is largely controlled by developers. Eager to ride the boom of the mid-1960's, the government imposed few restrictions on development. Real-estate entrepreneurs, in the words of a commentator who compared city planning to a self-service restaurant, were invited to help themselves to Paris. Such an arrangement rarely yields design quality.

This is a problem shared by the United States, yet the standard is even lower here. One reason may be the French bureaucracy, which seems to discourage any innovative design that does not fit into narrow building codes. A still deeper problem may be the strong hold the traditional Beaux-Arts academy held on architectural education for so much of this century; while the Beaux Arts exerted a powerful influence worldwide, it prevented France from developing a strong tradition of capable modern designers when other countries were doing so.

Modern architecture, in other words, was considered totally unacceptable for far too long, and now that it is in demand there is little the French seem to be able to do except lift examples from other countries and add a few surface frills.

All is not a wasteland architecturally. The new modern art museum, Centre Georges Pompidou, a structure of glass and steel trusses due for completion in 1977, will be of international significance. And the French continue strong in their odd talent for the creation of fascinating science-fiction–like modern spaces, most recently in the new Charles de Gaulle Airport, where Plexiglas people-moving tubes crisscross in a large central space. Lastly, there is a growing amount of pressure in Paris to halt careless speculative development before the special qualities of the city are lost.

What has happened in and around Paris is perhaps the ultimate irony, given the history of modern architecture. In 1925, Le Corbusier, the greatest French architect of modern times, proposed that much of Paris be demolished and a series of huge towers, widely spaced, be erected in its place. The misguided proposal, rejected as unthinkable, became the basis for the "tower in the park" approach to urban renewal around the world. Now, in the form of La Défense and the other developments, it has come to roost in Paris at last.

—*July 18, 1975*
Paris

The Jerusalem Skyline

The new Jerusalem

Not long ago Mayor Teddy Kollek enthusiastically showed visitors the new structures on the way up in this ancient city. Now he seems to point with as much pride to the projects he has helped to prevent. And he talks of the city's need to "learn from its mistakes."

Jerusalem, which a 1968 master plan foresaw as an American vision of skyscrapers and freeways, has now begun to change its mind. Plans for highways that were to cut through old residential neighborhoods are being dropped, permits to build high-rise structures are being less readily granted, and Mayor Kollek talks of his desire to make his multicultural city "a mosaic, not a melting pot."

The change in mood is due in part to the recession, in part to generally scaled-down ambitions since the 1973 war. But it is also a result of continued international criticism of the ways of city planning here.

In 1970 a group of international experts, known as the Jerusalem Committee, was invited by the city to evaluate its planning. The group denounced the master plan as appalling and, in so doing, made the physical future of Jerusalem an issue of world concern.

At that time, the Israelis of Jerusalem, eager to assert the new prosperity that came after the city's unification in 1967, were on a vast building spree. Skyscraper hotels altered its classic skyline; housing projects covered the once empty hillsides, aggressively injecting the Israeli presence into former Jordanian lands.

The recent turnaround has not been easy for Mayor Kollek, a jovial figure who might be called the La Guardia of Jerusalem. An ardent civic booster, he helped line up a great deal of the city's new construction. Now he seems to have conceded that much of the building has not been in Jerusalem's long-term interest. And he makes no secret of his distaste for the most conspicuous recent addition to the Jerusalem skyline, the 17-story Plaza Hotel, a bloated version of a Miami Beach tower that sits in Independence Park.

The Plaza is one of the saddest legacies of the city's 1960's planning approach: its land had been set aside for a city hall, and when that project was postponed, government officials, eager to promote the Israeli economy at any cost, turned the land over to hotel developers.

More towers are still on the way up in Jerusalem, so the skyline, dramatically altered since 1967, will change more. But city officials point out that building permits for these structures were issued years ago and cannot be rescinded, and they cite cases of other planned towers—such as a 24-story Hyatt House Hotel proposed for the top of Mount Scopus—that they were able to cancel.

The new humility in Jerusalem is by no means total, and the city is sharply divided on a number of planning questions. But there is an increasing sense here, as in the United States, that large-scale building and massive redevelopment often extract a price that is not worth paying—if not in dollars and cents, in the quality of urban life.

In Jerusalem this is particularly so. This is a city of low, small-scale buildings; even those on Jaffa Road, the main commercial street, are rarely more than three stories high.

Outside the walls of the Old City, which was in Jordanian hands until 1967, there are tranquil neighborhoods just a block or two from the central business district, with alleyways, old shops and houses, courtyards and gardens. Some quarters cover only a few square blocks, yet each retains a sense of identity— from Mahane Yehuda, a market that is a cross between an Arab bazaar and Covent Garden, to the religious community of Shaarei Hesed, a tight enclave of row houses with a common garden.

All buildings throughout the city are, by law, covered with Jerusalem stone, a rich, textured stone with a warm, pinkish hue. Together with the rich blue of the clear Jerusalem sky, the deep red of the old tile roofs, and the green trees, the stone gives the city a remarkable unity of color, subtle yet strong.

More impressive still is Jerusalem's topography, the hills and valleys over which this muted assemblage of color flows. The desert is to the east and the mountains are to the west, with the city providing the transition from one landscape to another.

It is—or was, before 1967—one of the most remarkable cases of city and nature in dialogue with each other. But it is all a very delicate balance, capable of being damaged far more seriously by insensitive building than more resilient urban landscapes such as that of New York or Los Angeles.

Jerusalem has not been destroyed by any means, and hysterical voices suggesting that it is already too late are not what the city needs now. But the city's critics have been important in reminding its leaders that, whatever their aspirations, they are dealing with a place that is not able to accommodate development on the American scale comfortably.

The problem of planning Jerusalem is made more complex by other factors. The city has a sacred role for three major religions, each with its own set of holy places. And Jerusalem's social problems are serious: there is a large welfare population; next year 22 percent of the budget, Mayor Kollek says, will go for debt service, a far higher proportion than in New York.

Most difficult of all is the unique situation of Arab East Jerusalem and Israeli West Jerusalem, now merged under one Israeli administration. This annexation is not the same as the absorption of immigrant cultures, as has happened for generations in New York, but presents an entirely different set of problems.

The Israeli government reacted to the unification of Jerusalem with zeal, thrusting enormous new housing projects into former Jordanian territory and, not incidentally, building for the first time on many of the unspoiled hills to the north and south. It was a cogent reminder that architecture is often at bottom a political tool; the government's desire was not so much to improve housing conditions as it was to establish a significant presence in captured territory.

As a result many of the projects were erected hastily and with little care, although there is a certain amount of variation among them. The best, oddly, was the first to be finished: Ramat Eshkol, to the northwest, occupied in 1970. It is a decent array of 4- and 5-story structures, faced in Jerusalem stone and arrayed around open space, with pedestrian areas separated from vehicular roads. Although it is not elegant, it is above the level of most publicly sponsored housing in the United States.

Less successful is the enormous French Hill development on a site to the northwest that still contains Jordanian battle trenches. From afar, French Hill

The new Jerusalem

reads as an inconspicuous low wall atop a mountain; close up it is more like Co-op City, lowered by a few stories and sheathed in Jerusalem stone. (The stone, incidentally, should be given some sort of citation by the Israeli architectural profession; it has succeeded in making a great deal of very bad architecture bearable.)

These projects, and the several others still going up around Jerusalem, are the works of the central government's Ministry of Housing, not of the city government. The city has protested against some of the more arrogant designs, but the central government has ultimate control over all Jerusalem planning matters, so the protests have been largely a matter of form and politics.

More significant, perhaps, was the ouster of five staff architects of the Ministry of Housing in 1971 for their involvement in public protests against an enormous project planned for a hill adjacent to Nebi Samuamuwil, the tomb of the Prophet Samuel. It was to no avail; the project is nearing completion.

In areas in which the city government has at least partial freedom to act, it has been planning with far more responsibility than in the past. Meron Benvenisti, a hulking, gruff-voiced historian who is Mayor Kollek's deputy mayor for planning, has played a large role in turning the city's planning philosophy around, dropping projected expressways—one was to have gone through the Mahane Yehuda market—and arguing against even the idea of a master plan.

"What you need is not a scheme based on projections for the year 2000 but a set of principles based on what people see from their windows," he said. "If this city teaches you anything it should teach you to have more modesty than any other city."

Mr. Benvenisti and the Planning Department have been working on neighborhood preservation. They rely heavily on the techniques New York and other American cities have been experimenting with: the transfer of development rights, the setting up of special funds for neighborhood improvement, and special zoning tailored to area needs.

In Jerusalem these needs have often been strikingly different from what they might be in New York. One neighborhood, Mea Shearim, a quarter inhabited by an extremely zealous Orthodox sect, has been troubled by the departure of its younger married couples, who want more space than their immigrant parents were used to. To keep the area together the city has waived zoning restrictions to permit the erection of a third floor on several buildings; in exchange the owners will combine lower floors to create larger apartments.

Even in its large-scale development the city seems now, five years after the Jerusalem Committee's denunciation, to have come to terms with a more modest approach. A project for the rebuilding of the Jewish Quarter of the Old City by the architects Shlomo Aronson and Peter Bugod is modest in scale and attempts to repeat the arches and light wells of the adjacent buildings, which date from the Crusades; if anything, its problem may be that it is too derivative and too romantic.

An attempt at a middle ground between new and old and large and small has been made in two proposals by Moshe Safdie, the Israel-born Canadian architect who designed Habitat, the housing at Expo '67 in Montreal. Both are up for public discussion and are proving controversial.

The first project is a large mixed-use urban-renewal development for the Mamilla area, a near-slum that crosses the former border near the Jaffa Gate to the walled Old City. Containing no high-rise elements, it is a set of buildings terraced downward to a central open space that will function as a spine through the area. Traffic is to be run underground through much of the project, and an artificial terrace is to be built over the depressed roadway next to the walls of the Old City. The structures themselves are simple and appropriate in scale, with a few modern details such as quarter-sphere glass domes.

Nonetheless, the project has been criticized in some Jerusalem circles, largely on the ground that at 1.5 million square feet it is too grandiose. Putting aside the obvious fact that if such criticism can be made of a low-rise project, the residents of this city have become a lot more sophisticated in the last few years, it is an interesting argument cutting to the very core of the problems facing Jerusalem.

For the people here, as in America, are beginning to question large-scale development in any form, even when it is as well-designed as the Safdie project. They may well reach a point where they will decide that at this moment in their city's history they would rather build nothing at all.

That would be unfortunate since Mamilla is a sensitive design that could probably be scaled down successfully. Mr. Safdie's other proposal, an enormous amphitheater-like array of terraced buildings to face the Western, or Wailing, Wall in the Old City, poses greater problems. The wall, a frequent site of prayer, is revered as the only remnant of the Jewish Temple destroyed by the Romans; until the 1967 war it was in Jordanian hands. Formerly, it was reached by a set of narrow alleys, an approach of tremendous drama. After the war Israel cleared blocks of Arab housing adjacent to the wall to create a huge temporary plaza—an unattractive space that the Safdie design was commissioned to replace.

Whether an elaborate set of terraces is the appropriate environment for this somber shrine is a question that remains. It brings to the fore all the problems of planning in Jerusalem: the sensitivity of holy places, the relation of new buildings to old, the difficulty of reworking an ancient environment to fit modern needs without destroying its essence. As is the case with most of the problems Jerusalem faces, there is no precedent.

—July 8, 1975
Jerusalem

New Orleans and the Fight
for a Livable City

The City Council here recently extended legislation halting demolition in several of this city's downtown sections, originally passed last year, through 1975. An active group of historic preservationists is working to establish historic districts. And the city government is exploring legal mechanisms, such as zoning, to assure the preservation of New Orleans's rich architectural heritage.

It would seem, given these signs, that this southern city has managed to avoid the cataclysmic effects of the large-scale urban development that ravaged so many American cities in recent years. But statistics show otherwise.

In New Orleans's central business district, one out of five buildings that stood in 1970 is gone now. Several modern skyscrapers, all of them undistinguished, break the scale. And 42 percent of all the land, not counting streets, is vacant—much of it cleared by developers before building plans were certain and now used for parking lots.

What makes New Orleans different from most American cities is the extent to which its citizens have joined together to stem the tide of speculative development— even though, as many of them admit, some of their efforts are now too late. But the climate of opinion has changed dramatically all the same.

A couple of years ago the main topic of discussion was the Superdome, New Orleans's attempt to overwhelm Houston's Astrodome. Now it is the demolition moratorium, a preservation move more drastic in the opinion of many preservationists than anything any other city government has yet tried.

The moratorium is intended merely as a stopgap mea-

One Shell Square
towers over
the French Quarter
(New Orleans)

69

sure to stem the tide of demolition in the city's central business district until more complex regulations can be instituted. Not long ago the downtown area was a splendid array of nineteenth-century Greek revival, Italianate, and cast-iron buildings, working together to form a superbly scaled streetscape and an outstanding urban whole.

The buildings began to go in the early 1970's, largely in response to development pressures released by the Superdome and by the fear of many of the city's business leaders that New Orleans, which had thus far seen almost none of the boom-town growth of so many American cities in the 1960's, was being passed by. Skyscrapers began to shoot up on Poydras Street, entire blocks were demolished purely to speculate against rising land values, and suddenly the essence of downtown New Orleans was gone.

"Those were the dark ages," recalls Roulhac Toledano, the wife of a leading lawyer and one of the city's most ardent preservationists. "No one valued anything unless it was in the French Quarter—the finest building in town could be across the street and there would be no way to save it."

The French Quarter, or Vieux Carré, has enjoyed legal protection since 1937. But its buildings, laced with the ironwork that has become a trademark of this city, are only a small part of New Orleans's valuable architectural inventory.

And in its brief "boom" period the city was, in fact, tearing down things right across the street from the French Quarter—such as a nine-square-block section of Treme, a black neighborhood of superb nineteenth-century wooden cottages. Treme was cleared between 1956 and 1973 for a citywide cultural center, an urban-renewal project that raised such protests that it was abandoned. Now, a park to be dedicated to Louis Armstrong is under construction on the site.

A similar attempt at a traditional sort of urban-renewal scheme, a riverfront expressway originally proposed for the city by Robert Moses, was defeated by citizen protest in 1971.

The battle over the expressway "had all the intensity of the segregation debates," said Bill Rushton, managing editor and architecture writer for the *Vieux Carré Courier*, a local weekly, "and it was the turning point in the city's mood."

Many New Orleanians consider Mr. Rushton, who has been writing about the local architecture scene since 1969, to have been a major factor himself in the change of public opinion in New Orleans. He was the city's first architecture critic, and has now been joined by Jack Davis, formerly an investigative reporter for *The New Orleans States-Item*.

The city's preservation effort is different from that of most American cities for two not unrelated reasons. One is the broad base of support it seems, quite suddenly, to enjoy. "Preservation is motherhood now," as Renna Godchaux, one of Mayor Moon Landrieu's staff members, puts it.

New Orleanians have long prided themselves on the fact that their city, by far the most European in feeling of all eastern cities, was not like other places, and the traditional Chamber of Commerce–type values of progress at any price have turned out to be less potent than expected here.

The other distinctive aspect to the New Orleans effort is that it has skipped the initial impulse to designate individual landmarks. The French Quarter has always been viewed as a *toute ensemble*, or an entire grouping, and this tradition has made itself felt in the desire to create historic districts.

The city is now on the verge of establishing its first two historic districts, which will incorporate the lower Garden district, a residential quarter rich in the gingerbread wood architecture characteristic of New Orleans, and St. Charles Avenue, where the great mansions that once defined the street have been disappearing at a rapid rate.

In the lower Garden district, middle-class families, often young professionals, are restoring the old frame houses. Much as in New York's restored brownstone areas, real-estate values are rising sharply, but with the improvements come problems—namely, the retention of the area's integrated population mix.

In conjunction with the Chamber of Commerce—"which once thought we were useless, and now thinks we're angels," in the words of one preservationist—the city government has commissioned Wallace, McHarg, Roberts & Todd of Philadelphia to prepare a $190,000 study, called the Growth Management Plan, to guide the development of downtown.

Perhaps the most telling indication of the new mood in New Orleans is the fact that builders—traditionally the enemies of historic preservation efforts—are now talking preservation. Joseph C. Canizaro, a major landowner who is planning a large mixed-use development at the foot of Canal Street adjacent to the French Quarter, says he wants it to work in with the low-rise quality of the quarter.

"Old buildings are one of our resources," Mr. Canizaro said recently. "They are how we keep the city livable."

—March 21, 1975
New Orleans

San Francisco: A Cliché Comes Home to Roost

It is not for nothing that this city likes to think of itself as the most beautiful in the nation. Even with the recent boom in construction of downtown skyscrapers, a boom that has turned the financial district into something that looks more like Chicago's Loop than anything San Franciscan, the city retains an aura of lightness and grace that distinguishes it from every other American metropolis.

San Francisco is whites and pastels and low stucco houses and views to the bay as much as it is cable cars and steep hills, and all of these things join to create the city's physical identity. But beautiful places, rather like beautiful people, often have crucial flaws, and San Francisco's might best be characterized as a certain coyness, an excessive cuteness. It is a quality that has been around for years, but lately it seems on the rise—perhaps because San Franciscans, concerned that their downtown was beginning to look like other places, are trying too hard to make the rest of their town look different.

Or perhaps it is because so much of the rest of the United States has become so homogeneous and dull that anything else stands out. In any case, one senses today that this city knows its beauty, and it tends more and more to be self-conscious about it.

These thoughts are occasioned by a visit to an enormous new development on this city's waterfront, a restaurant, shopping, and entertainment complex called Pier 39. The name, which comes from that of the old shipping pier that was in the complex's location, is the only matter-of-fact thing about the place. Pier 39 is a gaggle of overdesigned places, all with cute names ("Just in Case" is a leather shop, "Whittler's Mother" is a wood-carving shop) and architectural details that strain

Pier 39, San Francisco

73

so hard for cuteness and prettiness that they lead one to cry out for a fluorescent-lighted supermarket.

The construction of Pier 39, which was sponsored by a developer named Warren Simmons and designed by Walker Moody, aroused considerable controversy among San Franciscans concerned about the direction their city was taking. Their fears are justified. This place is an amusement pier, not a development that emerges naturally out of San Francisco's character. It is designed for crowds so large that it was necessary to build a 1,000-car parking garage just beside it—a huge concrete bunker that belies all the low-scale modesty of the place itself.

Pier 39's buildings, which jut far out into San Francisco Bay, are of wood, and they do try hard to establish an air of low-rise, village-like casualness. There is a long central walkway of wooden planks, nicely laid out so that you do not walk to the end of the pier in a straight line, but turn several times.

The central walk opens into wide spaces intended to function as village squares, where there is often such entertainment as high-divers and mimes. The stores and restaurants are on two levels, and there are frequent flights of wooden steps to allow an easy and natural up-and-down flow of people.

But layout is Pier 39's only strong point. The design of the development itself, with all its candy shops, glass shops, toy shops, T-shirt shops, and the like is not only too cute, it is all wrong for San Francisco. Wooden buildings that have the air of farmhouses and sea shanties might be right for Nantucket, but they have no more to do with San Francisco than they do with Los Angeles. One wonders if this whole place wasn't put on the wrong coast by mistake.

The wood is probably an attempt to get away from the cliché of exposed brick, which certainly has become trite in this kind of design. But wood is no better, at least not when it is so obviously faked up as it is at Pier 39. It just comes off as trying too hard, rather like the Kentucky Fried Chicken outlet across the bay in Mill Valley, Marin County. That establishment has been sheathed in redwood for "good taste."

It's in good taste, all right, and surely free of the vulgarity of the highway strip, but at the price of a lot of fakery. A redwood fast-food outlet may be earnest in its intentions, but it is about as convincing as a truck driver in Gucci loafers.

The ancestor of Pier 39, oddly enough, is just down the road—Ghiradelli Square, the deservedly acclaimed complex completed in 1967 to the designs of Wurster, Bernardi & Emmons and Lawrence Halprin & Associates. Ghiradelli Square, once the site of a chocolate factory, pioneered not only in the notion of "recycling" of older buildings for new uses, but it was also the original cute, in-town restaurant and shopping complex. When it was finished, it seemed dazzlingly fresh—candle shops and little restaurants, lots of exposed brick and old-fashioned lettering all around an open space that could function like a village square.

Ghiradelli Square itself still looks splendid. But it was too successful for its own good. It took no time at all for imitations to spring up all around the country, until exposed brick and flickering gaslights were enough to send one rushing toward Howard Johnson's. Ironically, the places that were intended to create a "sense of place" ended up being so copied that they became as anonymous as a Holiday Inn.

The final irony is Pier 39; the cliché has come home to roost in San Francisco, and the most trite imitator of Ghiradelli Square has turned up just down the road from the original. What few differences Pier 39 has are all negatives—the mistaken use of wood, the amusement section, which creates the air of a boardwalk (this section is called the "Palace of Fun Arts," a pun on the Palace of Fine Arts, the San Francisco landmark).

It is all an attempt to make the mass-produced place look individualized, and it fails. It is unfortunate that it should happen in San Francisco, a city that, these days, needs less cuteness, not more, if it is to save itself. The things that Pier 39 wants to celebrate—street life, human encounters, entertainment, eating, people-watching—are all valid and necessary, but San Francisco is already full of them.

The real city is right there, waiting to be experienced, and we are offered, instead, an artificial substitute. It is a case of the cute and the make-believe triumphing.

—April 2, 1979
San Francisco

Baltimore: An Urban Success Story

This seems to be the year of Baltimore. This old seaport city, which has had a relationship to Washington not unlike that of Oakland to San Francisco or Newark to New York, has put great effort into changing its image. It has built office, apartment, and hotel towers downtown, it has restored old townhouses, and it has turned the Inner Harbor, the portion of the shoreline closest to downtown, into a mixture of shopping, entertainment, and cultural facilities.

Baltimore has, in short, been trying to get on the bandwagon of such cities as Boston and San Francisco. It wants to be thought of not as a harsh, crime-ridden city, but as a community of middle-class professionals, all in love with the idea of living in a vibrant downtown.

National magazines, thrilled to discover another Cinderella among cities, have filled their pages with color photographs of Baltimoreans sitting in chic new cafes and shopping for exotic produce in expensive new markets. Most of the publicity has focused on one particular area, a development called Harborplace, right beside the water at the Inner Harbor. Harborplace is a mixture of restaurants, shops, boutiques, cafes, and food markets, all put together by the Rouse Company, one of the most prescient real-estate developers in the nation. Rouse built the "new town" of Columbia, Maryland, and a huge string of suburban shopping centers before discovering the potential of a certain kind of urban shopping area when it opened the Faneuil Hall Marketplace in Boston in August 1978.

Harborplace is an attempt to bring the success of the Faneuil Hall markets to Baltimore. There are many similarities. The architect, Benjamin Thompson, is the same, and so is the general drift of the design. And the goal is certainly the same: to provide a mixture of food, merchandise, and social experiences that will seem "urban" in a way that the mixture of food, merchandise, and social experiences in a shopping mall on a freeway does not.

At this, Harborplace is a stunning success. It was Rouse's genius to realize that Baltimore, although not as fabled a center of young professionals as Boston, was still full of urbanites with no place to go. People come to Harborplace not only to shop but also to promenade and to see one another.

In retrospect, it is no surprise that Harborplace had 7 million visitors in the first three months after its official opening last July, reaching in that period the visitor totals projected by Rouse for the entire year. The rents to merchants are high and the prices to consumers are hardly low, but there seems to be enough room for profit for everyone in this venture.

The place itself is handsome and understated, free of the exposed brick and gas lamps that are a feature of so many meccas for the new urbanites. The cuteness reflex seems to have been kept under control here, if not entirely eliminated.

Mr. Thompson's design of the two main pavilions that house all the shops and markets is admirably restrained. The pavilions are two stories high, with a lot of glass and with green metal shed roofs. There are tile floors and wonderful heavy-glass Holophane light sconces, and there is a dark-green trim to add a sense of dignity. Many of the restaurants and shops have harbor views, and, by extraordinary luck, an immense spice warehouse nearby adds the smell of spices to the air.

Harborplace, Baltimore

The aisles in the pavilions containing the shops are quite narrow, a deliberate device to enhance the sense of this place as a little, crowded village, a world apart from the suburban mall. Graphics are strictly limited to Rouse-approved signs.

It is all rampant good taste. There is a bit more variety at Harborplace than at some similar projects and relatively fewer stores with cute names that are puns on the merchandise sold. But visitors can still buy stuffed animals at "Embrace-able Zoo" and headgear at "Hats in the Belfry."

There is a sense that the environment is controlled, very controlled. This, in the end, is the real problem with places such as this. Harborplace takes conventional aspects of the urban experience, the little cafes and the energetic markets overflowing with produce, and turns them into something tame. It makes them easier than they are in the real world, more contained, more measured. Harborplace asserts that it is about spontaneity and variety, as real cities are; it is, in fact, about order and conformity.

It is hard not to wonder how Rouse will do when and if the company gets a similar project going at the South Street Seaport along the East River in lower Manhattan. The proposed project, part of a $203-million development plan that includes an office building and hotel complex, has received approval from New York's Board of Estimate.

Baltimore and Boston were understandably so eager to get a place of markets and cafes and fashionable shops that they could happily accept so tame a version of the urban experience. New York's situation is very different. It overflows with the real thing, the kinds of stores, restaurants, markets, and cafes that are the inspiration for such places as Faneuil Hall Marketplace and Harborplace. Rouse may, of course, change its formula in New York, but if it does not, the city will be faced with the curious situation of an imitation of urban life amidst the real thing.

As for the Baltimore project, it is difficult to argue that Harborplace has not been a positive addition, if only because it has done so well at getting people downtown. Psychology is a large part of the battle to keep cities alive. Baltimore was never so bad as its detractors would have had us believe. It has a truly impressive stock of early twentieth-century buildings and, in Mount Vernon Place, one of the finest downtown squares in the United States.

But neither is the city quite so extraordinary as its new boosters would tell us. It is not the nation's prettiest city, nor its most livable, nor its most energetic. What it is is an old American city that has begun to look at itself as a fairly healthy being, and that alone is worthy of praise.

—February 18, 1981
Baltimore

Chicago: Quality Architecture— At a Price

"It is a milestone of sorts to be invited from the provinces to America's first city of architecture."

That is how a prominent New York architect began an address to Chicago architects not long ago, and his choice of words underscored how much this city's accomplishments in modern architecture have impressed the world and, indeed, evoked considerable envy in that larger city on the East Coast.

Chicago is the city of Louis Sullivan, Frank Lloyd Wright, and John Welborn Root. It is the city of Daniel Burnham and the nation's first attempt at large-scale urban planning. And it is the city of Mies van der Rohe, Skidmore, Owings & Merrill, and the other more recent masters of the glass and steel tower.

It is also a city of passionate architectural interests. The average person on the street here can rattle off architects' names in a way that would bewilder his counterparts in other cities. James I. Freed, the New York architect who moved here last year to head the Mies van der Rohe–designed architecture school at the Illinois Institute of Technology, said, "Buildings are for Chicagoans what the nineteenth-century novel was to Parisians—everybody can, at least up to a point, talk intelligently about them."

But, for all its brilliance, the nineteenth-century French novel was essentially a single style, and so is architecture in Chicago. This is a city defined by the austere towers of Mies van der Rohe and the newer, bolder glass structures of Skidmore, Owings & Merrill and followers. It is a place of remarkable, even stunning, architectural quality—glass towers as good as the Mies-designed Seagram Building, the pride of Park Avenue in New York, are common sights here.

Chicagoans do not theorize about their architecture. But Bruce Graham, the partner in Skidmore, Owings & Merrill who designed both the Sears Tower and the John Hancock Building, said, "In the heartland we believe in a direct relationship between work and thought. We make real buildings; we are not abstract about life, as they are in New York."

In one sense this is nothing new. In the early days of the skyscraper, around the turn of the century, Chicago was making straightforward, structurally honest buildings by such designers as Sullivan and Root that were at the vanguards of modern design, while New York, never willing to be either so direct or so single-minded, was decorating its skyscrapers with historical allusions from dozens of different periods.

Lately, however, that quality has come under fire from a number of critics who suggest that it comes at the price of diversity. Earlier this year, a major exhibition at the Institute of Contemporary Art, "100 Years of Architecture in Chicago," celebrated the city's better-known architectural accomplishments.

Water Tower Place (left) and John Hancock Building, Chicago

At the same time, a "counter show" was mounted by a group of dissident architects who argued that the structural rationalism of the so-called Chicago School was too narrow an architecture.

But if the Miesian era is coming to a close and if Chicago is breaking out of its glass box into a greater diversity, that is another matter. The point right now is that this sort of architecture has had a tremendous effect on this city.

It is no exaggeration to say that, on the average, Chicago has the best downtown commercial buildings in the nation. The fact that they are all much the same in appearance, and are generally products of an ideology that has traditionally been taken as gospel in this city, does not disturb Chicago's partisans. To them, a city is judged by what it builds—and only by that.

But diversity is the price for this quality. It makes Chicago the architectural opposite of New York, a city of dozens of different philosophies, building styles, and general attitudes about architecture, a city of talkers, as much as builders. Chicago, on the other hand, prides itself on being tough, pragmatic, and successful. It likes to see itself as a city whose architects like to build before they talk.

The best New York architects build very little on their home turf. Major decisions are left to real-estate developers who tend to hire dull commercial firms.

In Chicago, on the other hand, the tradition of building well in a single style is so strong that the city government itself commissioned Jacques Brownson of C. F. Murphy Associates, a firm of the Miesian school, to design the Civic Center in 1965, a much acclaimed building, with a Picasso sculpture in front.

The federal government, at around the same time it was building a mediocre decorated cracker-box courthouse on New York's Foley Square, hired Mies van der Rohe himself to design Chicago's Federal Center.

More important, standards of even developer-built buildings are higher here. "In Chicago, developers wouldn't think of going to anybody but the top firms for a major downtown building," said John Burgee, a former Chicago architect who is now in New York as a partner in the firm of Johnson/Burgee.

There are other comparisons similar to the two federal projects in the two cities. New York has for years been getting some of the most mediocre luxury housing in the world on the Upper East Side, the result in part of high labor costs but due also to the insistence of developers on adhering to the white-brick Third Avenue formula. Chicago, in 1971, saw completion of Lake Point Tower, a 70-story curved-glass form designed by Schipporeit & Heinreich and based on a sketch by Mies van der Rohe from the 1920's and one of the most daring pieces of commercial housing design in the country.

—September 14, 1976
Chicago

Houston: A Skyscraper Laboratory

It is ten years since the completion of One Shell Plaza, the 50-story tower of travertine marble that was the tallest building west of the Mississippi and the first major sign to all the world that Houston meant its skyline to be taken seriously. Since then, Houston has grown so much that One Shell Plaza is barely visible amid the plethora of skyscrapers in this booming downtown. And it has lost its title of tallest to a new building, the 75-story Texas Commerce Tower.

Texas Commerce, designed by I. M. Pei & Partners of New York, will not be completed until spring. But the building reached its full height months ago, the first tenants are moving in, and Houstonians have already become accustomed to a new symbol of their city's phenomenal growth.

Houston remains one of the nation's most intriguing urban environments, a city in which growth is something of a religion and yet planning is something of an anathema. The oil business has made Houston so rich that it has built continuously through the last decade, even when things were slack in other cities. But, alone among major American cities, it has no zoning laws, and thus all of its growth has come in random fashion. This is the laissez-faire city, the boom of the Sun Belt joined to the freedom of the frontier.

In the decade between the building of One Shell Plaza and the Texas Commerce Tower, Houston began, awkwardly and slowly, to take on some of the look and feel of a mature city. As it has become more prosperous it has become more crowded, more crime-ridden, and more traffic-filled, but it has also become more culturally alive. Most of the skyscrapers are built now of more granite or marble and less metal or steel, attesting to the

The Post Oak area of Houston— the new urban center

city's desire to create an air of permanence.

In both the central business district downtown and the shopping and business district in the Post Oak section west of downtown, the skyline has become a kind of San Gimignano, the famous Italian hill town where families vied to build the house with the tallest tower. In Houston, developers hire fashionable architects who vie to design towers of new and different shapes that will strive to make their mark in the crowd of tall buildings.

The first of these new and different shapes was Philip Johnson and John Burgee's Pennzoil Place, a tower of twin trapezoids with sliced-off tops that was completed in 1975. Since then, Houston has liked to see itself as a laboratory of current skyscraper design. It will continue to be, with towers under construction or in the planning stage by architects such as Cesar Pelli; Kohn, Pederson, Fox; and Mr. Johnson and Mr. Burgee.

The last two will doubtless add to their reputation as the showmen of the skyscraper with the two projects they have under construction here: a glass tower with setbacks that recalls the New York skyscrapers of the 1920's and a bank tower that mixes such diverse historical influences as Dutch and Romanesque architecture.

But what Houston has not managed to do in this decade of explosive growth is give itself a cohesive urban form. The city has always lacked what planners call a fabric, a look that ties the city together and gives it identity, such as New York's brownstones in some areas and solid limestone buildings in others. Houston really has no such fabric, though the rich materials of its new granite and glass towers are beginning to give it a certain look that one might call a mix of sleekness and solidity.

The new skyscrapers rise with little if any relationship to one another. Downtown, each building is like an island, filling a city block, a complete and closed world in itself. Nothing seems to tie the buildings together—the streets have few pedestrians and fewer stores, since Houstonians tend to drive and do much of their downtown walking in a series of underground tunnels. Tranquility Park, created in 1979 as a public square in the center of downtown, is empty most of the time. Indeed, about all that marks this as different from other parts of town is the fact that the buildings are closer together here—it is propinquity that makes this downtown, not real urbanity.

The Post Oak area is something else altogether. Its rapid growth is largely the result of the vision of Gerald D. Hines, the Houston developer who was also responsible for One Shell Plaza, Texas Commerce Tower, and the Johnson/Burgee buildings. Out here, near the intersection of a pair of freeways, Mr. Hines a dozen years ago built a luxury shopping center called the Galleria, a hotel, and an office tower. One thing led to another, and now the area has five hotels, dozens of office buildings, and literally hundreds of stores and restaurants spread out over miles of west Houston. It is a second downtown.

But although there is much architecture of interest—such as Cesar Pelli's

Four Leaf Towers condominiums, a pair of towers that anticipate that same architect's design for the Museum of Modern Art condominium in New York, and a trio of buildings by Johnson/Burgee inspired by the streamlined architecture of the 1930's—there is even less order than in downtown Houston. Downtown, the old-fashioned grid of city blocks functions as a web, bringing buildings closer together; out on the freeways and boulevards of Post Oak, the buildings look as if they have been dropped at random across the landscape, stopped only by the ribbon of Interstate 610.

The result is a place without focus. It has an almost exhilarating sense of freedom—new things are tried here with an eagerness that would never be found in New York—but it is all at a price. There is every kind of building, from towers with sleek aluminum curves to those with prissy marble arches, from 40-story apartment towers to rundown gas stations, all fighting for a share of the landscape.

The coming of high-rise condominiums to Houston is a significant event, for it may signal the end of sprawl. For decades, Houston has grown by spreading out, across cheap land, developing farther west, for example, than Post Oak. But now it seems to be doubling back on itself. Development is coming back in, to land that was once filled with single-family houses, and is putting tall luxury apartment towers there instead.

It is a sign, perhaps, that Houston's rich do not wish to travel infinite distances, but it is also a sign that the city does not want to develop solely as suburb after suburb. Indeed, Mr. Pelli's reddish glass Four Leaf Towers are now a dominant presence on the Post Oak skyline, and they may foreshadow the transition from highway shopping mall to true urban center.

—October 10, 1981
Houston

Los Angeles, Scene I: Her Heart Isn't Downtown

For a long time the idea of a downtown in Los Angeles was only a bit more plausible than a beach in Omaha or a ski slope in Miami. It existed, mainly in the form of a few bank buildings huddled together at a freeway intersection, but it never seemed to belong to the rest of the city.

But for the last several years downtown Los Angeles has been trying to assert itself, and aggressively. There has been a boom in skyscraper construction here that rivals that of New York and Houston, and downtown is about to get the city's new Museum of Contemporary Art, slipped in beneath a skyscraper complex.

Yet all this growth has made this downtown feel less like a part of Los Angeles and more like anyplace else. That is, of course, both good and bad. This city has never had much in the way of conventional urbanism: density, street life, pedestrian activity, buildings tying together to make a whole. There are those who say that such things are inconsistent with the idea of Los Angeles in the first place, that just as street life enhances the essence of New York, it contradicts the essence of Los Angeles.

But no one need worry that Los Angeles is about to turn into a pedestrian city. For all the growth downtown, it is not, so far at least, turning into a particularly vibrant place.

There is an unquestionable zeal right now to give the city a "real" downtown, something its planners have always thought was a good idea but which its real-estate market never used to care about very much. But the intent and the results are different things altogether.

And the results of all this growth, so far, are dismal. They stand as a strong reminder that the mere act of

Downtown
Los Angeles

commitment to some sort of traditional, dense cityscape is not enough. Although there are now several hotels downtown, numerous brand-new skyscrapers and commercial complexes, and one vast commercial development in the planning stages, it all adds up to a kind of emptiness.

Downtown Los Angeles is not the city's real center—it is in the very essence of this sprawling city never to have a single center—and thus, despite its rapid growth, it does not have the symbolic importance that, say, downtown Houston has. It is mainly a financial center, and while it has some housing and the city's Music Center, a result of a 1960's effort to give downtown more importance, it remains a place apart from much of the city's life.

It is common to hear people who do not understand this unusual city criticize it for a lack of character, but in fact most of it has a considerable, and powerful, character. Curiously, it is downtown Los Angeles, the part that seems the most like other cities, that has the least character of all. For all the growth that has occurred here, there is almost nothing that ties this downtown together, almost nothing to give it a feeling of coherence and urbanity.

And if downtown Los Angeles does not have the coherence of a fine older downtown, it does not have the energy of a late twentieth-century downtown either. One still feels that the excitement, the sense of being in the center of things, is far stronger in West Los Angeles and Beverly Hills.

Downtown Los Angeles has neither the freewheeling, automobile-dominated ambience of the rest of the city nor the kind of dense, pedestrian-oriented excitement of a city like New York. It consists of a series of skyscrapers, virtually all of which look as if they had been designed to be somewhere else, that have been lined up side by side along long, dull streets.

In most cases the buildings are completely cut off from those streets, making downtown completely uninviting to pedestrians despite the closeness of the towers to each other. The Bonaventure Hotel by John Portman, for example, consists of a group of five glass cylinders atop a heavy concrete base; it looks rather handsome from the freeway, but the solid concrete walls make it seem nothing but a bunker from the sidewalk.

Not every building is so cut off from its surroundings, but almost all of the large buildings here have some aspect that makes them seem wrong for Los Angeles. The Arco and Bank of America headquarters, twin granite and glass boxes by the architectural firm of A. C. Martin, are not only jet black but have an underground shopping mall, cutting occupants off from sunlight in one of the few cities in the United States that is comfortable outdoors all year round.

To erect these towers, Arco demolished the Art Deco tower built by its predecessor company, Atlantic Richfield, thus putting an end to the one truly distinguished skyscraper Los Angeles has ever had. With that building gone, there is only one great work of architecture in the central section of downtown, the Los Angeles Central Library by Bertram Goodhue, architect of St. Bartholomew's Church in New York.

The library, a brilliant mix of Spanish, Byzantine, and Art Moderne architecture erected in the 1930's and one of the few pieces of important public architecture in this city of private houses, is itself threatened. The city considers it outdated and has indicated willingness to sell the valuable site to real-estate developers in exchange for the construction of a new library.

That would be a double tragedy, since the library building and its surrounding land, most of which is used for parking, could be turned into the focal point this downtown needs. A well-designed park and some kind of cultural and commercial complex could be a powerful force to pull together this aimless and dull downtown. Losing the library, then, would mean not only the loss of an important piece of American architecture but also the loss of a chance to help all of downtown.

As it is, the hopes for turning downtown into more than a set of buildings that look like refugees from Houston are pinned largely on Bunker Hill, a multi-tower commercial complex to be erected on the edge of downtown by the Canadian developer Cadillac-Fairview and designed by Arthur Erickson, the Vancouver-based architect. Mr. Erickson's sleek design is conservative by today's standards of skyscraper design, but it is certainly cohesive, and by virtue of its immense size and general stylistic uniformity it may well pull the disparate parts of downtown together in much the same way that Rockefeller Center did for midtown Manhattan.

As of now, however, there is only one completed building downtown that is any reason for celebration at all. The brand-new headquarters of the Wells Fargo Bank, a shiny aluminum skyscraper by A. C. Martin, has a base that is both dignified in itself and responsive to the neighborhood's needs.

The building is entered through a sort of portico of green marble columns cut into its base; it is a handsome outdoor room, with a kind of classicizing grandeur that calls to mind the lobby of the RCA Building at Rockefeller Center. Public passageways and escalators encourage pedestrians to use this space to cut through the hilly block on which the building is set. The passage is one of the few pleasing architectural experiences downtown Los Angeles can now offer.

—April 11, 1982
Los Angeles

Los Angeles, Scene II: The City as Stage Set

It is easy to think that the most real place in all of Southern California is that vast complex up the Hollywood Freeway known as Universal City. Here, sprawling across 450 acres of North Hollywood, are rows of storefronts, bodies of water, and one suburban street.

Nothing at Universal is really real, of course: this is the back lot of a movie studio, and thus the big houses on the suburban street are only fronts and the other buildings are only skin deep. Even the shark that starred in *Jaws* and is still activated to entertain tourists has no behind—its machinery is visible if one sneaks around to see it from the rear.

But everything at Universal seems real, and that is what makes it a key to Southern California's way of looking at architecture. Everything in this state's vast landscape of freeways, drive-ins, and Spanish colonial houses is a stage set of sorts, real buildings looking unreal; what the movie studio does is reverse that process, making unreal buildings look like real ones. It is all a kind of playland, you-can-have-any-kind-of-environment-you-want land—but then again, that is what Los Angeles itself is about.

After a number of visits, one is still more impressed with this stage set quality of Los Angeles than with anything else about the city's architectural environment. There are Tudor and colonial and Norman-inspired houses all over the East Coast, but they rarely have the brash, hedonistic quality of their Los Angeles counterparts, which seem to want not merely to employ history, but rather to possess it. It is as if, by building a house that recalls something of the style of the Second Empire, an owner might himself absorb some of that period's power. To have the Second Empire, and air-conditioning, swimming pools, and palm trees besides is the goal.

The stage set thus merges with the notion of the real building. The real places look, to an easterner, unreal—and the "unreal" places are, for all intents and purposes, real. Universal City is one example; the best, about which so much has been said that it seems pointless to add more, is Disneyland.

Disneyland succeeds masterfully at the creation of a setting for fantasy—a setting that depends for some of its effects, ironically, on using not extraordinary kinds of buildings but very conventional ones, like Main Street, which it then makes special by a slight change of scale and change of context. But theatricality prevails, always.

Of course, most of Los Angeles is not extravagant stage-set houses or places like Disneyland, but little suburban houses, freeways, and commercial strips with gas stations, McDonalds drive-ins, and car washes—a landscape that it has recently become fashionable to praise in certain architectural circles, but which is, if not the evil cancer some would call it, still pretty boring.

But such places exist everywhere; and the point is not that Southern California has them, or even that it has more of them than anyplace else. It is that Southern California's architectural environment is much more original and complex than the freeways and the roadside commercial strip would suggest.

A merging of the notion of the stage set with that of the so-called real building is crucial to an understanding of what this place is. Los Angeles encourages fantasy, be it in the common setting of a fast-food stand shaped like a hotdog, the extravagant setting of a house designed to look like a Spanish colonial mansion, or the extraordinary setting of Disneyland.

By stimulating fantasy, Los Angeles is not cutting itself off from the tradition of cities, it is joining it. Great cities have already been settings for theater. Balzac's descriptions of nineteenth-century Paris suggest a place in which

Beverly Hills

public acts and the exercise of fantasy were crucial; the New York of Edith Wharton or Damon Runyon or Truman Capote is a place in which private fantasies are stimulated and public ones are acted out.

New York has a somewhat less public environment than Paris—there was no Napoleon III to order vast boulevards and public squares, and we were left more to capitalism's devices. Los Angeles takes all of this one step further. It is a city made up almost entirely of private places, such as houses and restaurants. (Not surprisingly, virtually all of the major serious works of architecture here, like the buildings of Frank Lloyd Wright, R. M. Schindler, and Richard Neutra, are houses, not public buildings.)

Since the tradition of the physical environment here is more private than public, the fantasies have become more personal, more whimsical, more hedonistic—in every way more extreme. But the city they have created, and are in turn created by, is no less valid for this reason.

It could be said, in fact, that the ability to function as a certain kind of theater is one test of a great city. New York obviously does so, these days with an intensity unmatched anywhere. But cities like Atlanta, Houston, or Kansas City seem unable to—they are consumers, not creators, of culture, places in which the human spectacle seems always to lack a certain final crucial element. Los Angeles, for all its utter physical differences from New York, is more like it in this sense, a place of innovation and theatricality, where our culture, for better or for worse, is made as well as consumed.

Los Angeles residents seem generally to understand this fact about their city, and much of their building is consistent with the idea of exploiting Los Angeles's particular set of fantasies. Sometimes, however, the city's architects seem to miss the boat, as in the music center, a poor imitation of Lincoln Center in downtown Los Angeles; or more recently, in the Arco Towers, a pair of twin black skyscrapers housing the Atlantic Richfield Company.

Designed by Albert C. Martin and Associates, the towers are massive black boxes with a large pedestrian plaza in between. They are bland, but not really worse than much else that goes up around the country today; what is extraordinary about them is that they contain an underground shopping mall. In Los Angeles, the one major city in the country where it is neither too cold in the winter nor too hot in the summer to shop outside, the architects have thrown everyone underground.

The whole building looks like a desperate attempt to take an idea from the East Coast, without a single thought as to whether or not it makes any sense here—but then, that's what the architects of Los Angeles's fantasy buildings have been doing for generations, so maybe the Arco Plaza isn't so inappropriate after all. Like Georgian, Tudor, French, and Spanish architecture, Los Angeles brings an idea, the glass tower with its underground mall from, in this instance, the East, and grafts it onto the open landscape of the West.

—*June 23, 1977*
Los Angeles

Denver Fights Off Houstonitis

Nothing seems to frighten civic-minded residents of Denver more than the suggestion that the explosive growth of their city in the last few years has made it resemble that other energy boom town, Houston. Indeed, one senses that the people of Denver would rather hear their city by the Rockies compared to Calcutta than to the Texas city that has come to symbolize not only growth but also chaotic sprawl, overtaxed services, and choking traffic.

Far from increasing confidence in laissez-faire planning, the immense growth here seems to have decreased it, making this city more nervous and less assured about its future. The mood of Denver right now seems to be skeptical chauvinism, a self-critical boosterism.

Denver is halfway between Houston and Portland, Oregon, and both exert a pull on it, Houston representing a tempting but disturbing prosperity, a city of unbridled growth where real-estate developers control much of the city's destiny, and Portland looking like a model of restraint, a place characterized by the Northwest's traditions of limiting growth and preserving natural resources.

Three years ago downtown Denver consisted of not much more than a few undistinguished medium-size postwar high-rise buildings, an eccentric old tower modeled after the campanile of St. Mark's Church in Venice, and the ninety-year-old Brown Palace Hotel.

Now, Denver's downtown is jammed with new office buildings. Where there was eight million square feet of office space as recently as 1979, there is now 20 million square feet, and 15 million square feet is under construction. The old skyline has virtually disappeared amid a plethora of new skyscrapers; perhaps even more significant, the landscape around the city has filled with new residential and commercial construction.

But downtown Denver remains a disappointing collection of mediocre skyscrapers, different from the Denver of three years ago only in quantity, not in quality. There is little to pull the place together. And, with the exception of two recent buildings with silvery metal skins similar to the sheathing of Citicorp Center in New York, there are no buildings that seem designed specifically for Denver. Most of downtown Denver could be anywhere, even Houston.

There are some encouraging signs, however. One of them is the discontent that so many of this city's business people, architects, and civic leaders feel about the direction that downtown development has taken. Denver is still small enough to make it possible for decisions to be made by a single group of powerful people, and that is more or less the intention of the Denver Partnership, an activist group fighting for better urban design.

The Denver Partnership was a major force behind the creation of the 16th

Downtown Denver in 1982

Street Mall, a pedestrian mall designed by I. M. Pei & Partners that is nearing completion on one of the city's main downtown streets. The mall will be managed by the group under contract to the city. The organization has also acted as an advocate for more sophisticated downtown zoning laws, which have recently been adopted.

What neither this group nor Historic Denver Inc., the city's active preservationist organization, has thus far been able to do is get a substantial amount of housing built downtown. This is beginning to change under the guidance of Liebman, Ellis, Melting, a New York and Denver–based architectural firm, but it remains an area in which Denver lags badly. While the city is increasingly attracting young professionals who prefer city life, there is still virtually no housing available in the center.

In some ways, however, it is already too late for Denver to avoid all the problems of Houston. While sprawl is not so pervasive here, its effects are more dramatic, for in Denver there is an extraordinary landscape to be destroyed. Miles of small suburban houses cover nothing but flatland in Houston; in Denver, they nudge their way up mountainsides, fighting the beauty of the Rockies that is the city's real heritage.

Denver's current phase of growth can be said to have begun with the completion of the headquarters of Johns-Manville in 1978, a sleek metal building on a former ranch some miles out of town. When the company moved from New York to Denver, it brought 3,000 employees with it. Although these people work in an environment with views of a pristine mountain landscape, the views out of their office windows are increasingly the only untouched ones, for the coming of so many new households led to the development of miles of mountainside land with tract housing.

The problems here are truly regional ones, and population statistics show it. The population of the city of Denver remained relatively constant at 500,000 from the 1970 to the 1980 census, while that of the surrounding counties grew 31 percent, from 1.24 million to 1.62 million.

Much of the growth comes from an influx of young professionals for whom Denver, like Houston or Washington, D.C., has become a focus of migration. But virtually the only housing constructed in recent years downtown has been some flashy condominium towers, and there are few services for full-time living downtown.

The problems of downtown Denver and the region, then, are closely connected, for as Denver expands by covering up its mountains, it also weakens the downtown it is trying to promote. Every house built at the foot of the Rockies does double damage: it takes away a part of a virgin landscape, and it saps energy from the downtown it could have strengthened.

—April 26, 1982
Denver

The Johns-Manville
Headquarters

Johns-Manville
headquarters

Surely no building in the United States has as dramatic an approach as the new headquarters of the Johns-Manville Corporation on a 10,000-acre ranch twenty-two miles southwest of Denver. The last few miles are traveled along a country road that winds through a valley; the road makes a sudden turnoff through a mountain pass, then winds upward past great formations of red rock that sit beside the road like sculptures. Suddenly the road makes another turn, and there, set across the valley like a squared-off aluminum spaceship come to rest in the foothills of the Rockies, sits the building.

It is as sleek and gleaming an object as any architect ever dreamed of creating, and it sits in the rough mountain landscape with the self-assuredness of a Greek temple. The architect was the Architects Collaborative of Cambridge, Massachusetts, whose design was chosen in 1973 as the result of an architectural competition sponsored by Johns-Manville.

The building has absolutely nothing to do with its site—it is a machine-made object, and every detail of its precise, shiny facade shouts that fact. One's first instinct is to wonder why there was not more of an effort made to relate to the site, but then it becomes clear that the right route was taken—that this site is so extraordinarily beautiful that to "relate" in the usual way through the use of natural materials or a more modest physical form would have been futile. The only answer was to celebrate the site by also celebrating technology, and letting the machine-made object sit gently in the natural landscape.

Once-virgin
land near
Johns-Manville

That said, however, both the building itself and the philosophy behind the Johns-Manville headquarters raise serious questions, with relevance far beyond this splendid, stunning piece of land. The building is perhaps

97

the ultimate new corporate environment in the nation—it is the farthest extreme to which any major corporation has gone to create its own environment. This shiny structure in the foothills is sealed off, both literally and figuratively, from the world around it.

Johns-Manville had formerly been based in New York and New Jersey. Its executives, like those of so many corporations, grew tired of problems of the Northeast and chose to flee, not just out of the city but out of the region. And the company, once it had chosen to move to Colorado, made it clear that it did not want to try city life again, either—Johns-Manville not only didn't want to be in New York, it didn't think much more of Denver. So the company bought the former Ken-Caryl cattle ranch, a safe hour's drive from downtown Denver, and its officials talked excitedly about the problem-free land to which they were moving.

All well and good in theory. But the reality is a bit harder to accept. Much of the land between Johns-Manville's sprawling site and the city of Denver has been farmland until recently, but the coming of the corporation, with almost 2,000 workers—which means 2,000 households—has changed all that. Real-estate developers bought up the farmland in anticipation of Johns-Manville's arrival, and now much of the land has been built up with suburban subdivisions, just like those one would see anywhere else.

So Johns-Manville, which wanted to trade the crowded Northeast for the land where the buffalo roam, has ended up causing a lot of that land to be turned into something not so very different from the place it left. The company itself is apart from this suburban sprawl, of course—its enormous site affords it protection from the changed landscape. The views from the executives' windows are of a pure, perfect virgin landscape. But over the ridge, it is something else.

Company executives come and go by helicopter; others are forced to travel the long distance by car, so that here again, the company that sought to find a trouble-free environment has helped to seriously alter that environment. The question inevitably arises: is this the most socially responsible kind of architecture we can expect from a corporation with the vast resources of Johns-Manville?

If stealing away to a palace in the mountains is not the most responsible course of action Johns-Manville can take in terms of its overall effect on society, one wonders if it can be justified in terms of the company's own operations. Only Johns-Manville's employees know, of course, and the company naturally maintains official pleasure at the results of the move.

But it is hard not to wonder if the extreme isolation does not have some sort of effect on the people who work at Johns-Manville. They do not have anyplace to shop, and they do not have anyplace to eat except in company facilities. They have no one to talk to except fellow employees, and never in their work lives is there ever the chance for that sort of accidental encounter with a friend or a colleague or even a competitor that can yield a new idea. Johns-Manville is so isolated that it makes Greenwich, Connecticut, look like Times Square.

Curiously, it is these issues that come to mind after a visit to this headquarters complex, not questions of architecture. As pure architecture, the building is good—perhaps as good a structure as the Architects Collaborative has done—although it blazes no really new trails.

Like so many buildings of the 1960's and 1970's, the form traces its descent from La Tourette, Le Corbusier's famous monastery in France of 1955–61. As at La Tourette, there are horizontal floors set atop pillars, and the entire structure is set gracefully into the side of a hill.

Johns-Manville takes the La Tourette form, alters it, and stretches it to the point of near-absurdity—the building is more than 1,000 feet long, a fifth of a mile. Some corridors inside run for the full length, and they are astonishingly dramatic and powerful spaces—we almost never see that kind of space stretched out like a tunnel, and the effect is genuinely exciting.

The building breaks away from its La Tourette beginnings in other ways besides its size. It is sheathed entirely in aluminum, making it responsive to what is really an altogether different esthetic from Le Corbusier's harsh, raw concrete. Most of the other aspects of the design relate well to that sleek, aluminum esthetic—the major form of the building is shaped like a wedge so that there is one sharp corner that deftly jabs the sky, and there is an immense, drumlike wing of aluminum just behind the main wing that provides an important formal counterpoint to the larger form.

The inside is so enormous that there are floor plans every few hundred feet to help keep one's direction straight. The offices, designed by the Space Design Group, are comfortable and attractive and are laid out so that most employees get to share in at least a bit of the view. There are a number of fine modern prints on the walls—among them several etchings of New York buildings by Richard Haas, which seem like touching bits of nostalgia.

There are lavish facilities—gyms, dining rooms, a swimming pool—for the use of the employees. Indeed, the pleasures this building provides are such that it is difficult to imagine a worker not being relatively content. And after all, there is only one price he or she must pay for all of this—the lack of contact with the real world.

—April 27, 1978

Detroit's Renaissance Center

Renaissance Center,

Detroit

Renaissance Center is certainly in Detroit, but it is hardly of Detroit. The $337-million development, which includes four office towers and a 73-story hotel that is due to open today, is one of the largest privately financed real-estate projects in history. Its sleek, fresh forms stand out boldly against the dreary skyline of the rest of this sadly deteriorating city. It is a vision, its sponsors hope, of a new Detroit.

The commitment to a revived Detroit was so strong that the center's developer, a 51-member partnership led by the Ford Motor Company, managed to obtain a first mortgage loan of $200 million, said to have been the largest ever made for a single real-estate project. John Portman, the architect whose flamboyant and futuristic forms have become a staple of the revitalized American downtown, was hired to do the design.

But there is a problem with this project, one so serious that the pleasure the individual buildings bring—they are among Mr. Portman's better efforts—cannot make up for it. Renaissance Center sets itself apart from Detroit, so dramatically that one almost feels compelled to question the developer's assertion that the project represents a "vote of confidence" in the city.

The five towers are set on a multistory concrete base, which turns a massive wall to the rest of the city. Its site is on the edge of the Detroit River, across wide Jefferson Boulevard from the rest of downtown and from most pedestrian movement. And much of the center's heating system is contained within huge concrete structures that serve as a further barrier between Renaissance Center and "old" Detroit.

It is hard to find one's way in on foot, but as in suburban office developments, it is easy to get around by car. There is a sense that, conceptually at least, this is in fact a suburban development—it is just tall instead of short, and dropped within the city limits instead of set outside them. It wants to stand alone, and it fails to do the crucial thing that all good urban buildings do—relate carefully to what is around them.

Obviously, this is what a lot of people want. The center's 2.2 million square feet of office space is already 65 percent leased, and the sponsors believe that the rest of it will go rapidly. To many tenants, the chance to hop from car to elevator and never set foot on a city sidewalk is ideal.

All of this might be more acceptable if Renaissance Center billed itself as an alternate to the existing city, not as a savior of it. Detroit's downtown is old and tired; it calls to mind Newark more than Manhattan. It seems possible that the arrival of Renaissance Center on the market will entice tenants out of the older buildings, and thus hasten rather than slow the decline of the downtown district.

This basic conceptual failure is especially disappointing because there is so much that is visually attractive about the project. The centerpiece, the 73-story Detroit Plaza Hotel, is a much improved version of the sort of hotel Mr. Portman has been building lately. There is an 8-story atrium lobby with hanging plants, a central lake, and round projecting balconies, the futurist vocabulary the architect has been using successfully for some time.

In many of Mr. Portman's other recent hotels, such as the Bonaventure in Los Angeles, the arrangement of spaces is confusing. Here, the atrium lobby has been clarified, and happily this has not been done at the expense of its theatrical effect. We can find our rooms this time, but we have our Buck Rogers, too.

The hotel rooms are set in a round reflective glass cylinder that is the centerpiece of the complex. The four office towers are octagons, and they are set at the four corners of the grouping, with Mr. Portman's trademark, the glass elevator, used for access to all of the office floors. The views of the city and the river are superb from even the lower floors of both hotel and office towers.

Everything connects at the hotel atrium level, making the complex feel like the single development it is, not like a set of five separated towers. Getting from one building to another is somewhat confusing still, but it is so much clearer than Mr. Portman's other recent projects that this is hardly a major problem.

The hotel interiors were largely Mr. Portman's work, and they show a welcome restraint and taste. There is no fake Louis-the-this or Louis-the-that here, just good, honest modern furniture. And the simplest of the many restaurants, a buffet room called the Café Express, is designed in a combination of brass and natural woods that, for the first time, brings elegance and dignity to a hotel's budget eating area.

—March 15, 1977
Detroit

Seattle's Balance of Terror

Rainier Bank tower, Seattle

Frank Lloyd Wright used to talk about the need to "destroy the box," and by now, so many architects have come to agree that it is difficult to find a new skyscraper that does not have some sort of eccentric form to it. Pennzoil Place in Houston is a pair of trapezoidal towers, Transamerica in San Francisco is a pyramid, and John Hancock in Boston is a parallelogram.

Now, unorthodox shape has come to Seattle in the form of Rainier Square, a 40-story skyscraper that has people in this city not just talking, but looking up nervously as they pass near it. This building's eccentricity is all at the bottom; the 140-foot-wide tower is balanced on an 11-story concrete base that narrows to just 68 feet wide at street level, making the entire building look as if it is about to tip over. At ground level there is a plaza, and from there the concrete pedestal widens in an upward and outward slope from its tiny square base to the much larger tower, like a giant inflatable form that has just blown out from beneath the earth's surface.

The architect was Minoru Yamasaki, who ironically gave New York the biggest boxes of all in the World Trade Center, and it is difficult to know quite what he was doing here. The shape of the Rainier Square base is not visually pleasing or even amusing; it is in fact rather terrifying, since it is hard not to feel a considerable nervousness at the sight of a 40-story skyscraper looming overhead on a concrete pedestal that touches the ground only in the center.

One of the local newspapers here ran an article explaining the engineering principles to assure worried Seattlites that the building would not topple over on passersby. But the article missed the point. No one really thinks that the building will fall over; the much deeper problem of this building is that it suggests that there are certain forms against which we react almost instinctively and by which we are made to feel uneasy. If this is so, a natural question presents itself: why do architects like Mr. Yamasaki feel so free to use them? This building looks upside down, and all the technological savvy in the world will not make it look right side up. We may know that the building will not fall down, but that knowledge is not enough to make walking past it comfortable.

The tower's builder, Unico Properties Inc., talks in descriptive brochures about Rainier Square's base as "a place that welcomes people" and observes that Mr. Yamasaki has "opened up an entire city block" to make "space to breathe, to circulate, to explore." Freeing ground space, therefore, is the rationale of the tower that balances like a dancer on her toes, but the utterly disturbing quality the building's shape has as it hovers over its newly opened city block renders that argument absurd.

It is not a place that feels relaxing, and while only time is the final judge in such matters, it does not seem likely that it will become any more comfortable in the future; what is wrong with this building is not a mere quirk but the genuinely threatening face it presents to the city.

This is what differentiates Rainier Square—which, incidentally, is the new headquarters for Seattle's Rainier National Bank—from other flamboyant buildings like Transamerica in San Francisco. The much-mocked Transamerica pyramid is admittedly a bit silly, but it is altogether benign, and its effect on San Francisco's cityscape is in fact quite healthy: it is the only new building that brightens that city's now dreary skyline.

Similarly, Pennzoil Place in Houston, where twin towers of trapezoidal shape have their tops sliced off at a 45-degree angle, makes an effort to enliven the skyline, while at street level it relates carefully to what surrounds it. The best of the new generation of oddly shaped skyscrapers save their fun and games for the top where flamboyance is logical, and they present a more sober and responsible face to the city at street level. In this sense they recall the best of the skyscrapers of the 1920's and early 1930's, like the Empire State Building, which brings drama to the cityscape in its famous profile, but which is integrated carefully into the scale and surroundings of Fifth Avenue and 34th Street at ground level.

But Rainier Square does precisely the opposite. Its tower is mediocre, dulling an already dull skyline, and where the building should have calmed down, at the bottom, it suddenly went wild, breaking the line of connection with neighboring buildings and creating that looming, threatening shape. It is a self-aggrandizing narcissistic flamboyance, not an entertaining one, and it is ironic indeed that the whole thing should be presented in the rhetoric of "planning for people."

—*March 25, 1977*
Seattle

The Transamerica Building: What Was All the Fuss About?

When plans were announced in 1969 for the design of the Transamerica Building, the pyramid that stabs San Francisco's skyline with a point 853 feet in the air, there was an enormous public outcry. "It is a large and pretentious folly," said Allen Temko, the architectural historian. It is "insensitive, inappropriate and incongruous," wrote *Progressive Architecture* magazine. It would be "ideal for Las Vegas," complained an angry letter writer to the Transamerican Corporation, which planned the pyramid as its headquarters.

But the building was built—although its 853-foot height is somewhat shorter than what was originally planned, and now that it has been occupied for four years it is a bit difficult to understand what all the fuss was about. Transamerica may be flamboyant and a little silly, but it is also the most sensible new skyscraper in this city. Its shape may be bizarre, but it does less damage to San Francisco's skyline than almost any other large building that has been erected here in the last few years.

Transamerica's architect was William L. Pereira and Associates of Los Angeles, a commercial firm with a certain leaning to science-fiction futurism. That leaning has not always yielded the most sophisticated products, and even at Transamerica, there is a lot to be criticized in the way of details—the huge pyramid meets the ground in a confusing forest of columns, and the windows are precast concrete units that come together to create a facade of crashing mediocrity.

But these problems do not deny the basic validity of Mr. Pereira's idea—that there is reason for creating a skyscraper in a city like San Francisco that emphasizes height but not bulk, and that has an identifiable shape

Transamerica Building, San Francisco

which will add life to the skyline in the way that the elaborately topped towers of the early part of the century did. Lately the skyline of San Francisco has become a deadened mass of boxes, much as that of the southern tip of Manhattan has; Transamerica's pointed top is the one brightening element.

Transamerica's basic success is all the more intriguing because the building flies in the face of so many precepts we have come to accept as crucial in urban design. Its ground level is not largely devoted to retail space, for example, and it does not make much of an effort to relate itself to the context of the surrounding blocks—a context, interestingly, that includes both the somber buildings of San Francisco's financial district and the more casual structures of North Beach.

But since Transamerica occupies almost an entire block, the problem of its failure to relate closely to surrounding structures is less severe. It abuts directly on no other building on three sides and can thus stand alone more comfortably. And it does make one fine urbanistic gesture: it terminates the vista at the end of Columbus Avenue, a diagonal slashing across the city's grid, with considerable presence.

Still, the nagging question remains—why, at a time when most intelligent voices are calling for a less flamboyant, more modest architecture, can Transamerica be called acceptable? It draws attention to itself, perhaps too much of it, but if there is a simple answer, it is that the building's flamboyance is more than just architectural narcissism. Its form is derived from the logical desire to be high, yet not to block light and views. And the result of all this is a shape that also enlivens the skyline in a way that benefits the entire city.

—March 2, 1977
San Francisco

The A.T.&T. Tower—
A Monument to Postmodernism

A.T.&T. building

Is it an oddity, a trailblazing new design, or in the words of one architect, the world's first Chippendale skyscraper? The design was made public only yesterday, but the proposed new headquarters tower for the American Telephone & Telegraph Company at 550 Madison Avenue seems already on its way to becoming one of the city's most controversial buildings.

There is no surprise to that. The design, by Philip Johnson and John Burgee with Harry Simmons as associate architect, is surely the most provocative and daring—if disconcerting—skyscraper to be proposed for New York since the Chrysler Building shook up the traditionalists of the 1930's. Back then, the Chrysler Building's gleaming steel spire seemed shocking in a city full of formal towers of stone; now, with steel and glass as the norm, it is an ornamented stone building that provides the shock. The A.T.&T. building is intended as a deliberate rebuke to the towers of steel and glass that have turned midtown Manhattan into a city of boxes.

Mr. Johnson, as an apostle to Mies van der Rohe and an associate architect of the Seagram Building, was for years among the chief polemicists for the stark, purist lines of modernism. But he, like so many architects today, has been having second thoughts. He now talks more and more about the fact that the public never warmed up to the architects' style of steel and glass, and he has joined that group of so-called postmodern architects who seek an alternative.

The A.T.&T. building is clearly postmodernism's major monument. The building is to be sheathed in granite, with a heavy base into which is cut an open colonnade, so that the public may wander through a forest of columns in what amounts to a covered plaza. The building itself will be entered through a massive, 80-foot-high arch in the center, which opens to a smaller arch, above which is a round window.

There is to be a glass-enclosed lobby in the center of the covered colonnade. Behind the lobby, running from 55th to 56th Street parallel to Madison Avenue, will be a glass-covered arcade containing retail shops—a concession to the city's current zoning amendments—which offer added bulk to builders in exchange for such arcades.

The granite tower will rise with strong vertical lines from this base to the design's most startling element, the top. After another colonnade—this one just a row of columns extended across the facade for the top few floors—the facade breaks into a 30-foot-high pediment.

But this is not just any triangular pediment. It is broken in the center by an immense cutout circle, so that the tower top resembles nothing so much as the top of a grandfather's clock or a Chippendale highboy.

The instinct behind all of this deserves to be respected—there is no question that the flat tops of most postwar buildings are an esthetic disaster, boring levelers of the city's traditional erratic skyline. In the A.T.&T. plan, both an architect and, it should be stated, a supportive corporate client were eager to bring some romance back to the skyline, and they stand ready to go to extra expense to make that romantic element possible.

The particular device chosen, however, is not a little bit troubling—its very resemblance to a piece of furniture suggests that a joke is being played with scale that may not be quite so funny when the building, all 660 feet of it, is complete. On the other hand, if the architects really do go ahead with their plan to place the building s steam exhausts inside the round opening of the broken pediment and floodlight the steam, it could be a stunning visual experience—a vision of steam and light and stone right out of the eighteenth-century schemes of the great French architect Boullée.

All of this may suggest that what Mr. Johnson, Mr. Burgee, and Mr. Simmons are doing is playing a historical game, but it is surely more than that. Modern architecture rejected the use of historical forms, but until the mid-twentieth century, allusions to the architecture of the past were common. We are, curiously enough, now at a time in which the use of history, as in this building, is the most avant-garde thing to do—as the erection of a "modern" building of steel and glass would be the most conservative. So there is no problem with the basic philosophy behind this building—the question is simply whether the physical form that philosophy has yielded is going to work as well as it might in the cityscape.

Other questions remain as well. A.T.&T. is asking the city for an increase in allowable bulk in exchange for the inclusion of the midblock galleria behind the tower; some city planners have wondered whether or not the company should be required to include still more retail space in exchange for this gift of added size.

Retail space seems to be today's instant solution to all urban-design problems, and it would be unfortunate if it were applied in a formularized manner here. Shops are a vital ingredient of every streetscape, but they are not always necessary in every place.

It seems certain that the open public colonnade on the ground floor will constitute a real public benefit, too. It will be an unusual one—wandering about that forest of columns will be a lot different from being on the ground floor of any other New York skyscraper—but it will be a special architectural experience, surely as much public good as an extra boutique or two.

—*March 30, 1978*

Now that A.T.&T., if not finished, is nearly up, it is not difficult to observe that the earlier words were far too cautious—even though they represented the most favorable response to this design of any architecture critic writing at the time. A.T.&T. is shaping up as the finest new skyscraper in New York, and perhaps in the nation. Its pink granite is warm and rich, and the workmanship—something one could never guess at from the drawings and models—is as fine as anything that has been done in New York in a generation. The top does seem to work at city scale, in spite of how unusual it looked in its original presentation, and the base, for all the inappropriateness of putting a variation of the Pazzi Chapel on Madison Avenue, seems truly noble and sumptuous.

It is not easy to play with classical forms and end up with something as visually convincing as this building has turned out to be. The reason for its success—beyond the obvious facts of materials and workmanship—seems to lie as much in Philip Johnson and John Burgee's successful manipulation of compositional elements as anything else. This is not a building that conveys any real sense of commitment to classicism; it is an exercise in compositionalism, but in that sense it is joined more truly to the finest eclectic work of the 1920's than almost anything else being built today. It is a product of a strong intuitive design sense, and if it represents any powerful conviction, it is the belief that such design sense can make architecture as much as pure theory.

The one question that remains is that of this handsome object's relationship to what is around it. No one can question that it is too big a building for an already overcrowded part of New York. But it intrudes on one's sense of scale less, I think, than the neighboring I.B.M. Building by Edward Larrabee Barnes, and it seems less intrusive, despite the presence of its bulk on the street, than many a tower set behind a plaza.

It was fashionable for a time after the building's plans were made public in 1978 to say that the design was all right, but was stifled by its presence on Madison Avenue, and what A.T.&T. needed was a wide street—or better still, a huge plaza in front that could create a wide open, axial vista. It is now clear that nothing could have been worse—that part of the pleasure of this building comes from the drama of the huge expansion of scale on narrow Madison Avenue. To come upon A.T.&T. from a side street and have the immense entrance arch burst upon you is to experience a kind of drama that is common to baroque Rome, but rare indeed in twentieth-century Manhattan. Ironically, a wide, straight-on approach to A.T.&T. across an open plaza would have been dull—I don't think that the design is quite vibrant enough to hold such an axial vista. Its power comes in large part from the contrast of this overscaled classical entrance and the busier, littler, and sleeker streetscape that surrounds it. To lose that would be the same as having the Seagram Building lose the Racquet & Tennis Club across the street from it—in both cases, urban coherence is made by contrast.

Rear of A.T.&T. building at base

New Skyscrapers and Unfulfilled Promises

Not for half a century have as many skyscrapers with the pretense of architectural significance come to completion as now. There was a boom in construction in the 1950's, and a bigger one in the late 60's, but these periods were essentially without architectural aspirations, save for a few exceptional works. Now, however, the situation on the skyline is different. Every building seems to want to be architecture, though perhaps that word should be written Architecture, so desperate seem all of these buildings, from the best of them to the worst, to prove their value as objects of design.

Putting aside the fact—at least I believe it to be a fact—that intention is worth at least something, it is not too early to ask what all of this eagerness has gotten us. It is no longer news to hear that an architect has chosen to depart from the banality of the glass box; now that the seeds sown in the last few years have developed into full-fledged presences on the skyline, we are seeing all sorts of buildings that can be called "interesting," but we are seeing far fewer that can be called good. If the current wave of construction now reaching completion in Manhattan is an advance over the insipid and dull quality of the towers of the last generation, that does not, in itself, make it successful architecture.

Not every major new building is finished, of course, and the most conspicuous unfinished building in Manhattan, the A.T.&T. headquarters at 55th Street and Madison Avenue, is in fact the most promising of all the city's new towers. But of the recent crop of buildings that have reached completion, every one seems to fall short of the mark in at least some way.

The I.B.M. Building by Edward Larrabee Barnes is as good an example as any. Here is a 43-story tower of

I.B.M. Building, New York

green granite at the prominent corner of 57th Street and Madison Avenue that seems to do all the right things—or at least it sounds like it does when it is described in words. The tower is five-sided and sheathed in stone, to break away from the glass box. It rises straight up without setbacks to reinforce the even wall of buildings that is so important to the Manhattan cityscape. It even makes a social statement: behind the tower is a glass-covered public park filled with bamboo trees.

But the fact of the matter is that the I.B.M. Building is as heavy-handed and overbearing as any box from the 1960's. It is immense, and since it rises without setbacks it seems to bear down on the passerby, an effect that is intensified by the pretentious balancing act the building does at its main corner, where the entire tower is cantilevered out over the front door. That is structural exhibitionism, not architecture—it is a 43-story building trying to act like a ballet dancer on tiptoe.

So the unusual shape offers no real improvement over what the last generation gave us. Moreover, the granite is so thin and so highly polished it looks as if the architect really wanted it to be metal, making one question the whole point of sheathing the building in stone. And the glass-enclosed park is a cold and unwelcoming place, so far nothing like the public benefit that was promised.

If I.B.M. represents certain reasonable ideas gone awry, the same might be said of the new Philip Morris headquarters at 120 Park Avenue, by Ulrich Franzen. Here, as at I.B.M., a distinguished architect was given the chance to create a large corporate office building on an important site—in this case opposite Grand Central Terminal. And here, too, the architect was conscious of the failure of the isolated, austere, and excessively abstract modernist building of the past and earnestly sought to vary the form in such a way as to integrate it more successfully into the surrounding cityscape.

But once again these intentions fall short of the mark. In the case of Philip Morris, the problem is not bulk, as this 26-story tower is relatively modest by today's standards. It is in Mr. Franzen's rather odd conception of the idea of fitting in. The building is covered in gray granite, and it has two completely different kinds of facades—one of vertical stripes facing Park Avenue and two of horizontal stripes facing 42nd and 41st streets. The Park Avenue facade is intended to appear to stand slightly apart from the bulk of the building, almost like a formal screen, whereas the side-street fronts are set right into the mass of the building.

What is wrong is not in the idea of different kinds of facades for different sides—indeed, in principle that is a welcome change from the modernist preoccupation with the building as a purist and isolated form. The mistake—and it is, in my view, an enormous one—comes in the facades themselves. None of them is very handsome, and the 41st and 42nd street fronts are especially dreary, like industrial buildings given a fast overlay of granite. Moreover, the two types of facade clash with each other, which is a problem since the building is most often viewed from the corner. And the horizontals of the 42nd Street facade clash terribly with the strong verticality of the Lincoln Building next door to the west.

But even if one grants the idea of different designs for different sides, does it make sense for Park Avenue and 42nd Street to be treated so differently? They are not really such different streets at this intersection. They are both wide and important, almost monumental given their role as approach streets to Grand Central Terminal. To treat them differently does not seem any more logical than it would have been for Henry Hardenbergh to have designed completely different facades for the Fifth Avenue and Central Park South sides of the Plaza Hotel.

Once inside the doors of the Philip Morris Building, however, one is tempted to forgive all. The offices are handsome and contain the daring innovations of operable windows and old-fashioned ceiling fans to supplement the air-conditioning system. More important so far as the public is concerned, Mr. Franzen has designed a lovely space for the new midtown branch of the Whitney Museum, and this space surely represents the most significant advance on the idea of the public plaza in some time. The 45-foot-high windowed room fills the building's base; it is both lively and serene, at once involved with the city and a tranquil place apart from the hubbub. After the dreariness of most recent public plazas, this place feels like an oasis, and it could not be more appropriate for a company as identified with innovative corporate sponsorship of the arts as Philip Morris.

Across the street from Philip Morris is 101 Park Avenue, a tower of black glass by Attia & Perkins that seems like an all-too-desperate attempt to put some distance between the architect and the glass box. It is an excessively active form that looks like it has fins that will start the whole tower spinning at any moment; it pays no heed whatsoever to what is around it and should put to rest any naive belief that all architects who have departed from the dullness of the glass box have done so in search of forms that will relate more carefully to their surroundings.

The same can be said of 520 Madison Avenue, by Swanke Hayden Connell, a tower of polished brown granite that splays out at the bottom. It is 43 stories tall, rather too big to be wearing a skirt, particularly a skirt that makes the building break so arrogantly with everything around it. And like the I.B.M. Building, this building serves as a reminder that building in stone is no assurance of a solid and dignified result.

There is a far more urbane and civilized presence to the building at 535 Madison Avenue, diagonally across the street, than there is to number 520, and number 535 is a sleek structure of metal—designed, incidentally, by Edward Larrabee Barnes, who here has repeated at smaller scale virtually all of the ideas he used in the I.B.M. Building. But this time all his ideas work, and the comparison between Mr. Barnes's two buildings is a lesson in urban architecture in itself. The esthetic is similar—sleek and geometric, with a strong reliance on diagonals—and it makes more sense executed in metal than it does in polished stone. The little building has a welcome column over its recessed corner entrance, and since it is smaller, it is able to hold the street line without seeming to hover ominously. And it will have an open park beside it that looks to be vastly more pleasant than the icy I.B.M. plaza.

Just around the corner from this Madison Avenue jamboree is the 68-story Trump Tower, at 56th Street and Fifth Avenue—as awaited a building, surely, as any in midtown. The architects here were Der Scutt and the firm of Swanke Hayden Connell, and the external form is a tower of dark glass, full of setbacks and zigs and zags, though less nervously agitated than 101 Park Avenue. Trump Tower is slick, to be sure, and once again there is a sense that breaking out of the box and creating a form that would be visually lively in itself was seen as more important than tying the building gracefully into its surroundings, which in this case include such handsome limestone buildings as Tiffany & Co. But despite all of this, this is far from the most disappointing new skyscraper in New York—indeed, one might say that it is the one that has exceeded expectations instead of fallen short of them.

Trump Tower is rather too tall for its site, though this is to be blamed on the zoning code the city must live with rather than on the architects; if anything, the sawtooth form of the tower ameliorates the effect of the extreme height. What is most important about Trump Tower, however, is not the exterior but the shopping atrium within, a 6-story space lined with an unusual, and expensive, Italian marble that has a pinkish-orange tone to it. It is a lovely stone, and it exudes an air of contented affluence; combined with the brass trimmings, the effect is one of considerable warmth. The Trump Tower atrium makes no pretense of being devoted to anything but commerce, and it brings to New York a type of interior-mall shopping that is essentially uncharacteristic of this sidewalk-oriented city—but it is also among the pleasantest public spaces in any new building, and that success has to count for a great deal in this time of unfulfilled promise.

—April 10, 1983

What Makes a Civilized City?

It is odd to hear a real-estate developer describe buildings as "obscenities," but that is what happened not long ago at a symposium sponsored by the Architectural League of New York. The event, co-sponsored by the Museum of Modern Art, was entitled "New York's Hidden Designers: The Developers," and it was just what it sounds like—five prominent developers appeared before an audience of architects in a program designed to focus attention on the impact of certain powerful nonarchitects on the physical environment of the city.

The event was actually the first of a series; later programs included panels devoted to bankers and lawyers. Neither of those evenings attracted quite the overflow crowd the developers' panel brought, no doubt due at least in part to the fact that no banker or lawyer would ever dare to be as outspoken as Melvyn Kaufman, the builder who brought down the house with his denunciation of every building as an obscenity.

More about that in a moment. For now, it is worth observing only that architects and real-estate developers have always had curious relationships with one another, ones that in some ways almost resemble those of parents and children—full of resentment and pushing and pulling, yet mutual dependence as well. These relationships are rarely thought about, despite the fact that the interaction between the creativity of an architect and the aspirations of a builder is crucial to the shaping of the city.

The event got off to a somewhat slow start, with the developers beginning by saying essentially what they thought an audience of architects would want to hear. Of course, the deck was a bit stacked, since the league invited only developers who have publicly indicated at least some interest in architecture. On the panel were

Charles Shaw, co-developer of the Museum of Modern Art tower; George Klein, who has built numerous office buildings by well-known architects; Donald Trump, builder of Trump Tower; Harry Macklowe, builder of River Tower; and Mr. Kaufman, who has built several office buildings with unusual public space. Suzanne Stephens, editor of the magazine *Skyline*, served as moderator.

Mr. Shaw praised the Architectural League and his own architect at Museum Tower, Cesar Pelli, extolling Mr. Pelli's facade that he said will contain 600 different kinds of glass. "Great architecture can be profitable,". he said. The tone of homage became stronger still with Mr. Klein, who perhaps more than any other builder has based his reputation on commissioning works by prominent architects, including I. M. Pei, Philip Johnson and John Burgee, and Edward Larrabee Barnes. "Great architecture is an obligation," Mr. Klein said. "A developer has an obligation to be creative—he is leaving a mark, a statement of what he believes in."

It fell to Mr. Kaufman, who has always been something of an iconoclast in this business, to bring the discussion down to earth. After saying that "Before I accepted this invitation I consulted a psychiatrist"—a remark that caused the evening's first outbreak of applause—he did not defend architecture at all. Neither, as it turned out, did he defend the real-estate business. "Every building is an obscenity," Mr. Kaufman said. "It is an obscenity put where trees, grass, wildlife once were. I think every building carries with it an obligation that from the moment you begin to the day you die you must apologize."

He went on: "I am hard put to see any reasonably good architecture in the city of New York in the last fifty years. Form, shape, size—sheer nonsense. A city like New York has nothing to do with architecture—architecture is totally invisible. People cannot see architecture. The only people who have time for architecture are the developers, the architects, and the press."

Mr. Kaufman was not arguing for a laissez-faire city, for allowing builders such as himself to do as they please. What he was doing was defending his own unorthodox method of building, in which routine office towers are fancied up with lively and bright public spaces—his way of "apologizing" to the public. Now, any thoughtful critic would be hard-pressed to deny that Kaufman buildings like 747 Third Avenue, 127 John Street, and 77 Water Street are by far the most pleasing presences in their immediate neighborhoods—and what Mr. Kaufman was doing, in effect, was challenging both architects and his fellow developers to prove that "serious" works of architecture could bring any more pleasure and quality to the cityscape.

After Mr. Kaufman threw down that gauntlet, even Donald Trump—these days surely the New York developer best known as a public personality—seemed a bit upstaged. Mr. Trump presented his thinking mostly in terms of marketing concerns. For him, the building's shape, size, location, and general style were questions of marketing. And Harry Macklowe talked similarly of real-estate development in terms of process as much as of product, though he did at one point speak of the relationship between a builder and his architect as "like a marriage—there has to be an understanding and a rapport."

Whether architects and builders are like partners in marriage or like parents and children is not the point, of course; what matters is that their relationship is one that is basic to the shaping of the city. There are as many kinds of developers as there are architects, from George Klein, who has been commissioning office buildings by distinguished architects as a collector might assemble a group of paintings, to Harry Helmsley, who prides himself on building straightforward buildings that are seen as balance sheets more than as physical objects.

But to put the issue only in terms of whether a developer cares more about architecture, as Mr. Klein does, or less about architecture, as many other developers do, is to misunderstand it entirely. Architecture is not a single, simple scale of values; it is not a quantifiable thing—one cannot rate a building as 98 percent architecturally valid, or 37 percent, or 49 percent. Each and every building is a product of numerous forces—economic, social, cultural, political, functional, esthetic—and must be evaluated in terms of how well it has responded to all of these forces. It is not a pure object, whether its design was created by a famous architect or taken out of a file cabinet.

That, I think, is what Melvyn Kaufman was getting at, and that is why his remarks gave that symposium its most important moments. He was, in the end, asking the audience what makes a civilized city—is it objects by celebrated designers, or is it buildings that try to offer an easier kind of pleasure?

If there was any fallacy to Mr. Kaufman's challenge, it was in his implication that these things are mutually exclusive—that "serious" architecture cannot ever bring the kind of pleasure that his own relaxed and entertaining buildings give us, or at least that in this day and age we are incapable of creating the kind of serious architecture that does bring such pleasure. If one accepts that premise, of course, there is then no sense even in trying to create significant works of design—it becomes an excuse to opt only for a kind of superficial designing which, while undoubtedly superior to the attempts at more profound architecture that fall flat on their faces, nonetheless seems to bespeak a kind of cynicism and defeatism. If we cannot have great art, he is saying, let us not even try—let us be entertained instead.

So it comes down to a battle not between architects and developers but between developers who seem to want to attempt to further a kind of art and those who do not. We have seen so many wretched and uncivilized buildings built in New York that Mr. Kaufman's attitude is certainly tempting—let us just build decently and with a light heart, and stop all of this other nonsense. There is no question that a city of Kaufman buildings would be a pleasanter place to live in than a city of the kind of buildings most other developers put up. But it would also be a city that offers no real challenge to us, no inspiration, if I can use such a word. It would be a city without the valleys we now have, but without the peaks, either.

—July 18, 1982

The Philip A. Hart Senate Office Building

Why is it that the federal government always seems to be twenty years behind the times when it comes to architecture? The Everett McKinley Dirksen Senate Office Building, finished in 1958, has, inside, the air of a commercial building of the late 1930's. Now comes the new Philip A. Hart Senate Office Building, into which the first handful of an eventual fifty senators and their staffs are moving, some with no great enthusiasm.

It would have been quite the thing if it had turned up beside a Dallas freeway in 1962. For the Hart building, designed by the firm of John Carl Warnecke & Associates, working under the Architect of the Capitol, George M. White, looks just like the sort of commercial architecture that was beginning to fill the American landscape in the 1960's, and now looks so dated and dreary. There is an atrium on the inside, and the outside is a mix of masonry and glass with stark, boxy windows framed in marble.

Only two things make the Hart building different from the modern, sprawling suburban office buildings that are its real peers. The scale of this building is much grander—senators' offices have 16-foot ceilings—and everything that is not glass seems to be a bright, almost glaring, white Vermont marble.

It is the bigness and the marble, presumably, that are intended to make the Hart structure feel like a government building—to give it the air of permanence and civic importance that we expect from an office building intended to house members of the United States Senate. Unfortunately, they are not enough, particularly given the $137.7-million price tag.

That is not in itself so high a cost in this day and age, and the criticism this building has drawn for being too

Hart Senate Office Building

expensive and opulent seems misguided. The issue is not that the building is too costly. It is that all of that money seems to have bought so little. The Senate has spent $137.7 million, and certainly none of that money has gone for any ideas. For $137.7 million one would expect something other than dull, institutional ordinariness.

To be fair, the Hart building does avoid the vulgar, overblown pomposity of the Rayburn House Office Building, the inept escapade into classicism that was completed in the mid-1960's. But it also lacks that building's arrogant swagger. The Hart building seems to be trying hard to please, but in the process it has given up the real dignity of Washington's finest government buildings, and there are not many of them. A Hyatt Hotel–type atrium dropped into the middle of a building of government-issue marble does not a truly dignified environment make.

The most pleasing thing about the building, surely, is the offices themselves. So far as congressional work spaces are concerned, the Hart offices represent an important innovation in internal planning. Each suite is a self-contained duplex unit with one double-height space for the senator's office and the rest of the space divided into a low-ceilinged main floor and mezzanine. This avoids the awkward internal layouts of many Senate suites in the older office buildings, which consist of rooms strung out along a single corridor.

But even this plan, which makes each suite look like a bureaucratized version of the apartment layouts of Le Corbusier's celebrated Unité d'Habitation in Marseilles, has its problems. For while the senators' ceilings are unusually high, everyone else's ceilings are unusually low. And the structure of the building is such that it was necessary to place 16-foot ceilings in all the rooms along the front of the building and not just the senators' offices, giving every suite an awkward extra space as high and formal as the senators' own.

Because the building itself lacks any strong personality, the furnishings chosen by each senator play a much greater role in setting the tone here than they do in the older congressional office buildings. The most pleasing one by far, and the one office to be worth considering as a serious work of design, is that of Senator Mark Hatfield of Oregon. He has mixed antiques with an innovative office desk and partition system to create a space that is both handsome and comfortable. The system, manufactured by the Acoustical Screen Corporation, was intended for use throughout the building, but budgetary cutbacks led to the reuse of old furniture instead. It is unfortunate, for the partitions, consisting of speaker fabric stretched over stained oak frames, bring real warmth and style to this dull interior.

The rest of the interior is unexceptional. The architect has designed a pleasant curving staircase, but it is so awkwardly situated that it is easily missed. There are long walks to many of the office suites, making the Hart building little better in this respect than its older neighbors.

The atrium itself is stark and now gives the impression of emptiness more than anything else; funds set aside for a huge Calder sculpture were cut from the budget, as was money for lobby furnishings and plants. The glass roof lets in plenty of sunlight, but to little purpose, for almost no one ever seems to be in the atrium. The enormous marble space has neither furnishings nor much human traffic, and it seems mysteriously dead, as if every day were Sunday and no one had come to work.

So all of the labor that has gone into this—the hearings to discuss the need for new Senate office space that resulted in this building began as far back as 1967—has brought forth a mouse. The Hart building is not, in the end, the product of any real architectural convictions. It is not pure functionalism, for it is much too overblown for that; it is not pure visual pleasure, for it is too restrained and formal for that.

And it is most certainly not the result of any conviction about the classical style of architecture, and this is perhaps the saddest thing of all. The Russell Office Building, the old Senate office building completed in 1909, is an altogether splendid piece of Beaux-Arts classicism, full of both self-assurance and spirit. By the time of the Dirksen building in 1958, modernism had already become the style of the land, and the sense of conviction evident in the Russell building had begun to dilute. The Senate was unwilling to go all the way, however, and so the Dirksen turned out as a kind of uncomfortable cross between modernism and classicism.

And now, just as architects are coming around again to a genuine respect for classicism, all conviction about anything seems to have gone out the window. Congress has at last discovered modern architecture, but a generation too late, and in a form both dull and weak. The modernism of the Hart office building has neither the crispness nor the rigor of great modern buildings, nor the sumptuous dignity of real classical ones. What it tells us is that what really symbolizes the government now is a set of warmed-over ideas.

—January 25, 1983
Washington

The Vietnam Memorial

When a plan by Maya Yang Lin, a twenty-year-old Yale architecture student, was selected last year as the winner of a nationwide competition to find a design for the Vietnam Veterans Memorial on the Mall near the Lincoln Memorial in Washington, it was hailed by the architectural press with words such as "stunning," "dignified," and "eminently right."

The reaction was less enthusiastic from Vietnam veterans themselves, some of whom found the proposed memorial rather more cool and abstract than they would have liked. Nonetheless, Miss Lin's scheme, which is neither a building nor a sculpture but, rather, a pair of 200-foot-long black granite walls that join to form a V and embrace a gently sloping plot of ground between them, was approved rapidly by the Department of the Interior, the Fine Arts Commission, and other public agencies that have jurisdiction over what is built in official Washington.

Construction began last March. Next week, however, the Fine Arts Commission will hold a public hearing to consider a revised design for the memorial, despite the fact that by now the granite walls—on which are carved the names of all 57,692 Americans who were killed in Vietnam from 1963 to 1973—are nearly complete. Opposition to the scheme from Vietnam veterans, which was muted when Miss Lin's design was first announced, later grew so intense as to lead to the unusual step of a proposed design change in midconstruction.

The hearing is scheduled for October 13, and the battle lines have already been drawn fairly sharply. On one side, defending the changes, will be the Vietnam Veterans Memorial Fund, the organization that sponsored the architectural competition and had committed

itself to building the winning scheme, as well as an advisory committee of
Vietnam veterans who were among the more outspoken critics of the original
design.

On the other side is not only Miss Lin, the designer, but the American
Institute of Architects, which has taken a strong public position in defense of
the original design and which sees the move to change the memorial as a threat
to the integrity of the system of architectural competitions in general. Robert
M. Lawrence, the institute's president, wrote this summer to J. Carter Brown,
chairman of the Fine Arts Commission. "What we have here is nothing less
than a breach of faith. The effort to compromise the design breaks faith with the
designer who won the competition and all those who participated in this
competition."

What has provoked the heated emotions, however, is less the integrity of
architectural competition than the specifics of Miss Lin's design. To many of
the Vietnam veterans, her scheme was too abstract to reflect the emotion that
the Vietnam War symbolized to them, and too lacking in the symbols of
heroism that more conventional monuments contain. They saw in the simple
granite walls on which the names of the dead are inscribed not merely a means
of honoring the dead, but a way of declaring that the Vietnam War was in some
way different from past wars—from wars such as World War II, whose heroism
could be symbolized in such a vibrant and active memorial as the Iwo Jima
Monument just across the Potomac River, which contains a statue of marines
struggling to raise the American flag.

The changes in the Vietnam Memorial, therefore, have all been in the
direction of making it less of an abstraction and more realistic. When the
Vietnam Veterans Memorial Fund decided some months ago to give in to
criticism of the design from Vietnam veterans, it named an advisory committee
consisting entirely of Vietnam veterans, in contrast to the jury of internationally
known architects and design professionals who had selected Miss Lin's design.
That committee selected Frederick Hart, a thirty-eight-year-old sculptor who
had been a partner in a losing entry in the original competition, and commissioned him to create a realistic sculpture to act as the memorial's new centerpiece.

What Mr. Hart has created is an 8-foot-tall statue of three armed soldiers,
one black and two white, which would be placed within the triangular piece of
land between Miss Lin's granite walls. The revision of the design also includes a
50-foot-tall flagpole outside the granite walls, and thus it will change the view of
the observer who is looking at the memorial in any direction.

Mr. Hart claims that his statue will "preserve and enhance" Miss Lin's
design, and will "interact with the wall to form a unified totality." Miss Lin,
however, disagrees and in a letter to the Memorial Fund on September 20 she
called the changes an "intrusion" that "destroys the meaning of the design."

Ironically, it is the very strength of the original design—its ability to be interpreted in a variety of ways—that is making for the current controversy. Miss Lin's original scheme is, in a sense, a tabula rasa, a blank slate—not a room, not a building, not a plaza, not a park, not a conventional memorial at all. It is a place of reflection, where the gradually sloping land, the thousands of carved names on somber granite, and the view of the buildings of official Washington in the distance should combine to create an understated, yet powerful, presence.

It is a subtle design, like every great memorial capable of being given

Vietnam Veterans Memorial

different meanings by each of us. The anguish of the Vietnam War is present here, but not in a way that does any dishonor to veterans. To call this memorial a "black gash of shame," as Tom Carhart, a Vietnam veteran who was another losing entrant in the competition, has said, is to miss its point entirely, and to fail to see that this design gives every indication of being a place of extreme dignity that honors the veterans who served in Vietnam with more poignancy, surely, than any ordinary monument ever could.

The Lin design is discreet and quiet, and perhaps this is what bothers its opponents the most. It is certainly what bothers Mr. Carhart, whose own design was described as "a statue of an officer offering a dead soldier heavenward." By commissioning the Hart sculpture and the flagpole, the Vietnam Veterans Memorial Fund seems intent on converting a superb design into something that speaks of heroism and of absolute moral certainty. But there can be no such literalism and no such certainty where Vietnam is concerned; to try to represent a period of anguish and complexity in our history with a simple statue of armed soldiers is to misunderstand all that has happened, and to suggest that no lessons have been learned at all from the experience of Vietnam.

The Vietnam Veterans Memorial, as it now nears completion, could be one of the most important works of contemporary architecture in official Washington—and perhaps the only one that will provide a contemplative space equal to any in the past. The insertion of statues and a flagpole not only destroys the abstract beauty of that mystical, inside-outside kind of space that Maya Yang Lin has created; it also tries to shift this memorial away from its focus on the dead, and toward a kind of literal interpretation of heroism and patriotism that ultimately treats the war dead in only the most simplistic of terms.

For in the original design, the dead are remembered as individuals through the moving list of their names carved against the granite. It is the presence of the names, one after the other, that speaks. But if the statues are added, they will overpower the space and change the mood altogether. A symbol of loss, which Miss Lin's design is, will become instead a symbol of war. The names of the dead and the hushed granite wall will become merely a background for something else, and the chance for a very special kind of honor—and for a very special kind of architecture—will be lost.

—October 7, 1982

The Fine Arts Commission did approve the addition of the Hart sculpture and flagpole, although at greater distance from the main portion of the memorial than originally proposed. By the spring of 1983, however, these elements still had not been added, and the final outcome was uncertain.

The Kennedy Library: An Exhilarating Symbol

The years of John F. Kennedy's presidency were years of hope, of promise, of an almost unquestioning faith in the ability of technology and human intelligence to assure a noble future. It is an attitude that is far less characteristic of American culture today, yet it seems to have been recaptured, strikingly, in the new John Fitzgerald Kennedy Library here. The building has a quality of exhilaration to it, of confidence that strong, bold gestures will bring a better day, and in this sense it is a startlingly appropriate symbol of the Kennedy presidency.

This symbolic rightness is perhaps the best thing about the building, which was designed by I. M. Pei & Partners of New York. The library consists of several wings: a stark structure of white concrete, roughly triangular in its floor plan, that rises to a height of just over 100 feet; a box of glass, 70 feet long, 70 feet wide, and 112 feet high, that is set into the triangle, and a low, rounded wing of concrete containing a pair of theaters.

The theaters join with underground exhibition space to provide the tourist attraction for the library; the concrete tower is the storehouse, containing the Kennedy archives and space for scholars, and the glass box is a monumental pavilion intended to provide a respite for scholars and the general public from the more enclosed rooms.

It is this pavilion that is the design's real achievement. It is a soaring space, full of a kind of tensile, taut energy. The walls and ceiling are supported by a space-frame truss, a gridwork of three-inch metal pipes that form an interlocking frame, holding the large panes of glass in place. From within it gives a sense of technology turned into monumentality—of a grand, formal hall made of modern industrial elements.

The site of the library is remarkable—it is at Columbia Point, overlooking Boston Harbor, the harbor islands, and the city's skyline—and the placement of this great hall takes full advantage of this piece of land. The glorious views from the site are not visible as one approaches the library from land, past the harsh red-brick campus of the University of Massachusetts; the closeness to the water is revealed, with considerable drama, only after entering the main entrance on a mezzanine level that looks down into the great hall.

The hall itself remains just an enticement at this point: visitors do not descend into it but move first into the theaters and exhibit area. They end their tours by emerging into the grand space, its monumentality a reward, as it were, for going through the exhibit area.

The exhibits themselves, designed by Chermayeff & Geismar Associates of New York, do not fully escape from the dangers of presidential cultism to which all presidential libraries seem vulnerable, but they are at least dignified, entertaining, and reasonably frank in including material critical of their subject. And the design is coherent and handsome, logically organized throughout.

The building is most successful, unquestionably, on the interior. The outside lacks the nimble, tensile quality of the glass pavilion, and in fact seems not a little awkward. The set of strong geometric forms that make up the total

John F. Kennedy Library, Dorchester, Massachusetts

structure do not meld very gracefully into one another; they seem a bit disjointed, and it is hard to get a sense of the building's overriding order from any side except the waterfront.

Indeed, the whole structure seems to want to present its best face to the water, even though no one ever approaches it that way, leaving visitors with the feeling that, however grand the present entrance may be, it is still a kind of back door. And the high concrete wall of the archive wing, which faces inland, has an even stronger sense of being a backside.

The land has been reworked to permit the library to be placed at the water's edge, and this has brought both advantages and disadvantages. Obviously, there are the splendid views, which are so fine as to make the place a logical attraction for visitors with no interest in Kennedy memorabilia at all. But this waterfront point has heavy winds, which makes the decision to have a large open plaza beside the building curious, not to say pointless.

On the other hand, there is a welcome waterfront walkway, replete with dune grass, a recollection of the sort of landscape inevitably associated with John F. Kennedy. Indeed, the constant visibility of water, not to mention the skyline of the city of Boston, has great symbolic value as well as inherent beauty. It is a constant reminder that Mr. Kennedy loved both Boston and the sea.

This site is vastly preferable for these reasons to the original library site just off Harvard Square in Cambridge. It lacks Cambridge's panache—Columbia Point was a landfill site that was once used as a garbage dump—but in Cambridge the library would have emerged awkwardly with a university community that was, and is, inhospitable to it.

Here, it is welcome: this monument can command the point of land, spreading its wings as much as it wishes. Since the function of presidential libraries seems to have turned, for better or worse, into the making of tourist attractions, this seems a better place in which to put one.

It is for that very reason—that presidential libraries are, in fact, tourist attractions—that the symbolic role of their architecture is so important. The Lyndon Baines Johnson Library in Austin, Texas, suggested a pompous presidency; it may or may not have been so, but the mausoleum-like architecture makes it hard to believe that Mr. Johnson was anything but an emperor.

The Kennedy Library, on the other hand, makes it hard to believe that Mr. Kennedy was anything but a man of energy, of zest, of confidence. It is not the arrogance of this building that is striking, but the earnestness of it: how well it replicates the faith of a particular moment in history and convinces us that it was real.

—October 21, 1979
Boston

Mr. Venturi's Washington Plaza

Western Plaza,
Pennsylvania Avenue,
Washington, D.C.

"Washington is no place in which to carry out inventions," Alexander Graham Bell wrote in 1887, and his words have been carved in granite, along with thirty-eight other comments on this city, in an immense new public square, called Western Plaza, that is intended to be a centerpiece of a revived Pennsylvania Avenue. Bell was speaking of things mechanical, but his words could well refer to this much-heralded plaza. For Western Plaza, designed by the Philadelphia architectural firm of Venturi, Rauch & Scott Brown, was perhaps the most creative urban square proposed for any city in the United States. In its original conception, unveiled in 1978, it managed to be witty, ironic, and monumental, all at once. But what was built is only a shadow of the original design, and it stands as a reminder to architects that Bell knew whereof he spoke.

The $5.5-million plaza, which was dedicated last month, is a project of the quasi-public Pennsylvania Avenue Development Corporation. The plaza occupies an area 600 feet long by 160 feet wide on Pennsylvania Avenue from 13th Street to 14th Street, a crucial site in Washington. It is right in the middle of the great axis that Pierre Charles L'Enfant, the city's designer, envisioned connecting the Capitol at one end of the avenue with the White House at the other. That view has not been as L'Enfant intended it for some time, since the construction of the Treasury Building in the 1830's partly blocked the clear vista to the White House. Making things worse was the fact that the site of the plaza had become over the years a confusing muddle of small islands and traffic lanes.

The new design was intended to clear up the confusion and provide a symbolic focus, and to do as much as possible to direct attention to the partly blocked view. The plaza is primarily a vast walk-on map of L'Enfant's plan for the city, rendered in marble and granite.

The map consists of "streets," roughly a yard wide, indicated by white marble, and "city blocks" of black granite. Where the real Washington contains open spaces such as the Mall and the Ellipse, this make-believe version has small plots of grass.

Because the plaza reproduces L'Enfant's original design, there is no Treasury Building, and visitors can see in miniature the clear vista the planner intended to link the Capitol and the White House. The two buildings are marked in the plaza by outlines of their floor plans in brass set into the granite. The thirty-nine quotations about Washington are carved into the granite surface of the plaza here and there throughout the area.

It is all quite pleasant, as far as it goes. The problem is that the design originally accepted by the development corporation was vastly better. It contained two significant elements missing from the completed plaza: a pair of freestanding marble pylons, 86 feet high, a 20-foot-high model of the Capitol, and a 6-foot-high model of the White House. These were intended both to be sculptural elements in themselves and to enhance other aspects of the plaza. The pylons would have framed and focused the view in each direction along the avenue, and the miniature buildings would have turned the two-dimensional map of the city into a three-dimensional adventure.

As it is, the plaza is entirely flat; it has no three-dimensional elements at all, and to an observer passing by in a car, there is nothing to suggest that this place is anything but an austere, empty stretch of granite. The plantings are few and sparse, and there is relatively little seating. All of that would have been fine had the plaza had the three-dimensional activity it was expected to have. But without the pylons and the little buildings, the absence of trees and seating suddenly becomes conspicuous.

The problem, as sources within the development corporation explain it, was last minute cold feet. The board of directors of the corporation had always found the plaza design a bit extreme for official Washington, which indeed it was. This is a city of mundane modern architecture and empty, unimaginative public spaces; the notion of a plaza that plays the sort of visual games this one would have obviously did not sit well in many quarters.

The pylons were attacked by some as too stark, too close themselves to the totalitarian architecture that the city's critics so often state is Washington's official style—their role as frames, not to mention their irony as pseudoclassical elements, was ignored. The models, on the other hand, were seen as too whimsical, which in itself helps make clear what is wrong with attitudes toward architecture in this city.

So the plaza was built without the elements that would have turned it into something magical. It is still, despite its castration, a significant public work, and the ideas Robert Venturi, Venturi, Rauch & Scott Brown's chief design partner, was trying to get across still came through, if weakly. What Western Plaza is about is scale. The miniature version of the city teaches us, more clearly than any words could, about the difference between big and little things, about the relationships of parts of a city to the whole. We feel the shape of things more clearly on Mr. Venturi's map of stone than we ever could by reading a map on paper.

Indeed, perhaps the most pleasing experience is standing on the miniature Pennsylvania Avenue, a diagonal corresponding precisely to the "real" Pennsylvania Avenue. One can stand on the little marble strip and look straight down both the miniature avenue and the real one, with the real Capitol in the distance; it is a vista that intensely conveys the meaning of the ideas behind L'Enfant's plan. We can see instantly here how this was intended as a city of great, formal boulevards and long vistas.

The L'Enfant plan was fundamentally an abstraction, and Mr. Venturi has understood this, too. The pattern of the diagonal streets intersecting is attractive, and there has been a general tone of abstraction in keeping with this. So there is nothing suffocatingly literal about the reproduction of the L'Enfant plan—this is not a classical plaza in its details, but quite a modern one.

The public seems to have taken well to Western Plaza, though it is the carved quotations that seem to have been the chief attraction. Even in cold weather, the plaza is filled with people reading them; the notion of a public place that deals in words is itself pleasing, obviously, to people who are used to stark architecture that plays dumb.

The quotations demonstrate a variety of attitudes toward the capital city, but the one that seems to summarize best the story of this plaza is this line that Charles Dickens wrote in 1842: "It is sometimes called the City of Magnificent Distance, but it might with greater propriety be termed the City of Magnificent Intentions."

December 18, 1980
Washington

As of mid-1983, there remained some possibility that a more enlightened Pennsylvania Avenue Development Corporation would choose to complete the plaza as designed.

A Wild, Mad Vision in Downtown New Orleans

The Piazza d'Italia is poised at the edge of this city's growing business district, between colorful old warehouses and banal glass skyscrapers, but even in this mixed environment it comes as something of a shock. For while downtown plazas in most cities are mere expanses of empty concrete, this new one has as its centerpiece a set of curving walls containing an array of classical columns, arches, entablatures, and friezes, all painted brilliant rust, yellow, and orange and awash with water spouting, flowing, rushing, and gurgling around and about and above and below every part of it.

As if that were not enough, the structure is lit up with blue and orange neon ornamentation at night. And the fountains all empty into the central pool with an island of cobblestone, slate, and marble that clearly and unquestionably turns out to be the shape of a map of Italy.

The whole thing is a wild, mad vision, as if the Roman Forum were re-erected in Las Vegas. One's first instinct is to say it is all a rather vulgar slap in the face of classicism—how could Corinthian columns painted yellow and lit up at night with neon be anything but vulgar?

But this place, which may be the most significant new urban plaza any American city has erected in years, is in fact so boundlessly good natured, so utterly full of goodwill and eagerness to please, that you soon realize that it is not a mockery of classicism at all. It is a laughing, almost hysterically joyous embrace of the classical tradition.

The architects for this most extraordinary exclamation point in the center of New Orleans were August Perez and Associates, a large, corporate firm that heretofore has not done unusually well in the area of imaginative design. The firm did better here because of an unusual partnership arrangement with Charles W. Moore, the

Los Angeles architect whose exuberant houses and public buildings have been among the most important small-scale architectural works of the last decade.

The fountain was Mr. Moore's design, and it came about in a strange way. When the city of New Orleans decided a few years back that it wanted to honor its Italian citizens with a $1.65-million plaza, it opened the project to an architectural competition. Mr. Moore entered with a proposal containing a wild adventure of a classical fountain; the Perez firm offered a design that concentrated on renovating the old buildings around the Plaza instead of dealing with the center. Perez won, but public pressure led to the Perez firm's agreeing to merge its plan with Mr. Moore's. The result is that New Orleans is getting the best of both worlds: the extraordinary Moore fountain and the Perez renovations and surrounding structures, most of which remain to be built.

Piazza d'Italia, New Orleans

Charles Moore has talked for years about his fascination with water and the way it was used in classical fountains. With the Piazza d'Italia, he shows that he at once understands historical precedent and is able to go beyond it.

The fountain not only spurts water up and washes it down; it also uses water as a sculptural element. There is one section that drops tiny streams of water in a circular pattern that turns the water into a fluted Doric column and another section with specially designed fountain jets that sculpture water into something resembling the egg-and-dart classical moldings of old.

This spirit of exuberance pervades the entire structure. It is a wonderful spatial experience—one can slip in and out of arcades of columns, in between walls, up and down over the stone islands of Italy in the central pool, making this a participatory plaza in the best sense. It is also a fine composition. The structure has a high central arch as its anchor, with arcades curving out from it like welcoming arms.

And there is splendid wit here. One section contains a pair of heads of Charles Moore spouting water. They were designed without the architect's knowledge by his associate Ed Perez as a surprise tribute.

Still, for all the joy of this place, questions remain. The Piazza d'Italia has a serious lack of seating space. There are just a handful of benches at the edge, far from the fountain. And the city of New Orleans has done a miserable job of maintenance. The fountain is only a few months old, and already lights are out and some water jets malfunction.

There is, of course, a more serious question. What differentiates something like this from the cheap classical columns in front of a place like Caesars Palace in Las Vegas? Both take classical forms and play with them, turning them into something easy and entertaining. The Piazza d'Italia was designed by a famous architect and is considered worthy of our attention. Caesars Palace is considered kitsch. Why?

Part of the answer lies in intent. In the New Orleans fountain, Charles Moore was operating on the level of exploring the meaning of classical elements; he wanted to make us think about what a classical column is and how it does its job, as well as entertain us. To do so, he created an intricate, subtle composition, full of wit and inventiveness.

Caesars Palace, on the other hand, is just a simple, quick-and-easy rip-off of classical elements in the belief that their very use, no matter how simplistic, connotes class. The Piazza d'Italia has no such naive aspirations toward "class." It is itself, its own thing, its own creation—like all real works of art.

—February 9, 1979
New Orleans

A Startling, Soft Green Lawn in Central Park

There is an extraordinary sight now to be seen in Central Park, a vision more remarkable in its way than almost anything on that 843 acres. And it is not, strictly speaking, an alteration to the park at all. It is simply the Sheep Meadow, the vast open area that has over the years been the site for rock concerts, symphonic performances, operas and political rallies, looking for the first time in many, many years as it was intended to look—like a great, rolling, soft, and brilliant green lawn.

The meadow, which sits in the mid-Sixties just a bit east of Tavern on the Green and west of the Mall, has been completely resodded. For years now it has been more brown than green, worn by literally thousands of pairs of feet; now it has been transformed, and the vision of green it offers in the middle of the park is truly startling. We are not used to seeing a real lawn in Central Park, which more often than not tends to look like a rundown vacant lot, despite the efforts of the parks commissioner, Gordon J. Davis, and the Central Park administrator, Elizabeth B. Barlow, to maintain the park in the face of diminishing city resources.

It is the lushness of the new green sod that is so astonishing. For despite the fact that the park is a landscape, it has become over the years a harsher physical environment than it was intended to be, with far too much paved area and far too many brown spots amid the green. It is not the soft place it once was, and the incredible softness of the Sheep Meadow now, juxtaposed against the hard edges of the buildings surrounding the park, has a great drama to it, far more powerful than anything that was there in the past.

The Sheep Meadow is now lined with signs that cheerfully urge park users to keep off the grass until it grows, and chain-link fencing that makes the same point rather less graciously. But the fencing is a good idea, if rather inconsistent with the park's democratic ideals.

Without it there is not a chance of this new lawn's survival. Indeed, when a section of the park near Fifth Avenue opposite the Frick Collection was resodded a year or so back, it was surrounded by light, temporary wooden fences, which were torn down by people eager to use the new lawn as a playing field. The result was the complete destruction of the sod, and there is now nothing in that section of the park except a messy brown expanse.

Indeed, the vista across the Sheep Meadow is so splendid now that one is tempted half seriously to suggest that the fence might be left up permanently, on the theory that the people of New York will derive more pleasure from being able to stare at the miracle of a real lawn in the midst of the park than they would from walking on it and, ultimately, destroying it. As things now stand, Mrs. Barlow, the park administrator, expects that the fencing will stay up well into the summer, since the roots of the new sod are only beginning to weave themselves into the underlying ground. Several early summer concerts that traditionally take place on the Sheep Meadow have been moved to the Great Lawn.

The current state of the Sheep Meadow raises a crucial question about just what the park should be used for, and it is not a new issue at all. For a hundred years the park has been the center of a struggle between those who see it more as a great public gathering place, sort of a public square for civic events, and those who see it more as a tranquil retreat from city life.

Frederick Law Olmsted, the landscape architect who, with Calvert Vaux, created the park (and with it gave birth to the modern profession of landscape architecture), was firmly in the latter camp: he envisioned Central Park as a piece of the country, as a place in which those who could not leave the city could briefly escape its tensions. But Olmsted was hardly what we would today call an elitist; quite the contrary. His very notion was that the park could further the democratic ideal by permitting the various social classes to mix together, on equal footing, in this great open space. To this end he insisted that the park contain the greatest variety possible of different landscape experiences.

What he argued zealously against was the intrusion of much organized activity into the park. To Olmsted, the park was a pastoral experience, a quiet retreat from other tensions, and the meaning of that experience was diminished if the park became a place of athletic contests, musical events, and huge crowds attending organized festivals.

Not that these did not exist in Olmsted's time. Indeed, one of the most surprising things his writings offer us is the constant reminder of how similar the park's problems were in the nineteenth century to those faced today. Here is Olmsted in 1875 on the problems of maintaining the grass:

"During the dry weather fully a quarter of all the turf of the larger open spaces of the south park was trodden out and eradicated; the soil having no protection was pulverized by those walking on it and blew away in dust," he wrote in a letter to the Board of Park Commissioners.

Olmsted argued in favor of a brief closing of a section, as has been done with the Sheep Meadow: "If the public can be kept off and the turf be allowed a few months' respite from wear, it may recover a tolerable condition. If such use cannot be discontinued it is certain to present a dreary and stultifying appearance, and to bring discredit to the government of the city by midsummer."

Olmsted's foresight in this, as in so many other areas, was remarkable. He fully recognized that the park would become the province of many different ethnic groups. In 1863 the board of commissioners, following Olmsted's own ideas, wrote that the park's population "was reared in different climes, and bringing to the metropolis ideas of social enjoyment differing as wildly as the temperature of the various countries of their origin. The amusements and routine of the daily life of the Sicilian and the Scotsman are dissimilar. Each brings with him the traditions and habits of his own country."

Each group was entitled to use the park as it wished, Olmsted believed, so long as its activities did not interfere with the enjoyment of others. It is a position the park's administrators seem now to be beginning to return to. After many years of believing that the park was best used as a center for festivals and concerts and all sorts of activities, the parks department now, under Commissioner Davis, has begun to urge civic groups to hold activities involving large crowds elsewhere.

Such decisions are difficult, but probably necessary, for without some reduction in the present heavy usage, there may be no Central Park at all in a few years. There are some summer Sundays these days when the heavy crowds using the park make a mockery of the original vision of this open space as a pastoral escape from city tensions; the noise and tension within the park can be so severe that relaxation comes when one goes back onto the city streets.

The park is in troubled physical condition; the exquisite green blanket of the Sheep Meadow is misleading, for there is serious deterioration throughout the park. To discourage the sort of heavy public use that has come to the park in the last ten or fifteen years is an uncomfortable task, surely, but it is doubtless in the park's best interests in the long run. Without some kind of moderation in use, this brilliant creation—New York's greatest work of architecture, in some ways—may not survive.

—June 5, 1980

The Freeway as an Art Form

When Seattle decided a few years ago to turn an old gasworks into a monumental sculptural centerpiece for a new park, it thrust itself into the vanguard of American park design. Now this city has confirmed its position with another unusual park, this one a 5.4-acre mass of concrete completely covering a stretch of downtown freeway. Called simply Freeway Park, it does triple duty: it provides downtown open space, eliminates freeway noise, and links together two segments of town that the highway had cut apart from each other.

Freeway Park was created, in other words, to counter the effect the freeway had on the cityscape. Downtown highways have been ruthless destroyers of the urban fabric, cutting neighborhoods in two and drastically altering the ambiance of older cities. We may not be building many more of them any longer, but plenty are there, and Freeway Park is one of the few sensible responses any designer has yet offered to the problem.

Lawrance Halprin and Associates of San Francisco were the designers of the $3.5-million park, which is tied into a new office building by Van Slyck, Callison, Nelson of Seattle and a garage by Narramore, Bain, Brody and Johnson of Seattle. The overall project cost was $24 million.

The park consists of several flat, open, planted areas, grouped largely at the ends of a site that rambles in a rough diagonal across the freeway. The central visual element, however, is a dramatic 32-foot-deep concrete canyon, filled with waterfalls.

The canyon drops from the elevated park level to ground level over the median strip of the freeway. Like many of Mr. Halprin's designs, the canyon relies heavily on concrete—it is boxy and hard-edged, a configuration that poses some safety hazard. But Mr. Halprin believes the canyon discourages visitors from taking chances and thus poses little real physical danger. A similar concrete fountain area of a Halprin park in Portland, Oregon, has had an extremely good safety record.

At Seattle, terraces and irregular stairs and passageways bring the visitor into what feels like a deep crevasse. The view of the city disappears, the planting of the park's upper levels falls away, and the visitor is left in a concrete chasm, with water tumbling powerfully down all around him.

It is a striking place, far removed from the feeling of the surrounding city. But Mr. Halprin skillfully brings back the sense of the city with one splendid gesture—at the bottom of the canyon, behind the largest of the several waterfalls, is a vast window onto the freeway. The cars glide by, their sound hidden by the water, their movement framed by the windows. Suddenly the freeway becomes like a segment of an abstract movie.

The window is so successful that one can only wish that Mr. Halprin had done more with the idea of letting the park use the freeway as a design element. Most of the park is fairly conventional, as current park design goes, its major excitement emerging from what it does rather than how it does it, but the window onto the freeway is something altogether new. It transforms the mad onrush of cars not by denying their existence, but by catching their movement in a frame.

"I don't think we gain much by perceiving freeways as ugly monsters," Mr. Halprin said the other day. "We should deal with the freeway as a modern art form, integrating it into the city, taming it rather than complaining about it."

That is essentially what he has done, in a way that is far more sophisticated than most other such efforts, like the mediocre apartment towers dropped over the approach to the George Washington Bridge in Manhattan.

Indeed, Freeway Park recalls the very finest attempts to integrate urban highways into neighborhoods; it deserves to rank with such pioneering efforts as the Brooklyn Heights Esplanade over the Brooklyn-Queens Expressway or the integration of Carl Schurz Park into the F.D.R. Drive on the Upper East Side of Manhattan.

—March 9, 1977
Seattle

Georgetown Park: The Stage Set as Retail Environment

The most talked-about new building in Washington, D.C., right now is not another museum or government building or embassy or office block. It is a $93-million complex of stores and condominium apartments, and it is shoehorned tightly into a block just above the Potomac River in fashionable Georgetown.

The project is called Georgetown Park, and most Washingtonians seem rather unsure of what to make of it, for it is a strange hybrid in this city of generally rather bland and straightforward architecture. Georgetown Park is a combination of nineteenth-century decoration and twentieth-century merchandising—a three-level, in-town shopping mall with a triple-tiered marble fountain at its center, cast-iron railings, a large octagonal glass dome, patterned tile floors, and lights set in vast glass urns.

The entire complex is enclosed in a set of red-brick walls, some of which are remnants of the nineteenth-century industrial buildings that once filled the site, while others are twentieth-century reproductions, done in the hope of blending this large project gracefully into the old, small-scale Georgetown streetscape. Parking for 500 cars is hidden underground, and 128 condominium apartments are spread across the roof in the form of a small hill village.

Inside, instead of Muzak, Mozart is piped through the sound system, and scattered in and around all of the Victoriana of the interior mall are such establishments as Mark Cross, F.A.O. Schwarz, Godiva Chocolates, and Crabtree & Evelyn. There are more than ninety shops in all, and most of them are aimed clearly at the well-to-do professionals who now make up so much of the Washington retail market.

Georgetown Park,
Washington, D.C.

143

Georgetown Park is surely not like anything Washington or any other city has seen. It is a far cry from the sleek icebox of Chicago's Water Tower Place, perhaps its closest equivalent as an in-town version of the covered suburban mall, and it is farther still from the artificial street-fair atmosphere of Boston's Faneuil Hall Market or Baltimore's Harborplace.

Georgetown Park seems to have been designed with absolute seriousness to make us think that it is what would have resulted had the Victorians known about our modern concept of enclosed interior malls. It is a modern urban mall in its layout, in its design, in its accommodation to the automobile, and in its cleverly merchandised mix of shops and condominium residences. But in all of its interior decoration, it is an earnest, and very self-conscious, Victorian stage set.

The fact of the matter is that the Victorians did know about the enclosed mall, and that knowledge resulted in such landmark works of nineteenth-century architecture as the covered arcades in Cleveland and Providence. These are both natural, easy places, grand and self-assured, without any of the sense of self-consciousness that marks this design.

But if Georgetown Park is a bit precious, it is also a lot pleasanter than almost any other urban shopping mall in the nation. Its builder, the Western Development Corporation of Washington, is a group of fairly young, alert real-estate operators who are not locked into the formulas of an earlier generation.

It is not for nothing, then, that Washingtonians are flocking to this place. The profusion of decoration and detail, the colors, the sunlight that floods in through the glass dome, all contribute to a far more relaxed shopping environment than virtually any other large-scale mall has yet been able to provide. Whatever else can be said about it, it is hard to deny that ersatz Victorian is better than an honest suburban mall.

And the architects of this project, Alan Lockman & Associates, Clark, Harris, Tribble & Li Associates, Roger Sherman & Associates, and Wah Yee & Associates, have had not only a good sense of detail, but they understand planning and movement as well. The main entrance to the retail mall is on Georgetown's busy M Street, from which we are deposited not at the bottom of the three-story atrium, but at the top. The view down enhances the drama of the space considerably; it makes us want to explore the complex space entirely. And the overall layout is also skillful. The apartment units have been fully separated from the shopping mall, so that there is no sense of living over the store. Instead, they are broken into small groups for privacy and arrayed across the roof of the project, which will itself be turned into a garden.

The apartments, which sell for $170,000 to $250,000, are somewhat more conventional. But they are hardly standard: the layout of the complex yields not only unusually shaped rooms but also a number of large, private roof terraces. And inside there are moldings and fireplace mantels which, though mass-produced and hardly of custom quality, are nonetheless a clear attempt to extend the idea of period detail from the mall into the houses.

This entire complex, then, from its Victorian lamps to its mock-Georgian kitchen doors, is something of an event in the evolution of popular taste. It is hard to be quite sure, however, whether this is low art gone fancy or high art gone popular. Serious architects in the last few years have been moving more and more toward the reuse of historical styles; a lot of inexpensive commercial projects never gave up copying the past, and Georgetown Park seems to be a place in which these two types meet. It is clearly serious design, not cheap commercialism, and yet it carries the notion of the stage set as a retail environment farther than we have yet seen it go.

The project raises other issues beyond those of architecture and taste, and it may be that these, in the end, will be the most important determinants of its success. Whatever its garb, Georgetown Park is at base a regional shopping mall, and there is a real question as to whether that is what Georgetown needs. For the neighborhood is already crowded beyond reason; traffic is heavy and the sidewalks of M Street and Wisconsin Avenue are often so full that pedestrians are forced off the curb.

It may be that the presence of Georgetown Park will pull some of these people off the streets and into the mall, relieving crowding. But it may simply bring more people and more cars into Georgetown, adding to the congestion and, most importantly, taking Georgetown farther from being a residential neighborhood. It has been something of a tourist magnet, not to mention a shopping center, for much of metropolitan Washington for some time now, and the opening of Georgetown Park can only increase this trend.

—October 19, 1981
Washington

The East Building

It could not, at first glance, be more different from the building it adjoins: the new East Building of the National Gallery by I. M. Pei & Partners is sharp and geometric, a trapezoid sliced into triangles, while beside it the original gallery of 1941 by John Russell Pope is a neoclassical palace, serene and sumptuous. But the two buildings are more similar than they at first suggest. Not only are they both constructed of marble from the same Tennessee quarry; much more important, they are buildings that respond to a similar set of attitudes. Both buildings are monumental, intended to provide a sense of grandeur and permanence, yet both represent endeavors to make their monumentality serve, not fight, the art they house.

Both are conservative buildings. By the time the Pope building was constructed, a literally classical building such as that columned, low-domed structure struck many as reactionary, for modern architecture by then had become an accepted style. Now, curiously, taste has changed again; literal reproduction is not so quickly condemned, and it is the sharp and powerful geometrics of modernism that seem conservative.

So the gallery has made a choice that is, ironically, not so very different from the one it made thirty-seven years ago. It has opted not to stand at the advance guard, but to seek to create the very best building it could in an established style. And by these standards the new building is not merely a success, it is a work of considerable distinction.

The East Building represents a kind of quality we will rarely see again in our time. The generous gifts of the Mellon family and its foundation, underwriters of most of the $94.4-million cost, have made possible a structure

Main entry,
East Building,
National Gallery,
Washington, D.C.

147

of lavish appointments, impeccable detail, and splendid workmanship. The East Building is surely the finest piece of contemporary architecture in official Washington; it is equally certainly the most distinguished structure to come out of the Pei office in many years. And it is among the very best buildings of the current generation of museum structures.

The building occupies a trapezoidal site, and unlike the ponderous Hirshhorn Museum across the Mall, it responds to its context by allowing the site's geometries to determine the form of the building. Thus the trapezoid, which was sliced in two to divide the structure into a public museum, the larger triangle; and a study center, the smaller one. There are three high towers at each corner of the public triangle, and between them is a 60-foot-high glass-covered court.

The galleries—about which more in a moment—are set within the towers and around the court. The court itself is one of the more successful such spaces in any museum, new or old; it is every bit as noble as, yet a good bit more welcoming than, the rotunda, its symbolic partner in the original National Gallery next door.

The court serves as both orientation space and as display space. It contains several works commissioned especially for it, most conspicuously an immense Calder mobile that hangs beneath the tetrahedronal skylight and a Miró tapestry that adorns a high, stark marble wall. The court is punctuated by bridges that cross it to connect various gallery spaces, and by a grand staircase, balconies, windows, and trees.

What is most impressive is the subtle balance of elements Mr. Pei and his associates, Leonard Jacobson and Thomas Schmitt, have achieved here: the space is at once active and serene. There are constantly changing patterns of light and shadow and form and void, yet there is never the sense of busyness. The strong, silent, marble walls provide the perfect counterpoint to the slow, gliding motion of the Calder and the faster movements of people back and forth across the bridges. The solid, confident enclosures the marble walls create extend up beyond the skylights, making the three towers visible up through the glass ceiling and giving the central space an important vertical dimension.

More important than the effect that watching the movements of others has on one's perception of this space is the effect of one's own movement, and here, too, Mr. Pei has orchestrated everything with skill. The entrance from the street brings one into a low vestibule space under a coffered concrete ceiling just 10 feet high, enhancing the drama of movement beyond into the great court. Better still is the entrance from the underground concourse that connects the East Building with the original building; from here, the elements of the court reveal themselves in a gradual and wonderful sequence as one moves slowly up a great marble stair into the space.

The building offers a wide variety of gallery areas, most of which were deliberately left unfinished by the architect, like loft spaces. The National

Gallery's own design staff then took over to design the exhibition installations, which, while technically temporary, are so elaborate and complex that they feel like finished rooms. The galleries of twentieth-century art are the best—superb rooms that are both interesting spaces in themselves and entirely at the service of the art they contain. There is amphitheater-like space for David Smith sculptures, a multisided room of de Kooning pictures, a rectangular room of Rothkos, and a squared-off spiral space for Barnett Newmans; in each case the installation both enhances the viewer's ability to see each work and permits the works themselves to engage in dialogue with one another.

One does lose a sense of the building itself within these rooms; they are creations apart from Mr. Pei's, and it is only on a return to the great court that one feels again a sense of where one is.

The facade itself is not, by any means, a lively one, and the long marble wall on Pennsylvania Avenue is especially somber. Of course, that may not mean much in Washington, where no one ever seems to walk, and this facade is seen mostly from moving automobiles; that way, the angled masses at least play off against one another to provide some life.

The building's insistent geometry—almost everything is based on a triangle—occasionally becomes a bit obsessive, as in the case of the stairwells in the study-center wing that rise not straight but along an angle, making it difficult to ascend comfortably. There seems to have been a sense here that consistency was everything, an unnecessary belief that any break whatsoever from the triangular motif would somehow weaken the overall design.

But that is a minor problem. What is more important is the allegiance Mr. Pei has paid both to the art within the East Building and to the urban context surrounding it. In an age in which it is fashionable to relate to existing buildings by reproducing their forms literally, the East Building stands as an important lesson that architecture can communicate across the generations in other ways as well.

—*May 30, 1978*
Washington

Louis Kahn's Legacy of Silence and Light

Louis Kahn spoke often of his love for the elements of silence and light, and there is a room in the new Yale Center for British Art that explains this love more clearly, perhaps, than anything else the architect ever made. This room is a great interior court, three stories high, with walls of oak set as panels within the building's exposed concrete frame. Skylights admit diffused light, which tumbles down softly through the space, like a gentle snow. The walls are hung with just a few large paintings, and to one side of the room sits a massive concrete cylinder within which is contained a stair; it sits silently, not an intruder but a form that plays off gently against the other elements of the room and brings just the right amount of movement and power to the space.

If the Center for British Art contained this room alone, it would rank as a significant building of our time. But the new museum—the last major building Kahn designed before his death in 1974—is a set of rooms that also includes distinguished public spaces and some of the finest settings for the display of paintings constructed in any modern museum. The galleries are at once intimate and grand and perhaps because of the special attention paid to light, they are always—as few modern galleries are—serene.

The building is radical in some ways, conservative in others. There are commercial shops on the ground floor, as the result of pressure from the city of New Haven, which wanted tax revenue, and the students of Yale, who wanted a lively street, and the stores do their job well without detracting from the sense of overall dignity. The facade is made up largely of panels of stainless steel in a dark, pewter finish that are set within a frame of concrete, much as the wood is set within the concrete frame

Yale Center for British Art and British Studies, New Haven

inside the building. The overall effect is perhaps a bit too somber, in spite of the occasional glass areas set into the stainless steel; moreover, the combination of metal and concrete does not feel quite as comfortable as that of the wood and concrete used inside.

But the facade has a rhythm that is the perfect counterpoint to the stone arches of the old Yale Art Gallery and the solid brick facade of Kahn's own "new" Yale Art Gallery, both of which are across Chapel Street from the new building. Kahn's Yale Art Gallery, which was completed in 1953, was the architect's first major building, and it is an extraordinary trick of fate that it should be across the street from his last. The buildings carry on a dialogue with each other that is exciting and moving; elements such as Kahn's use of exposed concrete and movable panels for picture display exist as daring, fresh ideas in the first building, as refined concepts in the second.

The new building is entered through a corner portico, a low space that gives with splendid surprise into a fine four-story lobby court. This court is a higher version of the one containing the stair; it is different also in that it is roofed in clear glass rather than the special sunlight diffusers used elsewhere in the building, so it reminds us that we are not quite inside yet—that the glare of natural light has not yet been replaced by the softness of diffused light that we will feel elsewhere.

The visitor moves ahead to elevators or to the round stair tower, and the plan of the building becomes clear: it is a rectangular shape with two courts cutting through around which galleries, libraries, and offices are arranged. Elevators are in the middle, and so is the stairway, which projects its round housing into one of the courts. The stair that sits within that concrete cylinder is harsh and strong, a square object inside a round container, its powerful geometries softened by natural light from above and by the use of travertine steps set into the concrete. It ennobles the act of ascending, yet since it is enclosed it never overwhelms other more important aspects of the building.

Two square mechanical shafts cut their way upward through the building; they are sheathed in the stainless steel of the outside panels and set at 45 degrees to the building's grid to emphasize their different role. As in all of Kahn's work, structure and mechanical systems are left exposed, not so much because the architect liked their appearance as because he felt it was false to hide either the process of construction or the mechanical processes by which the building operates. At the Yale Center, the vertical shafts and air ducts of aluminum left uncovered in all of the galleries are the main means by which we are made to feel the building's pulse, and their visual effect is one of unexpected dignity.

There are exquisite details too numerous to mention, many of which were from Kahn's own hand and many of which are the work of Anthony Pellechia and Marshall Meyers, two former Kahn employees whose own firm was named as successor architect after Kahn's death, which came at a point when some interior details were still incomplete. In each case, an attempt has been made to stay close to the Kahn spirit; the elegant wood doors with hints of panels in them were modeled after those Kahn had used for the Kimbell Art Museum in Fort Worth, for example.

Kahn's death led to a certain caution; no one could have been absolutely certain what the architect would have done with some of the unfinished details, and it was doubtless wisest to take the most conservative course—although one wonders what Kahn would have thought of the misguided desire to pursue "good taste" in the galleries by hiding the signs to the rest rooms. But much more important is that the galleries themselves welcome the visitor with a graciousness few museum spaces created in our time have been able to achieve.

The galleries are divided into 20-foot bays that are expressed by strips of travertine on the floor, by the placement of linen-covered panels on which pictures are hung, and by the arrangement of the concrete ceiling beams. The colors are soft and the material rich; Kahn understood that it is pleasurable to view art in a room rather than an institutional space, especially when the art has come largely from British country houses. But he could never indulge in anything so literal as the vulgar imitation rooms of the Lehman collection at the Metropolitan Museum; his solution effectively creates the aura of a room while never denying its existence as a gallery.

But in the end, it is the light that makes the building so extraordinary. The top-floor galleries are lit by an elaborate diffusing system in the skylights, a joint effort of the architect, the lighting consultant, Richard Kelly, and the Macomber Construction Company. The skylights brilliantly soften natural light and spread it evenly but permit the quality of light to change as clouds pass overhead. Thus we are ever aware of the sun's movements, tying our perceptions into the greater world and reminding us always that we are in a special place.

—April 18, 1977

The Getty Museum: A Roman Villa in Malibu

It isn't every day that they build a Roman villa beside the highway, even in Southern California, so when the J. Paul Getty Museum was finished in 1974 eyebrows were raised in art and architecture circles across the country. A number of critics were scandalized at the idea of erecting a fake Roman villa in the 1970's. Others accepted the basic premise but quibbled about the building's authenticity. But the public loved it, and while the controversy still rages in professional circles, attendance at the museum has been so high that visitors are now being accepted only by reservation.

In this land where popular taste is king, one is tempted to let the Getty's attendance figures be its judgment. But the building does raise a number of real questions of architectural propriety, and it is only fair to deal seriously with them.

In 1941 the opening of the National Gallery, John Russell Pope's classical mausoleum in Washington, provoked a similar controversy, as the righteous forces of modernism clashed with the equally righteous forces of good taste who strove to defend Pope's use of antiquated forms. Today, our belief in modernism is less fervent, and our views of architecture less ideologically rigid in general, and thus there have been some voices raised in defense of the Getty Museum not as something proper and noble but merely as a building that is fun and pleasant to be in.

This line of reasoning is surely the most avant-garde of the various defenses put forth; it has become somewhat fashionable in California circles to praise the Getty as one might, say, praise Disneyland. But the Getty is not Disneyland; it is a serious attempt to reproduce, as accurately as possible, a Roman villa, and as such it must be judged. The Getty's ostensible model was the Villa dei Papyri, a villa at Herculaneum near Pompeii buried in the eruption of Mount Vesuvius.

Unfortunately only an incomplete floor plan by the Swiss engineer Karl Weber, who excavated Herculaneum in 1750, exists for guidance, and the rest of the Getty's design was completed by a Los Angeles architectural archeologist, Dr. Norman Neuerberg, who selected details and facades from other villas. Working with Dr. Neuerberg were Los Angeles architects Langdon and Wilson, a large commercial firm whose previous experience had run more to steel-and-glass office buildings than to Roman villas.

The result of Dr. Neuerberg's labors is a heavy, formal building, full of bright colors and *trompe l'oeil* murals, an accurate reminder that Roman taste was never quite as refined as the Beaux Arts always made it out to be. There are elaborate formal gardens and a huge colonnaded central court surrounded by galleries. The level of craftsmanship is remarkable: there is marble and plasterwork of a sort rarely seen today, and much of it was done, ironically, by California stage-set craftspeople.

In true California style, the building departs most sharply from precedent in order to service the automobile. The entire structure sits on a basement platform that contains a garage. Moreover, the building is entered from the garage, an appropriate homage to the California drive-in tradition if not to the Romans.

The building, it should be said, is by far the most pleasant museum in which to view art in Southern California. The gardens and fountains that surround it make the experience relaxed and even joyous, and the galleries themselves are for the most part attractive, well-scaled rooms.

There are some problems, however. An excess of marble in some galleries provides a loud and insensitive background for marble busts, and it can well be argued that the appropriateness of a Roman-style structure is lessened somewhat by the fact that most of the Getty collection consists not of Roman art at all, but of European paintings and furniture.

One wonders, given all of this, why the museum's creators have wasted so much energy trying to prove that the building is authentic. We will never know precisely what the Villa dei Papyri looked like, and any attempt to reconstruct it must rely heavily on conjecture. That is all right; there is no real need to be literal, and the strongest failing of this building is the pretentious and somewhat sterile air that its strivings for literal reproduction seem to have created.

But for all of this, the Getty Museum is nonetheless a pleasurable place to be in, and it deserves credit as such. A false building is not likely to achieve the very highest level of architectural sophistication, and one wishes the designers of the Getty had only realized this, relaxed a bit, and let the museum be more of what it seems, even now, to have always wanted to be: a California stage set.

—August 26, 1975
Malibu, Calif.

The Albany Mall: Clichés of Modern Architecture

There is a strong temptation to view the Albany Mall as a grandiose, utter folly, and while it is not merely that, there is a lot of that aspect to it. The buildings of the mall are so foolish, so silly, so impractical as to be indefensible on serious architectural grounds, yet they do come together to make a totality with a certain futuristic tone to it, as if Buck Rogers were creating a seat of government.

But while acknowledging that the buildings of the mall have a powerful sense of place to them—even if that place appears to be more the planet Krypton than the capital of the state of New York—we are entitled, one suspects, to a bit more reality for $2-billion worth of public funds. And reality is in short supply in this complex.

It was intended, former Governor Nelson A. Rockefeller said, to symbolize the vitality of the state and its government. Vitality the mall has precious little of: its characteristics are pomposity and banality, qualities that, in their own way, perhaps, to many people symbolize government just as well.

The chief architect was Wallace K. Harrison of Harrison & Abramovitz, and what Mr. Harrison has wrought, in brief, is a quarter-mile-long open space containing a reflecting pool and surrounded on three sides by new buildings (the fourth side is open to the State Capitol). One long side is filled by a low office building and four identical 23-story towers, behind which runs a stretched-out low marble building; the opposite side contains another low marble building, a 44-story tower, and a bizarre upside-down dome like a half-grapefruit that contains a meeting center. A massive library-museum complex fills the far end opposite the Capitol.

Underneath the whole business is a multistory plat-

Albany Mall
(Empire State Plaza)

form containing a concourse and underground parking. The concourse is the kind of space that makes an airport corridor look warm; it is white, fluorescent-lit, and runs for the full quarter-mile length. And the parking assures that every mall occupant can live out the suburban dream of never having to set foot on a city street.

The buildings themselves are a compendium of clichés of modern architecture. The four identical towers each consist of a wedge of marble around which is wrapped a steel and glass form, cantilevered for dramatic effect. Here the mall's futuristic yearnings are at their best, and in their similarity, the four towers, taken together, are not unimpressive as a piece of minimal sculpture.

But as buildings they are absurd—they are so small (only 12,000 square feet a floor) that they cannot begin to approach practicality, and it is obvious that efficiency here—as in so much of this complex—was put aside in favor of architecture, or in favor of what someone thought was architecture. But peek behind the curtain and there is no architecture, really—there is some structural razzle-dazzle as a means to futurist imagery, and that is all.

Across the mall, the larger tower, its mass presumably intended to provide some sort of balance for the four smaller ones, lacks even the little towers' benign silliness. It is merely a huge glass wedge, with a badly detailed skin and interiors that suggest dreary bureaucracy in the extreme.

Any thought that the whole place, in its almost innocent way, might be sort of fun disappears with the low-rise buildings, which can only be called an invitation to grieve. The library-museum at the termination of the mall, its horizontal floors sitting atop marble piers, traces its descent—like so many buildings—from Le Corbusier's great monastery at La Tourette, France. But here Le Corbusier's forms are frozen into a useless symmetry, clad in marble and trying desperately to appear pretty and delicate, as if an obese woman chose to dress herself in a tutu.

Here, too, sensible design has been put aside in favor of someone's—was it Mr. Harrison's or Mr. Rockefeller's?—misguided notion of art. An immense stair connects the end of the mall to the library entrance; it is so big it bridges a street. The museum section of the building is entered from underneath the stairs, as in a service entrance. So one enters one section like a character in a Cecil B. De Mille movie, and the other one like a delivery person.

The *pièce de résistance*, however, is the Legislative Office Building, ironically the one facility in the complex for which the need was undeniable. Here again, glaring white marble covers all—even, at what must have been extraordinary expenses, the fire stairs.

Buildings communicate messages, and it is hard to look at this one and not think of a government obsessed with power and monumentality, but utterly lacking in any sort of imagination or ideas. The form of the building is a sloppy attempt at classicism; it is basically a marble box with a wider marble box on top of it and a lot of vertical openings that appear to be windows.

The inside is expansive and confusing. So much space is wasted that one is tempted to say, like the mothers who tell their children that the poor could be fed with the food they wasted, that all the poor could be housed with the square feet wasted in this building alone.

One example will suffice. There is a huge, three-story marble hall in this building, with an enormous staircase. The hall goes from nowhere to nowhere; it is not an entrance hall, or a central hall, or anything. The pathetic space has come to be known around Albany as "the well," and indeed it is so badly proportioned it looked more like a hole than a hall. It has no reason to exist, and its design is so inept that the bulbs in its ceiling can only be changed with special scaffolding.

The list of such strange design decisions goes on and on—why, for example, the computer services of the Motor Vehicles Department are housed in an elongated marble sarcophagus may never be explained. Neither, probably, will the architect's belief that an upside-down dome was in some way an appropriate form for an auditorium.

Ultimately, of course, one realizes that the entire mall complex is not so much a vision of the future as of the past. The ideas here were dead before they left the drawing board, and every design decision, from the space allocations to the overall concept, emerges from an outdated notion of what modern architecture, not to mention modern government, should stand for.

The mall may look like Buck Rogers, but it is important to remember that the Buck Rogers comic-book visions were all drawn decades ago. Now they have become a comfortable part of our popular past, and it is only a tragically misguided kind of thinking that could turn them into icons for the present.

—July 2, 1976
Albany

The Portland Building

Michael Graves is a forty-eight-year-old native of Indianapolis who has practiced architecture in the shadow of Princeton University for the last eighteen years. For most of that time, he attracted little attention beyond architecture's academic salons, where his work has been the subject of interest for at least a decade. In the last few years, however, Graves has burst into a kind of celebrity shared by no other architect of his generation—and, indeed, probably by no other architect practicing today except Philip Johnson, who has been cultivating his own persona since before Graves was even born. Michael Graves's latest building, a 15-story office and municipal-services building for the city of Portland, Oregon, has been more eagerly awaited than any new building in the country except perhaps the Johnson and Burgee firm's American Telephone & Telegraph Company headquarters in New York, and it is at least as controversial.

Today, Graves is interviewed on talk shows when he travels. He is asked to design fabrics, furniture, and teapots as well as buildings. His drawings command prices in the thousands of dollars at a fashionable 57th Street gallery, and a signed Graves poster—not even an original drawing—recently changed hands for $1,000.

Graves's popularity—which has startled many of his students and strained his relationship with architectural colleagues—has led him to be praised in some circles as the greatest architect of his time and denounced in others as a mere creature of fashion. But the fact of the matter is that Graves, if he is not an epoch-making figure, is the most truly original voice that American architecture has produced in some time. His architecture is a kind of collage, an assemblage of parts, that speaks simultaneously to a public eager for easy visual delight, and to a profession that wants an architecture that seems grounded in a theoretical and academic base. His work is dazzling to look at, and yet it deals in issues more profound than simply the decoration of construction.

The Portland Building, as the new Graves building in Oregon has been named, typifies the Graves style—and has been, in and of itself, the source of much of the architect's recent fame. It is a hulk-like, somewhat squat mass that resembles neither a typical modern office building nor the sort of classical civic structure the Beaux Arts brought to the American downtown. Its facade, brightly colored in hues of deep terra-cotta and blue and ivory, is an assemblage of abstract interpretations of classical forms. It has hints of Art Deco to it, and suggestions of the mystical work of the great eighteenth-century French visionaries Etienne-Louis Boullée and Claude-Nicolas Ledoux. But the finished building looks like nothing so much as a wildly decorated version of one of those large, vertical storage buildings with blank fronts and classical ornamentation that exist in odd corners of Manhattan and other older cities.

The Portland Building is Graves's first fairly large-scale work to move from paper to reality. Although it may look strange and a trifle awkward at first impression, it is no exaggeration to say that, so far as the development of American architecture is concerned, it is the most important public building to open thus far in this decade. It is a monument of postmodernism, a determined rejection of the cool, unadorned forms of orthodox modern architecture. There have been postmodern houses, apartments, showrooms, and offices by the dozen, but Graves is bringing this attitude to a major public building.

The choice of Graves to design the Portland Building—over such established architects of large office buildings as Romaldo Giurgola and Arthur Erickson, who also submitted designs—was denounced as ridiculous by a figure as esteemed in American architecture as Pietro Belluschi and defended as a noble gesture by Philip Johnson, who had advised the city of Portland on its decision. The controversy between two of American architecture's most venerable practitioners—one saw Graves as a traitor to modern architecture; the other saw him as representing the best hope for the future—guaranteed that the building would become Portland's most famous work of contemporary architecture while it was still a set of elegantly colored drawings. And it helped set Michael Graves—by then already the object of increasing, if puzzled, interest in architectural circles—on the way to his general celebrity.

Portland decided to go ahead with the building in part because of Philip Johnson's enthusiasm, in part because the city government, led by Mayor Francis Ivancie, genuinely preferred the Graves design. The preference was not merely esthetic—the city hired the Morse-Diesel project management company to rate all three architects' schemes on practical aspects, such as mechanical systems, efficiency of offices, and operating cost. The Graves design came out on top. Earl Bradfish, director of Portland's office of general services, said that the Graves building "better met our specifications for space than the others, was cheaper to build, and was more energy efficient."

The suggestion that such an unusual building might in the end be more, rather than less, practical than the dreary glass box has done little to silence Graves's critics. Now that the building is complete, opinions seem sharper than ever. Wolf Von Eckardt, *Time* magazine's architecture critic, journeyed to Portland and produced one of the most violent denunciations of an American

Sketches for the Portland Building by Michael Graves

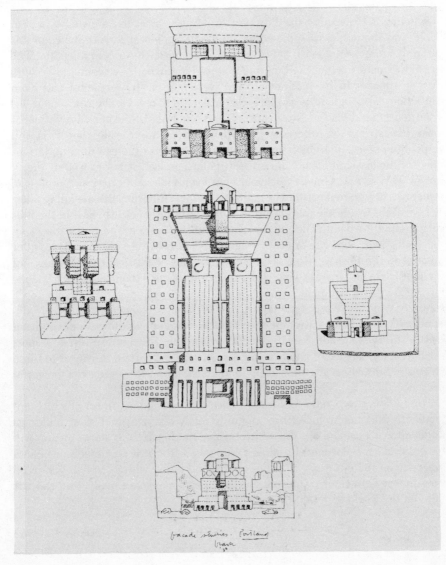

building ever written by an architecture critic. Von Eckardt called the Portland Building "pop surrealism" and then went on to say he found the prospect of other architects following in the direction set by Graves "dangerous," a word almost unprecedented in architectural criticism.

On the other hand, Vincent Scully, the Yale architectural historian, has written that the finished Portland Building "is of Portland and for Portland, a victory of mind and spirit in this place," and he spoke of it as having "a totally unexpected cultural assurance. One is at home there, as one had never expected to be in a modern office building."

If Scully is generous—the Portland Building is a bit too unusual to feel at home in without at least some adjustment—his enlightened acceptance of it is certainly more on the mark than Von Eckardt's nearly hysterical rejection. The fact of the matter is that the building is considerably more welcoming in reality than it appears to be in drawing and model form. It is fanciful and even exuberant, although it is far less classical than Graves's rhetoric about his intentions would lead one to expect. It is a touch garish, especially with what looks like stripes of reflecting glass that run up the facade, but it is still respectful of certain architectural conventions that are the essential underpinnings of the classical ideal. The greatest failing, in fact, is not in what is there, but in what is not: Graves's original plan for a village of classical temple-like structures on the roof was never realized, and it diminishes the overall results.

The offices inside are quite routine, but they offer generous views of the hills surrounding Portland. The public rooms and the sequence of entry spaces on the main floor, which were all designed by Graves, are superb. They offer homage to the formal, two-story entry vestibules of classical courthouses, but the motifs are all Graves's own. Like the series of showrooms Graves has done for the furniture company Sunar, these interiors rely heavily on color, on a carefully controlled processional sequence through changing and tightly defined spaces, and on an attempt to use fabric, wooden moldings, and wood and plaster to evoke traditional forms of ornament. The end result is a most extraordinary balance of nobility and ease. There is a certain sternness to these Graves rooms. For all their color and decoration, they create a powerful presence.

The building pays only minor obeisance to its neighbors, most of which are mediocre works of architecture. The only really distinguished older buildings in downtown Portland are the white terra-cotta department stores a couple of blocks away, the Portland Building's true peers. But it is an altogether benign presence on the cityscape. If it does not blend easily with its neighbors, in no way does it fight them. The building is both gracious and lively, and the last thing in the world it should be called is silly.

—October 10, 1982

James Stirling Builds at Rice

For some years now, architects have been expressing concern for the way in which a new building relates to its surroundings. Whereas modern buildings once tended to be conceived as pure, abstract objects, independent of what was beside them, there is now much more attention paid to the notion of fitting a building into its architectural context—trying, in other words, to make certain that the building echoes many of the architectural themes of its neighbors. It is a philosophy of design that suggests, by implication at least, that it may be better to be discreet than to be original.

Perhaps the ultimate example of such contextual architecture has now been completed here, in this city of generally large and very uncontextual buildings. It is the new building of the School of Architecture at Rice University, and it is the first American work to be completed by James Stirling, the British architect who was the 1981 recipient of the Pritzker Prize, the $100,000 international architectural award that has come to be one of architecture's most significant honors.

Mr. Stirling's reputation, made large by his sleek buildings of glass and brick in England and larger still by his anticipated structures on the campuses of Columbia and Harvard universities, will lead most observers to expect something other than what he has produced in Houston. The new and fairly modest Rice building is as contextual as architecture can be—its facades virtually reproduce the elements making up the exterior of the old architecture building to which it is joined. It is, save for certain details, an almost direct imitation of the older buildings of the Rice campus.

Now, this is not a normal debut at all—one of the most eminent architects in the world, trying his hand for the first time in the United States, doing nothing but imitating the older building next door? What could be going on here?

But this building, while it may shock and dismay those who have seen in Mr. Stirling some sort of answer to the current trend back toward re-use of historical forms—a trend that he has now joined with a vengeance, despite the different priorities of his earlier work—is in fact a far more thoughtful work of architecture than it first appears to be. It is, in fact, both original and joyful, and it is difficult to spend any significant amount of time in the building and on the Rice campus and believe that Mr. Stirling should have done much of anything else.

Rice's main buildings were designed in the 1920's by Ralph Adams Cram, one of the great eclectic architects of the early twentieth century, in a style that seems a curious mix of Romanesque and Spanish mission architecture. The university has required that all later building use a pale orange brick and limestone details to conform to the Cram buildings, and although it has not required that Cram's ornate detailing or even his hybrid style be repeated, it has demanded a certain sense of continuity.

In some of the buildings, this is successful; in others, less so. It was Mr. Stirling's wisdom to realize, as few other architects who have worked on the Rice campus in recent years have done, that the buildings which sought originality the most have been the ones that succeeded the least. So this is, if nothing else, a lesson in restraint—a reminder that one sign of great talent is the knowledge of when to hold back, a reminder that hubris is not always the solution in architecture.

But to leave it at that would be to sell this building short. The fact of the matter is that Mr. Stirling was hardly doing nothing, or literally reproducing the older buildings of Rice. His new architecture school is full of subtle variations, of tiny changes that show the presence of his hand. It is a work that provides immense visual pleasure—it is quirky and warm and affectionate, taking the older building's themes and giving them a kind of life that they never before had.

There is a first floor of high arched windows and a second floor of square ones, and there is limestone trim within which are set stripes of orange brick— all details that come from Rice's older buildings, but here composed and arranged in Mr. Stirling's own way. The facade that is most eccentric is at the far end of this L-shaped building; it is of orange brick, with a two-story arch within which is set a round window off center. At the base is a doorway bisected by a column and at the top are lines of brick serving as ornament. None of this is without purpose, though the column in the midst of the doorway is mannerism gone a bit perverse. But the overall form of this facade gracefully and subtly echoes the arches of a lovely little building just across the road from this one.

Within the L-shape that the building's plan takes, Mr. Stirling has created a pleasant garden court, like many of the aspects of this building something that one might think had been there for a generation. But once again, the goal is not to create a sustained illusion—there are curious cone-shaped skylight towers, like little rockets, on the roof, and the entrances are through round bays of glass, all of which make it clear that this is not a building constructed in the 1920's. But these details never take over and control the building—the central idea is the continuity with what has come before.

The interior consists mainly of pleasant, matter-of-fact drafting rooms, unfortunately with all-too-institutional lighting. There is a two-story central space which is used as a display gallery, but that is the only interior area that has any aspirations toward monumentality. The rooms are comfortable and logical without being insistent, and interesting without being shrill.

It is no surprise that the building is fairly popular with students—it is far pleasanter to be in than most architectural schools, and indeed, in its restraint it offers a lesson that most buildings in which architecture is taught eschew. Mr. Stirling's building at Rice is, in a sense, as far as we could come from Paul Rudolph's epoch-making Art and Architecture Building at Yale of 1963, the monumental concrete structure that summed up the heroic aspirations of a generation, and in its modernity was in deliberate and complete contrast to the Gothic architecture of the rest of the Yale campus.

But of course both buildings seek to teach architecture by example. At Yale, the example was grand and sweeping and dogmatic; it evoked both great admiration and great anguish in those who came in contact with it. At Rice, the example is modest and restrained and altogether discreet. It will be interesting to see what effect Mr. Stirling's lesson has on the teaching of architecture in Houston.

—December 3, 1981
Houston

School of Architecture, Rice University, Houston

A "Refuge" for the Retarded?

"This is a place of refuge, a sanctuary," said John Hejduk, dean of the School of Architecture at Cooper Union, of the new Bronx Developmental Center designed by Richard Meier. To Mr. Hejduk, the center—a long, low building sheathed in aluminum panels—is "a masterwork," a place where "architecture can lift up the spirit and make life a little better." To Anthony Pitto, a parent active in the parents' organization of the Willowbrook State School for the retarded, the new building is "an architect's nightmare of a submarine."

The two comments are a world apart, and the story of this building is not nearly so simple as either one would suggest. The Developmental Center, a residence, school, and outpatient facility for the mentally retarded, was constructed by the state's Facilities Development Corporation as part of a program to improve the quality and sensitivity of the architecture of state mental-hygiene facilities.

It is a sprawling facility just off the Hutchinson River Parkway in the northern Bronx, a group of low building sections arranged around two large courtyards and several smaller ones. An innovative aluminum panel system, which permits a large number of variations in window shape and size, gives the building a cool, almost futuristic air.

There is a long service wing four stories high containing educational facilities and administrative offices; it is the largest section of the complex and serves as a formal entrance and as a shield for the courtyards and, behind them, the smaller sections that contain residential quarters.

Bronx Developmental Center

It is a breathtakingly beautiful structure—in terms of its visual impact, one of the most attractive buildings

169

erected in the city of New York in a decade. Moreover, it achieves a serenity that few buildings that make use of its architectural vocabulary—a set of forms that combine modernist influences with recent technological ones—have been able to achieve. Most such buildings are tense; this one, for all its power, seems more relaxed.

However, in the years since this project left its architect's drawing board in 1970, the trend in teaching and housing retarded people has moved away from large institutions such as this one and toward smaller ones, and often toward ones that are physically connected to existing residential communities rather than isolated, as the Developmental Center is. Moreover, there has been a growing interest in providing environments for the retarded that take as their design theme the images of conventional houses in the hope that this will be an aid to the adjustment of the retarded residents.

"We must try to replicate the familiar environment from which the retarded come," says Kiyo Izumi, an architect who has done considerable research on the subject of environments for the retarded.

And the Bronx Developmental Center is nothing like home—its sleek, austere forms are utterly elegant, but they do not symbolize any kind of home. The building is clearly a work of art; the question that must be faced is whether that is enough in this case. It is a question that this building, because of its remarkable quality as an esthetic object, puts before us with an urgency, and even a poignancy, that almost no other structure of recent years has had.

The problem this building poses becomes even more difficult when one realizes how much concern Mr. Meier has shown for the well-being of the residents. There are soft and rich pastel colors on many of the interior walls, graceful proportions that help erase the tension caused by the technological imagery, and careful arrangement of living space in small-group units. Even such details as the building's rounded corners or the rounded corners of the windows set into the aluminum panels go a long way toward creating a sense of serenity.

Mr. Meier's well-known "white" houses show that he is a superb maker of compositions, and this is surely his finest composition ever. Such aspects of this building as the view from the two-story lobby into the courtyard, where a freestanding outside stair perfectly balances its opposite number inside, are architectural experiences of a truly high order. But what it comes down to is that the stylistic vocabulary at use here is the correct one for this most unusual and troubling of architectural challenges.

The profession is by no means in complete agreement. Mr. Izumi's writings suggest a problem with Mr. Meier's stylistic choice. On the other hand, Dr. Hans Esser, a psychiatrist who has also done a great deal of research in the area, says that the major problem "is ambiguity in the physical environment."

"I think an austere environment need not disturb retarded or disturbed people," Dr. Esser said. "What is much more serious is confusion. Complicated arrangements which we might find beautiful, they do not always understand."

The Bronx building is fairly good on that score—its large size makes for a certain amount of complexity, of course, but an effort has been made to arrange the wings of the building in such a way as to provide clear orientation as well as esthetic pleasure. The site, unfortunately, is bounded by industrial buildings and a highway, but even this has been turned to some advantage by the focusing of the building around interior courts. The view from many windows is of the distant highway, and it is surprisingly relaxing—the cars stream by like the flow of a river.

Ultimately, there is no absolute certainty as to what sort of environment is the correct one for this function, or even if there is such a thing as a single right way. The architect, with good reason, points out that even with the trend to decentralized mental-health facilities, certain functions can only be handled in larger institutions.

And Dr. David Kliegler, deputy director of the center, noted at the recent symposium that "there is beginning to be some backlash against the trend" toward small-scale, homelike institutions. "I don't know that it isn't better for at least some people to be in a more monastic setting," he said. "I don't know that we really know what's better for people."

If psychiatrists do not know, of course, it is hard to expect architects to. Here, an architect has practiced his art with immense sensitivity, listening to the recommendations of the medical profession as they came to him even nine years ago and joining them with his own knowledge of the nature of physical form. What that process has yielded is a building that is serene and beautiful to sophisticated eyes; one can only hope that to its occupants, it will appear the same.

—May 3, 1977

An Architectural Triumph for the Handicapped

There has been an undeclared war going on for some time between the nation's high-design architects and the advocates of better buildings for the handicapped. Architects have tended to think that the myriad of special requirements for the handicapped, like ramps and railings and special materials, get in the way of their design freedom. The handicapped retort that design freedom doesn't mean much if you're blind or in a wheelchair, and they have argued persuasively for buildings that are sensitive to their special needs. Most of these buildings, unfortunately, are designed by architects whose special concern is the handicapped and, while they serve the purpose, they do little to make a mark on broader design fronts.

Into this battleground has stepped Stanley Tigerman, one of Chicago's liveliest and most design-conscious architects. Mr. Tigerman was asked to join Chicago's city architect, Jerome R. Butler, Jr., on a new building for the Illinois Regional Library for the Blind and Physically Handicapped, and he set out to prove that a building designed to serve the special needs of the handicapped could still be an eloquent work of architecture on its own, in spite of its demanding requirements.

The building was finished last winter and dedicated last month, and the result is positive enough to make one wonder why architects and the handicapped had been such antagonists in the first place. Mr. Tigerman has succeeded in his double goal: the building, situated on West Roosevelt Road in the near-west side of this city, is a strong and handsome piece of design. Yet its esthetic themes come not just from Mr. Tigerman's imagination, but from the special nature of the problem at hand.

The location is in a desolate part of Chicago, with the

red-brick towers of public housing rising to one side and empty lots on the other, and a view of the 110-story Sears Tower looming off in the distance. The site is roughly triangular, and the building more or less echoes that shape, with the long side of the triangle a gray wall of concrete and the shorter side a brash combination of bright red and bright yellow steel panels.

The colors serve two purposes. First, they provide library users who are not completely sightless with a strong visual experience. But perhaps more important, the bright red and yellow exterior brings some liveliness into the drab neighborhood for the sighted, and stands as a reminder to them that this is not a facility to be shunned, like a prison, but one to be considered an active part of the community. (Since there is a conventional neighborhood branch library tucked into the second floor of this new building, the notion that it not appear too unwelcoming from the outside was especially important.)

While the long wall of the triangle lacks color, it has something to make up for it—a 165-foot-long continuous undulating window that begins as a narrow horizontal band, swoops up into one great arc of glass, then moves up and down gently for the rest of its distance. It looks like a radio-wave pattern moving along a graph, and it has become, like an eccentric ornament, the symbol of the building.

The window is not, in fact, as eccentric as it appears; its height was chosen to allow wheelchair patrons a continuous view, and the high section opens the view to staff members in the book delivery area. The long window is also a map of a long corridor that runs inside the long wall for the length of the building; it is a floor plan transposed onto a wall.

The floor plan, too, is logic masquerading as whimsy. The book delivery areas are all lined up on that long wall since, according to Mr. Tigerman, blind people remember linear arrangement better than other kinds of floor plans. This floor plan is simple indeed: there is an entrance lobby with circulation desk and a Braille card catalogue beside it, and from there the book delivery areas stretch out along the long wall for the length of the building.

To orient the blind further, the white Formica counters undulate gently in a pattern similar to that of the window. Blind users know that they are approaching the book station because the countertop dips down at that point; it also curves inward to accommodate wheelchair users.

The floors are all of round studded Pirelli rubber tile, an elegant material visually, but an excellent one for both blind and handicapped users because it is strongly tactile and prevents slipping and sliding. The choice of Pirelli tile seems to symbolize the intelligent design decisions made throughout this building; Mr. Tigerman was searching constantly for materials and form that would satisfy his own visual sense of duty, yet somehow convey the idea of beauty equally well to users who could understand it only through shape and texture.

The parts of the building that are not for blind users, such as the office and work areas and the local library branch, are more conventional but indicate similar design sensitivity. A tight budget ruled out any extravagances, but Mr. Tigerman did manage to work in a number of appealing gestures, the best of which is a preschool play area of carpeted steps and blocks building up to a high central point, with tunnels beneath and a view to the outdoors through three round portholes cut into the bright red walls.

In such an unusual building, the pleasure a nonhandicapped visitor takes can count for only so much, of course; the only real measure of success is the attitude of the users. And that, happily, is overwhelmingly positive. According to Donna Dziedzic, the library director, walk-in patronage is five times what it was before the library for the blind and handicapped moved to these Tigerman-designed quarters, and library circulation is twice what it had been. There could be no more convincing indication, it would seem, of the value of putting good architects to work on the problem of designing for the handicapped.

—August 9, 1978
Chicago

A Building Without Pretense

"I was taught that before you design a building you talk to the future users. Talk to the dying! What do I say? How do I avoid becoming tongue-tied by the fears of death which our society has given me as it gives nearly everyone?"

So wrote the architect Lo-Yi Chan in 1976, describing the emotions that confronted him as he began to do what no architect had done before in this country—to design a facility in which people die. The building is called the Connecticut Hospice, and it is an institution for the terminally ill. It is not a hospital, though it has many of the facilities of one, and it is not a nursing home, though it bears some resemblance to one of those. It is a 44-bed residence and medical-care center that exists to provide a physically and emotionally comfortable setting for the final days, weeks, or months of a patient's life.

The hospice's building, which has been in design and construction for seven years, has just opened, and it ranks as a significant event in the annals of social architecture. Although there are several similar facilities operating as units of large hospitals or in smaller structures converted from other uses, this is the first structure in the United States erected solely for this use. It came about after Cicely Saunders, an English physician who founded a facility for the dying in London in 1967, lectured at Yale University; in her audience was Florence Wald, former dean of the Yale School of Nursing, who became the initial moving force behind the creation of a hospice in Connecticut.

Mr. Chan had never designed any kind of hospital before he was offered this commission, which was a major reason he was hired. The planning committee, headed by Mrs. Wald, did not want anything resembling a traditional hospital.

It is clear, even after a brief visit to the completed structure, that Mr. Chan's hesitancy in his 1976 comments was misplaced; he has turned out to be an architect of uncommon sensitivity, and he has brought to this architectural problem a set of values rarely seen in any buildings constructed today, and almost never seen at all in buildings related to health care.

The hospice is thoughtful. It is not particularly elegant, and it is surely not the sort of building that prompts extended musings on the nature of architectural form. It is relatively simple as a structure. But it is responsive to the unusual needs of its users in a way that is impressive indeed—a way that helps remind us that architecture does not exist as pure form, that it is inevitably tied to certain social experiences and to certain social goals.

Mr. Chan, who is the senior design partner in the New York firm of Prentice & Chan, Olhausen, took as his central objective the creation of an environment that would be both serene and familiar to its occupants. The basic layout is simple. Institutional functions, such as offices and kitchens, are in a long straight wing, like a spine, while patients' rooms and common rooms are in sections placed diagonally off one side of the institutional spine.

There is, thus, a symbolic separation between the service areas of the building, which are treated as a kind of straightforward background, and the patients' areas, which are a more idiosyncratic foreground. The distinction is occasionally taken to extremes—the red brick in the patients' section is a shade lighter than in the service section, for example—but its basis is in the altogether sensible notion of making the patient areas the focus of the building.

From the outside, the Connecticut Hospice could be a suburban school—the mix of red brick, wood, and glass in a low structure calls to mind many a small-town elementary school. And the surroundings in this community near New Haven, a newer section of town containing many condominium residences, look like just the sort to have a school at their center.

But the building's failure to reveal its unusual function quickly is, of course, part of the architect's objective. The stigma of the architecture of health-care facilities is so severe that nothing could have been less desirable than permitting this building to look, at first glance, like a hospital. Instead, it is surrounded by small gardens and patios, and the side that faces the approach road is an active composition of the ins and outs of the diagonal walls of the patient wings.

Mr. Chan quite intentionally located the entrance around the far side, forcing visitors—and arriving patients—to circle the building, removing some of the sense of mystery and apprehension that such an arrival inevitably entails. A similar kind of reasoning led to the placement of a day-care center for children of the staff at the far end of the main corridor—permitting children to see the elderly patients and the patients to see children, reminders that neither group exists in a world without the other.

The entrance lobby is simple and modest, with the unusual details of a fireplace and a constantly brewing coffee urn, deliberate symbols of domestic life. The patient rooms, most of which accommodate four persons, are set into two 22-bed wings, each of which has a central living room with a fireplace. A common room and chapel are in between the two wings.

The layout of the rooms is itself unusual. Each room can be entered from a glass-enclosed, greenhouse-like corridor, which offers natural light and views of the gardens and patios. In good weather, nurses wheel patients out to the patios, in fact. Making the rooms pleasanter still are clerestory windows and slanted wood-paneled ceilings. The obvious comfort of these rooms was borne out on a recent visit, when several family groups—which are permitted, incidentally, to visit patients twenty-four hours a day—were sitting in the living-room areas chatting informally.

The architect's attention was not devoted solely to patient comfort, however. There was also concern throughout for the families of dying patients—and for the staff, too. There is one unusual room, lined in carpet and lighted only by a round skylight, that was created for staff members as a place in which to escape the tensions of caring for the fatally ill.

Still, for all the attempts to break away from the design of conventional health-care facilities, the hospice is not without a certain institutional air. Some of this is understandable—the really soft materials that connote an extreme air of comfort are often impractical for an enterprise that must, after all, contain 44 residents and a staff of 160. Such materials tend also to be quite expensive, beyond the range of a building constructed at a $2.9-million cost.

But had the budget been unlimited, one wonders if this building should have been permitted to take on a more residential feeling anyway. Perhaps not; this is, in the end, an institution, not a house. It is a place of comfort for the dying, but not a place of illusion; to have pretended that this building was a house and not a hospital might well have been patronizing to its occupants. As it is, the Connecticut Hospice is without pretense. It is comfortable and thoughtful, but above all, its architecture is honest in its intentions, and that is its greatest gift of all.

—December 4, 1980
Branford, Conn.

A Controversial Giant Cast from a 1960's Mold

The Woodhull Medical and Mental Health Center in North Brooklyn is a rust-colored machine of steel and glass that rises out of the urban jumble of Flushing Avenue with immense self-assurance and power. While it opened just yesterday, it is a monument to a different time—it recalls the days when the stark and often harsh lines of modernist architecture seemed to hold a promise of urban salvation.

Woodhull was designed in the late 1960's by the architectural firm of Kallmann & McKinnell and finished in 1978; it was to be New York City's great leap into modern hospital design. Great leaps are often expensive, and the political controversy over the cost of operating Woodhull—which was designed to have 60 percent of its patient rooms as private rooms—was so substantial that the hospital sat, structurally complete but empty and unused, from 1978 until this year.

Woodhull is like no other hospital in New York City, and like few in the United States. It is not only its enormous size—the building is so long that inside corridors stretch to nearly 700 feet—but also every fact of its interior layout that indicated a desire to rethink the ways in which hospitals should be designed. It is a rethinking that seems now, in light of the years since Woodhull was first conceived, to be in some ways dated and in other ways remarkably advanced.

For whatever its faults—and they are many—this building is one of the monuments of modern architecture in New York City. It was designed with genuine concern for both its occupants and staff, and its failures seem very much the failures of the years from which Woodhull's basic design came.

The first of these failures, surely, is size. Woodhull

Woodhull Hospital

contains more than 600 patient beds, and it is far and away the largest building in its neighborhood; its ten stories tower over everything around it and can be seen from blocks around. When such vast size is combined with such commitment to the modernist architectural vocabulary, the result is a building that looks something like a cross between a 1920's factory and the Centre Pompidou in Paris, rendered in rust-colored Cor-ten steel.

Whether this is the right image for a health-care facility is not the sort of question that was raised very often in the late 1960's, but it is one that it is impossible not to raise now. The trend in hospital design has moved toward smaller, more intimate facilities, toward the sort of buildings that can be understood easily by the people who will use them.

Woodhull is so enormous that even the clearest layout causes some confusion, not to mention a tendency toward signs like "To Concourse C," which give the visitor the feeling that he is in an airport, not a place intended to heal the sick.

These problems are more than incidental, since the physical image a health-care facility projects can play a real role in the success with which it is able to serve a community. Woodhull looks every inch an institution, at least as much as any old hospital facility in this city does. And if size is part of this, the austere modernism of its design contributes to it further.

Today, as the trend in architecture has moved toward more familiar, warmer buildings that rely, at least in part, on more traditional architectural elements, we would be less likely to see Woodhull's determined modernism as the ideal style for the image a health-care institution should project. But all of that said, this is still a strong and in some ways deeply impressive design, both in terms of the image it projects and in the way it will actually function.

So far as image is concerned, the positive aspect is a simple one to understand—most of this city's hospitals, both public and private, are so old and physically decrepit that there is a real appeal to anything that is new, light, and clean. Even if Woodhull does not strike the kind of note we would consider ideal for a hospital today, no one could possibly consider it anything but an improvement over the kind of hospital building most New Yorkers are used to.

Indeed, it is an improvement even over several new hospital structures, such as the Annenberg Building at Mount Sinai Hospital, another monolith of rust-colored steel. Where Annenberg is an actively hostile presence on the cityscape—with a confusing warren of unpleasant spaces inside—Woodhull is at least visually appealing. And it has numerous interior features that represent real advances in hospital design, at least for New York City.

The public spaces on the average are brighter and more welcoming than those of virtually any other New York hospital. But the most important feature of the interior is the use of a triple corridor system on the patient floors—one corridor in the middle for staff, deliveries, and the movement of patients, and corridors along each wall for visitors.

The peripheral corridors are window-lined, and the patient rooms have a door at each end to provide access to one of these corridors as well as the central corridor. The rooms have windows on the visitor corridor to permit natural light.

It is a system used originally in the Kaiser Medical Center in Oakland, California, but never in New York until Woodhull, and it has both clear advantages and disadvantages. By creating what is in effect a "backstage," efficiency can presumably increase, and visitors are spared awkward confrontations with patients on stretchers. On the other hand, since the only windows patients have are on the windowed corridors, patients desiring privacy can only get it by closing the curtains on the corridor, thus cutting off all their natural light.

Although Woodhull's high ratio of private rooms seems luxurious, it emerged from the belief, which underlay most of the design decisions in the entire building, that a higher initial cost would be repaid by decreased operating costs—a view that seems contradicted by the city's assumption that operating costs would be high, which led to the long delay in the hospital's opening.

So far as the private rooms are concerned, the hospital's planners have argued that private rooms yield economy by permitting a more flexible distribution of patients, since beds do not have to go empty if there are no male patients to match with other males, or females to match with other females, in shared rooms.

In any event, there is certainly no sense of extravagance to these private rooms—they are very small, more like large cubicles than real rooms. While they are handsome and efficiently laid out, there is one crucial flaw—in many rooms, the bed is positioned in such a way as to make it impossible for the patient lying in bed to look out the window.

On balance, however, Woodhull is a kind of achievement—certainly a determined attempt to respond seriously to the weaknesses of New York's older hospital buildings. There is even a kind of nobility to this structure, commanding North Brooklyn as it seems to do. If machines for healing were what hospitals were supposed to look like, Woodhull would be ideal.

—November 4, 1982

Philip Johnson's Crystal Cathedral

It was probably the most exciting event in Orange County since the completion of Disneyland. Roger Williams played "The Impossible Dream," Ronald Reagan sent greetings, and a Goodyear blimp hovered overhead. It was the dedication of the Crystal Cathedral, the $18-million glass church that will be the headquarters for the 10,000-member congregation of the Reverend Dr. Robert Schuller, the television evangelist. The cathedral, designed by Philip Johnson and John Burgee, was nearly finished last spring when Beverly Sills came and gave a recital. Now it is completely done, and yesterday Dr. Schuller's producers moved the cameras for their nation-wide broadcast hookup inside, and the congregation began to worship in its new home.

The church is surely the most talked-about new edifice, religious or otherwise, in Southern California in years. Dr. Schuller, who began his Orange County ministries preaching in a drive-in theater in 1955, is nothing if not theatrical in his approach to religion; he has made it clear that he sees this building as the culmination of his career, and he made it the center of attention in his preaching. At the two services of dedication yesterday morning, he delivered a sermon entitled "Why Did God Want the Crystal Cathedral to Be Built?"

The church is a spectacular structure. It is built of reflective glass in the shape of a stretched-out four-pointed star so that it is 415 feet from point to point in one direction and 207 feet from point to point in the other. There is a marble pulpit in one of the points of the star and balconies in the others. The walls and roofs are all glass—10,900 panes in all, supported by a network of white-painted metal trusses. The cathedral can seat 2,890 people.

Garden Grove
Community Church,
Orange County,
California

The building has already begun to attract the tourists who flock to this part of California in search of Disneyland and Knott's Berry Farm, and although this is a more serious work of architecture by far, it seems able to speak to the desires of Orange County every bit as well as the kitsch places. Yesterday, the church was filled for both services, and thousands more sat on the lawn outside, viewing Dr. Schuller through a pair of 90-foot-high glass doors, which opened dramatically as the service began. The congregants flocked to Mr. Johnson afterward for autographs, treating the architect as if he were a movie star.

The ability of this architecture to excite the average churchgoer is perhaps as interesting as the architecture itself. The Crystal Cathedral is an abstract object, very much in the tradition of late modern architecture—it uses sleek, industrial materials, and the goal is the creation of pure forms. What is supposed to make the Crystal Cathedral pleasing is not the symbolic association it brings to mind, as would be the case in a modern church—it is intended to be pleasing as a pure object in itself.

Rarely does that kind of abstract building communicate well to the public. But this one does have many things going for it that the average piece of sculpture in glass does not. First, there is the space itself, which is truly noble. It is 128 feet high, the sort of monumental space that is rarely made in this age of mean 8-foot ceilings. But the space is also well crafted. The angles of the star give it an energetic motion. Moreover, the metal trusses that hold the glass in place create a vibrant texture and rhythm.

The room is full of a kind of flowing energy, an energy that is ideally suited to the sort of joyful worship that Dr. Schuller's liturgy entails. And because the sun and the clouds and the sky are all visible through the glass, there is a sense of nature present at all times—this is not a church in which one withdraws from the world, but one in which one embraces it.

That is the best thing about this glass tent, this huge glass gathering place. What it lacks, what prevents it from being more than just a spectacular piece of theater, is that certain sense of mystery, of the unknown, that has marked most of the great religious structures of the past. Le Corbusier called it "ineffable space"—a quality of space that we cannot fully understand or grasp. Here, the simple geometries make it all clear from the beginning, and after an initial gasp, even the least sophisticated visitor is likely to comprehend the spatial qualities fully.

Perhaps that is as it should be, for it is clear that this was intended less as deep architecture than as a stage set—the bugle flourishes at the beginning of the service, the dancing fountain leaping up in the midst of the sanctuary on cue and the line of eager Boy Scouts marching down the aisles bearing flags are proof enough of that. Dr. Schuller's services here are as precisely regimented as a military parade, and they occasionally have a tone not too different from that. And without getting into the arena of religion, it is clear that Dr. Schuller's theology is not that of mystery—he preaches that all things are visible, that all things are understandable, and the architecture Mr. Johnson has given him is intended to be a perfect expression of this.

There are some aspects of the building that are less than pleasing—the expensive marbles and woods used on the altar are, for all their elegance, conventional materials, and they feel at odds with the refined abstraction of the building itself. They are crutches that the building does not need, and they take away from the overall effect of the architecture. The same might be said of the excessive amounts of greenery, or the rather tacky Mylar stars that hang from the ceiling like tinsel.

On the practical side, there are also some problems. The acoustics, improved since the night last May when Miss Sills's voice echoed embarrassingly, are still not perfect—although the echo is certainly more pleasing when it comes to preaching, for it seems to enhance the drama of the words coming from the pulpit. More of a real problem is the elaborate amplification system that has speakers placed behind every seat, creating an effect that makes every voice sound as if it is coming from a movie sound track.

The dedication took place on a reasonably cool and cloudy day, so it was not possible to see how the building, which is not air-conditioned, performs under the hottest California sun. It is supposed to get no hotter than the outside temperature, thanks to the reflective glass and to convection currents set up by open panes of glass; it was surely comfortable in yesterday's mid-70's.

The least interesting part of the building is the exterior—all of that mirror glass could be mistaken, from a distance at least, for a jazzy corporate headquarters. It is curious that Mr. Johnson, who has been such a champion of symbolism in architecture, would choose to design a church without any of the traditional symbols of religion. But then again Mr. Johnson has never been bound by any narrow dogma; this has always been one of his strengths—his priorities are architecture, not theory, and no one can accuse him of having been untrue to that tradition here.

If this is not the deepest or the most profound religious building of our time, it is at least among the most entertaining—one that will do much to interest a public that has grown accustomed to thinking of churches as banal works of architecture and not as uplifting ones. Here at Garden Grove, the goals of religion and the goals of architecture are united, as earnestly as they were in ages past; the result tells more than a little about the priorities of each of these pursuits in our time.

—September 16, 1980
Garden Grove, Calif.

A $15-Million Conversation Piece

To the motorist passing on Interstate 495, the fantasy form of the new Mormon Temple here appears to rise out of the woods like a mirage. A 120-foot-high hexagonal mass of marble topped by six gold spires, the $15-million structure is no normal building. Understandably, its fantasy form has been the talk of the Washington area since its completion last September.

The building would have been a conversation piece under any circumstances. But Washingtonians have been all the more interested in it since the Mormons, who normally close their temples not only to unbelievers but also to the less qualified of their own faith, opened this one to the public for several weeks between completion and dedication. The visiting period is over, but more than 800,000 tickets were issued, and the curious came in such droves that visiting hours were extended to 10:30 P.M.

The almost Disneyland-like form of the temple itself was reflected in the ambiance that surrounded it. Crowds seemed to view the experience as an amusement outing as much as a visit to a religious shrine, and the eager guides posted throughout the building and the parking lot attendants waving lighted flashlights only added to the tourist atmosphere.

This is not surprising, for while the visitors were undoubtedly attracted in part by the chance to learn something about Mormon ritual, it is the building itself that was the real drawing card. Designed by a specially assembled team of four Mormon architects from Salt Lake City, Harold K. Beecher, Henry P. Fetzer, Fred L. Markham, and Keith W. Wilcox, there is probably nothing quite like it anywhere in the United States.

Unfortunately, the temple is a grandiose building of little real imagination. Its huge, boxy base and six gold spires (one of which is topped with a statue of an angel) suggest nothing so much as the awkward forms that were always supposed to indicate "modern building" in old comic strips. It is as if the architects had tried to design Buck Rogers's church.

There is a myriad of small rooms inside the huge hexagonal mass—since Mormons use temples only for special ceremonies, not for regular worship, there was no need for a single great assembly space. It is an indication of how huge the structure is that the 1,600-seat hall on the top floor, while the largest room, is by no means a dominant architectural element in the building.

The futuristic aura disappears inside, replaced by what tries desperately to be "good taste"—and if good taste consists of ringing a crystal chandelier with fluorescent lighting, then it succeeds. The crystal and fluorescent combination is a favorite of the architects here—as are powder-blue carpets, walnut panel-

Mormon Temple, Kensington, Maryland

ing, small Miami Beach–type lobby fountains, and pointed arches.

The pointed Gothic arch is, in fact, a theme carried thoughout the interiors of this most un-Gothic building to give the place more of the feeling of a church, one of the architects explained. Thus the doors, stairway railings, doorknob plates, and altars, among other details, all carry the pointed arch theme. Its use in these areas suggests nothing so much as those corporate headquarters that endeavor to work their trademark into every possible aspect of their design— only here the trademark is Gothic architecture.

From an architectural standpoint, none of the rooms is particularly interesting, although they do seem to come together to express a certain philosophy of interior design. There are nine "sealing rooms," or marriage chapels, so called because of the Mormon belief that marriages are sealed for eternity.

Some of the sealing rooms are decorated in powder blue; the rest are in apricot, and they are all small carpeted rooms lined with heavy draperies. A marble altar with a pointed arch sits in the middle of each, and there are mirrors on opposite walls, reflecting each other indefinitely—"to symbolize eternity," according to the architect.

The ultimate impression all of this gives is not so much one of vulgarity as banality. Inside, at least, it is a very dull building, striving to awe and, in the end, able to do so only by creating in the visitor a sense of incredulity that so much money could yield so much dullness. The inside is a bizarre cross between a Holiday Inn and Forest Lawn.

But it is not without significance that a major, and rapidly growing, religion should choose this sort of building as its architectural embodiment—and that so many people should be so eager to experience this building for themselves. The Mormon Temple, pedestrian as it may be, probably comes closer to reflecting the architectural ideal of many Americans than do buildings of far more serious interest to architects. Like its Washington neighbor, the Kennedy Center, the Mormon Temple has an ersatz sort of grandeur—it is a kind of para-architecture that has great pretensions but is at bottom rather empty.

There is an increasing interest in such architecture among architectural scholars these days, and it is certain that the Mormon Temple will become a landmark in what Charles Jencks has called, not entirely pejoratively, "ersatz architecture." For the temple is a superb blend of the images of church and of a kind of futuristic fantasy, with an end result that, if nothing else, is unique and fascinating. And if studying such a building, for all its silliness, can make architects even a bit more aware of the gap between their own profession and the tastes of the general public, then perhaps all the attention the Mormon Temple is getting will be worthwhile.

—November 12, 1974
Kensington, Md.

An Eloquent Rejection of Modernism

It is no news that architects have been edging, slowly and fearfully, away from the glass boxes of modernism. They have not always had a sense of where they were going, but they have been absolutely certain of what they were leaving behind. Buildings like the new Asia Society on Park Avenue at 70th Street, the American Telephone & Telegraph building on Madison Avenue at 55th Street or the addition to the Frick Collection on East 70th Street do little to suggest to us a clear new direction—but they do a great deal to show us how widespread the rejection of orthodox modernism has become.

The annex to the Park Avenue Synagogue at the corner of Madison Avenue and East 87th Street, completed recently, is more modest than any of the other three buildings, but it clearly deserves to be given a place among the significant buildings of the last few years in Manhattan, if only because it underscores with particular eloquence the extent to which talented architects have abandoned the modernist mode. The synagogue's design is by the architect James Jarrett, working in association with the firm of Schuman, Lichtenstein, Claman & Efron, and it is unabashedly revivalist. Like the Frick addition, it is the sort of building that seems designed to make us think that it had stood on its corner since late in the last century, or at least since the golden period of eclecticism in the 1920's.

The $6-million Park Avenue Synagogue addition, which houses classrooms, a chapel, and an auditorium, is not in fact a literal work in a past architectural style. It is not really classical, though there are strong elements of classicism to it, and it is certainly not Romanesque, though there are hints of Romanesque architecture to it as well. The building is sheathed entirely in Mankato stone, a Minnesota limestone that has a rich, golden color not unlike the color of the stone of Jerusalem. The stone is rusticated, which is to say it is set in blocks separated by ridges and does not look like a single, smooth surface.

The synagogue building is a 5-story box, with four bays of windows on Madison Avenue and three bays on East 87th Street, each rising to the structure's full height and topped by a semicircular or arched window. There is a 2-story entrance arcade cut into the facade at the corner of Madison Avenue and 87th Street, and there are two additional bays of windows farther east on 87th Street; these lack arches and are intended to provide a simple, understated transition between the new building and the main synagogue building on East 87th Street.

The facades are in the best tradition of New York eclecticism, in that they merge elements from different historical styles into a new and coherent whole. The priorities are twofold: the establishment of a firm and dignified presence on the street, and the creation of an easy and articulate relationship between this new building and its older neighbors. These things were more important to Mr. Jarrett than "style" as such—as they have been more important to generations of the best makers of the New York streetscape.

As style goes, however, this building is a curious hybrid. The rusticated tone and the calm, definite order of these facades suggest the classicism of a Renaissance palazzo, but the specific design of the window bays and their arched tops calls to mind such masterpieces of early Chicago modernism as

Park Avenue Synagogue, New York

Henry Hobson Richardson's Marshall Field warehouse or Louis Sullivan's Auditorium. The Park Avenue Synagogue is more delicate than these harsh, powerful buildings—it is more concerned with being a gentle neighbor—but it seems, despite its classical overlay, to be within their tradition.

Precise lettering announcing the synagogue's name and the new building's memorial purpose—it honors Jewish children who died in the Holocaust—enhances the air of classical dignity this building brings to Madison Avenue. If there is any real problem with this facade, it is the absence of the strong cornice that such a building calls for. As a result, this box meets the sky weakly, while it meets the ground with strength. The reason for this is simple—the steel structure of this building could not support a more elaborate top.

Logic would suggest that the architects could just have called for more steel, and the reason they could not brings us to a crucial fact about the history of this unusual project. Mr. Jarrett and Schuman, Lichtenstein, Claman & Efron designed this building after steel had already been erected for a different synagogue design by other architects. The earlier scheme was a harsher, more aggressive, more "modern" building, more in the tradition of recent public institutional architecture than religious architecture. The leadership of the synagogue changed its mind about the initial design after construction had already begun, and the new architects were called in to create a design that could be constructed on the steelwork that had been already erected.

This is, thus, a clear case of a passage from one way of seeing buildings to another. The initial design was mediocre and thoroughly insensitive to its surroundings, but to be fair, this was not so much for the fact of its modernism as for the utter banality of its execution. The realization on the part of the congregation of the Park Avenue Synagogue that they owed the streets of New York something else—and the congregation's willingness to shift gears at a late moment—deserves to be remembered as an act of civic generosity. Here, a religious congregation has taken the view that one of the ways in which it can serve the community is to offer a distinguished architectural presence—an attitude opposite to that of those parishioners of St. Bartholomew's Church on Park Avenue who are arguing that they can serve the city best by turning part of their complex over to office-building development.

No building, particularly a building used by large numbers of people, can be judged on the basis of its facade alone. Happily, the interiors of the new building continue a high level of quality. There is a low, vaulted ceiling in the lobby, where the Mankato stone of the exterior is used in polished form, and there are pleasant, if unexceptional, classroom buildings on the upper floors. And in an utterly sensible gesture not done frequently enough elsewhere, the roof space is given over to playground uses.

—July 11, 1981

The Slow Finishing Touch

The construction that began yesterday on the Cathedral of St. John the Divine was full of promise for the future of New York City. It represents not merely the continued growth of one of the city's greatest works of architecture, but also the success of a remarkable work program: the cathedral's decision in 1978 to give young residents of Morningside Heights, Harlem, and Newark employment by training them in the ancient art of stonecutting.

The cathedral is being built by a crew of roughly two dozen artisans who have been apprenticed under James Bambridge, the master mason who came to Morningside Heights in 1979 from Liverpool, England, to oversee the construction. Nothing would seem, on its face, more outlandish—the notion of giving neighborhood youths employment by training them in an ancient art—but it has in fact turned out to be an absolutely natural marriage between the needs of the cathedral and the needs of the surrounding community.

The cathedral had stopped building during World War II, and work was not resumed after the war largely because the Episcopal Diocese of New York felt that the erection of a lavish structure would be symbolically inappropriate until the poverty of its upper Manhattan neighborhood could be alleviated.

It was the Reverend James Parks Morton, dean of the cathedral since 1973, who realized that perhaps construction itself could provide some help for the troubled city—that far from suggesting indifference to poverty, it might stand for community concern if it provided jobs and training in valuable skills. If community residents were taught to build the cathedral themselves, Dean Morton sensed, they would acquire skills that could be used elsewhere in this age of more and more masonry

Drawing for
West Front,
Cathedral of
St. John the Divine

construction, and their participation might well serve to knit together the cathedral and a community from which it has been distant on many occasions in its history.

The unusual idea has proved correct: it is difficult, watching the work that goes on in the huge metal stonecutting shed beside the cathedral on Amsterdam Avenue, to imagine a more appropriate blending of the needs of community and the values of architecture. The apprentices have been doing the preliminary work of cutting stone for two years now, building an inventory to prepare for yesterday's start of construction. They are a diverse group, ranging from Nelson Otero, who has worked as a maintenance man at an East Harlem church, to Timothy Smith, a stonecutter from Vermont, who is one of the few apprentices not to come from the inner city.

Some have experience in crafts or sculpture, another worked for the South Bronx Poor People's Development Corporation, and another was a forklift operator. All have, according to Mr. Bambridge, "learned faster than I would have expected—they are really more mature than the younger apprentices I have trained in England, and that makes all the difference."

The resumption of construction on St. John the Divine is thus an event that, far more than the building of the cathedral's earlier sections, represents a return to the making of cathedrals as they were in the Middle Ages—not in terms of technical methods, for this stone is cut by modern saws and hoisted by modern derricks, but in the way that it is a product of an entire community, joining to build itself a symbolic center.

The cathedrals of the Middle Ages were community centers as much as they were purely religious edifices, structures that represented a city's commitment to a public realm, as opposed to a private one. And so it is with the continuation of St. John the Divine, which can stand on Morningside Heights as a reminder that there remains a place in this city for a noble public building.

The stone mortared into place yesterday was the cornerstone of the cathedral's southwest tower, a Gothic spire designed by Ralph Adams Cram that eventually will rise 152 feet over the present high point of the building and 291 feet above the cathedral floor. The pace will be steady but slow. If all goes well, there will be about four feet of the tower in place by the time the first frost requires a suspension of outdoor construction, according to Mr. Bambridge. He declined to measure the work in years. When the tower is finished, his crew of two dozen stonemasons will begin to work on its twin at the north corner.

The cathedral is being completed according to the plans of Cram, the second architect of St. John the Divine and probably this nation's most ardent proponent of the Gothic style. But the architectural history of this massive building—which, even in its incomplete state, is larger than any Gothic cathedral in Europe—is not a simple story. The erection of a huge cathedral on Morningside Heights was a dream of Bishop Horatio Potter, who sponsored a competition to find a design. The firm of Heins & LaFarge won with a scheme for a

Byzantine-Romanesque cathedral, and in 1892 construction began on a cathedral in that style.

By 1911, when the apse, choir, and crossing were complete, both the
architects and Bishop Potter had died, and Cram managed to persuade the
succeeding bishop to allow him to take over the job and switch the style to
Gothic. Thus the 601-foot-long, 320-foot-wide nave is Gothic, as is the huge
facade. The size is, in a sense, a blessing, since it reduces the sense of stylistic
clash. The interior is so large that when one is in one section, one can barely see
the other.

The interior was largely complete by the time construction ceased in 1941,
but the exterior, where the absence of any towers creates a harsh, cutoff look, is
much more obviously unfinished. Cram left drawings for the two front towers,
as well as for a still larger central tower over the cathedral's crossing, and it is
these that provide the basic outline for the work now going on.

The process is complex, however, since the designs Cram left were never
detailed or converted into the actual working drawings from which the building
can be constructed. Since the size, shape, and placement of each stone must be
determined in advance, Mr. Bambridge's role in design is as crucial as Cram's.

Mr. Bambridge's nerve center is a room in the cathedral's basement, under
the existing nave, where he works, crouched on the floor, turning the Cram
drawings into programs for stonecutting. He does small drawings first, then
expands them to full-scale; these are then turned into metal templates from
which the stones are actually cut in the stoneworks in the cathedral yard.

Mr. Bambridge is also in charge of fleshing out ornamental details that Cram
had left unfinished. He is in the midst of designing floral carvings for stone
capitals, trying to follow the wish of Dean Morton that the cathedral have
details that make it "truly American, truly of New York." This, too, is in the
tradition of Gothic architecture, in which artisans created, often spontaneously,
certain ornaments to reflect the culture of their surrounding region.

The seriousness with which the cathedral's officials, Mr. Bambridge, and his
crew of apprentices approach the job inevitably invites comparison with Gothic
precedent—and raises the obvious question as to whether the erection of a
Gothic building makes any sense in this city at this time. It is a question that
would almost certainly have been answered negatively a decade or so ago,
when the creation of any building other than a purely modern one seemed a
foolish anachronism. Now, however, modernism has lost not a little of its
appeal, and we are seeing a substantial return to classical styles in both public
and private architecture.

If there is a difference between the attitudes of the current builders and that
of Ralph Adams Cram, it is that we do not today see the Gothic style as any sort
of moral imperative—it is not, as Cram felt it to be, an ecclesiastical necessity.
Rather, it is noble tradition that was for too long disdained, or seen only as part
of history, and the sense now is that there is no reason that Gothic building

cannot be built seriously and earnestly today. But if what is going on now in Morningside Heights has any meaning, it is not so much that Gothic architecture is important, as that the builders of the cathedral recognize that there still remains in our age a way in which monumental architecture can glorify the community that surrounds it.

—September 30, 1982

Substandard Luxury Towers

Philip Birnbaum, Schuman Lichtenstein Claman, and Horace Ginsbern & Associates are not names well known to even the most architecture-conscious segments of the general public. In fact, the three firms are hardly known to many architects. But these firms, and a handful of others, are playing at least as big a role in shaping the design of Manhattan as any architects of more note. They are the apartment-house specialists—the firms that have created their architectural practices largely on the design of the luxury towers which continue to sprout up throughout midtown.

Since luxury-apartment construction is virtually the only kind of building going on at a large scale in today's depressed New York construction market, these architects are as busy as ever. And their work covers more of Manhattan every day.

With a few exceptions, their output is appallingly mediocre. Architecturally, New York has what may well be the lowest standard of new luxury housing in the United States—and while the apartments are generally well supplied with such amenities as bathrooms and closets, quality of construction often falls below the standards required for more simple units in public housing projects.

The reasons most new luxury housing is so poor are purely economic: architectural quality costs money. In the heyday of New York apartment construction in the 1920's, labor was cheap enough to permit the large rooms, solid walls, and elegant detailing that made the typical Park Avenue or West End Avenue building desirable.

But today, with costs of land, labor, materials, and interest at all-time highs, it is difficult for a builder to turn a profit even from a cheap building—and even with the ten-year tax-abatement program, which is, in effect, a luxury-housing subsidy.

"Architectural amenities are sheer nonsense," H. R. Shapiro, a major housing developer, said recently—and he was probably speaking for most of his colleagues.

The sheer, unadorned tower, rising without setbacks for thirty or more stories, has become the staple of New York luxury-housing design, and it has had a significant impact on the cityscape, shattering the scale of residential neighborhoods. The present form has its origins in the 1961 zoning ordinance, which encouraged isolated towers set away from the street as an alternative to the squat buildings with catty-cornered penthouses. These buildings were the common high-rise form of the 1950's.

But while the buildings in the new wave of high-rises may take their general form from the zoning ordinance, their enormous size is, again, purely economic: with costs as high as they are today, developers can maximize profit if they spread out fixed costs such as land over a large number of apartments. So it has become commonplace for builders to build as big as possible, and even to argue before the city's Board of Standards and Appeals for still larger buildings than zoning would normally permit. Builder Paul Milstein is doing that now with his plan to erect a 43-story building at Broadway and 62nd Street, a tower that will have 50 percent more bulk than zoning allows.

Mr. Milstein's architect is Philip Birnbaum, who built an earlier Milstein building at Broadway and 64th Street and who has created a successful practice out of helping builders through the tangled web of economics and zoning. Mr. Birnbaum is skillful at maximizing the number of apartments that can be fitted onto a site, and his office is able to produce plans quickly to reduce costly construction delays.

Mr. Birnbaum's office is efficient, of course, because it rarely slows down to consider questions of esthetics. It is a seemingly casual operation run out of quarters in the Excelsior, a 47-story white-brick Birnbaum tower at Second Avenue and 57th Street. Stock plans are used, and the designs are often so similar that recently a staff architect, showing a visitor around the office, was unable to identify some of the firm's buildings that were displayed in rendering on the wall.

Even in unusual situations, like the triangular site of the Birnbaum-designed Nevada apartments at Broadway and 69th Street, the simplest possible solution is used. In this case, a floor plan contains only dull, rectangular rooms in spite of the opportunity of the odd site, and places only tiny bathroom and kitchen windows at the point of the triangle looking up Broadway, denying tenants what could have been a truly spectacular view.

Among Mr. Birnbaum's other recent buildings are the Bristol, at 300 East 56th Street, and the Brevard at Second Avenue and 54th Street (which, with its travertine base, dark brick facing, and small windows, looks just like the

Nevada squared off), and the Murray Hill Mews at Third Avenue and 38th Street, which is doubtless the only 37-story mews in the history of architecture. In all of the buildings, the apartments are virtually identical, and they are almost all one-bedrooms, since that size rents fastest.

They are only slightly better at the Park 900, Mr. Birnbaum's super-luxury tower at Park Avenue and 79th Street. Here, the facade is dressed up with a few curves and a Henry Moore sculpture. But even with rents at $750 up, the dull room arrangements remain the same.

Schuman, Lichtenstein, Claman, the other luxury apartment-design standby, is a bit more versatile in its nearly completed building, 2 Lincoln Square at Columbus Avenue and 66th Street. In compliance with the Lincoln Square Special Zoning District, the architects have created a set of arcades which may well prove an asset to the surrounding neighborhood.

But the tower itself is as undistinguished as they come—and its east wall facing Central Park rises for thirty-five stories without any windows, a frigid gesture to the building's surroundings. (The blank wall is a result of city building codes, which have stringent requirements for windows on a building's property line but not facing a street. Rather than reorient the building, the architects found it easier to build the windowless wall.)

There are three recent towers that, from the standpoint of pure design, rise at least somewhat over the low standard of the others. They are the Lincoln Plaza Tower, designed by Horace Ginsbern & Associates at Columbus Avenue and 62nd Street, the Landmark by Liebman & Liebman at Second Avenue and 59th Street, and the Sovereign by Emery Roth & Sons at 425 East 58th Street.

Lincoln Plaza Tower, whose architect designed many of the splendid Art Deco apartment houses of the Bronx in the 1930's, is built of striated concrete with rounded balconies and bay windows. Its facade seems clearly to be based on the architecture of Paul Rudolph, and this is one of the few instances in which the designs of a major architect have filtered down to imitation in the luxury-housing market.

The Landmark was not so titled to save the Landmarks Preservation Commission the trouble; its name comes from a nineteenth-century house next door that the commission has already designated. The builders of the Landmark, the Kalikow Realty Company, purchased the house's air rights to give their building greater bulk. The Landmark has a simple facade of exposed concrete and glass which, while not innovative, is a refreshing change from the banal brick and aluminum windows of the Birnbaum style.

Both buildings are renting fairly well, and the builder of Lincoln Plaza Tower, Marvin Greenfield, says he attributes at least part of his success to the building's architecture—which he claims cost him "only slightly" more than a more ordinary design.

The distinction of the Sovereign, one of the few recent residential efforts of Emery Roth & Sons, the firm that has produced so many of midtown's faceless glass office towers, is all on the inside. Outside, the 48-story building is brutally destructive of the scale of 58th Street and Sutton Place; in spite of its efforts to be neighborly by means of a poorly landscaped park, the building cannot help rendering absurd the old townhouses nearby.

Like the Park 900, the Sovereign is in the super-luxury category. (Rents run from $765 to $2,130.) The apartments themselves are generous in size, with 9-foot ceilings, and better planned than in most recent buildings.

The lobby extends under the entire building, and there are four separate elevator banks serving four semiprivate halls per floor—a welcome (and expensive) alternative to the long, double-loaded corridor. Such an arrangement has probably not been used in any New York building since the 1930's.

So the rich are getting at least something for their money here. But the rest of the city is not, since this is not architecture: fancy lobbies, plentiful plumbing, and skyline views do not make a good building.

Since the Sovereign and most of the other recent towers are recipients of tax-abatement programs, they are, in a way, subsidized by the taxpayers. Only two of the current wave of buildings, the Landmark and Lincoln Plaza Tower, repay this subsidy with any sort of responsible urbanism. A city like New York deserves better than that.

—*November 1, 1974*

The Invasion of the "Sliver" Houses

Sliver building,
Upper East Side,
Manhattan

They are sprouting like weeds in odd corners of the Upper East Side, and at least one seems imminent on the West Side. They are not particularly large, but they are, in their own way, as destructive of the city's ambiance as the vast monoliths of midtown.

It is a new building type—a thin, narrow apartment tower, sometimes no bigger than a townhouse, but reaching upward for 15 or 20 or more stories. They have become known as "sliver," or "needle," buildings; sliver is a better name, for there is none of the romance of the skyline in these structures that the word "needle" conveys. These new slivers are like awkward pieces of other structures forced at random into the streetscape; they break rather than enhance the order of the neighborhoods of which they are a part.

They usually contain no more than a single, tightly laid-out apartment per floor, and in some slivers the floors are so tiny that each apartment fills two levels. They are significant, however, not because of the living space they create on the inside, but because of the urban disruption they create on the outside. The slivers indicate as strongly as any midtown office building how the explosion in Manhattan real-estate values has made almost any kind of land exploitation possible.

There have been slivers recently finished at 350 East 86th Street, 344 East 63rd Street, and 266 East 78th Street, among other parts of Manhattan, and another is now nearing completion on 71st Street between Park and Lexington avenues. Others have been planned for 96th Street just off Fifth Avenue, 81st and Lexington, and Park Avenue in the Murray Hill section.

A near-sliver, which is to say a tower that is larger than these others but still far narrower than a conventional apartment house, is nearly complete at 49th Street and Second Avenue, and a similarly thin tower will soon squeeze itself onto Columbus Avenue at 79th Street. In virtually every instance the neighbors of these buildings have expressed strong opposition—but the buildings still seem to be going ahead.

The sliver came into existence as a building type for a simple reason—apartment values in Manhattan have gotten so high that it can be profitable for a builder to go to the expense of erecting a high-rise structure on a tiny plot. The city's zoning laws, which treat a number of the planned sliver sites differently, rarely prohibit such buildings outright.

But they do make slivers difficult to build, particularly in midblock sites. It is these projects—the slivers inserted into the middle of a block of low and architecturally compatible townhouses—that are by far the most destructive, for they shatter the pattern of building that is the basic order of Manhattan: high buildings on avenues and major cross streets and low buildings on side streets.

As the slivers seem to sneak almost sideways into the physical fabric of the city, so they seem to slip furtively into its political process, too. Few slivers have been built with much advance notice, and few have been planned by the city's major real-estate developers or designed by its better-known architects. The established firms seem to be eschewing this new building type, leaving the sliver to become, instead, a means by which lesser-known builders and architects establish a foothold in the city.

Not surprisingly, the strongest fights against slivers have broken out in parts of the Upper East Side, in which the classic pattern of side streets of handsome townhouses has remained largely intact. The slivers proposed for 81st Street and Lexington Avenue and for the middle of the block between 95th and 96th streets are examples: it is too early to tell whether they will be stopped, but neighbors and local community boards are opposing the new projects.

At 81st Street the proposed sliver, called Lexington House, is designed by Noah Greenberg and would be built by a development company named 177 East 79 Sponsors Corporation, after an earlier sliver that it built around the corner. But where the 22-foot-wide 79th Street sliver was squeezed between two conventional tall apartment buildings, and thus had a minimal impact, the 81st Street building would rise to 20 stories on a block that now contains mostly townhouses.

As designed, the 81st Street sliver could not be built under the city's present zoning code, and here is where the story becomes both complicated and ironic. The developer's site runs roughly 34 feet on Lexington Avenue and 55 feet on 81st Street. Existing zoning permits a building that fills out the site for the first 9 stories, then sets back 15 feet on Lexington Avenue and 20 feet on the side streets as it rises for 11 more floors.

Now, it is no secret that such a tiny tower, even more of a sliver than the proposed building, makes no economic sense—one could barely fit even a studio apartment onto each of its floors. The framers of the city's zoning ordinances understood this, and they assumed that builders, faced with the inability to build large apartment houses on such little plots of land, would naturally not attempt to purchase such plots with intent to develop them.

For a long time that rationale worked. But what is happening on East 81st Street is a clear sign that it works no longer. That development company has now applied to the Board of Standards and Appeals, the city agency with power to overrule zoning laws, for a variance on the ground that the site's small size creates an economic hardship. Since the "as of right" building—the one permitted under regular zoning—is uneconomical, the company has asked that it be permitted to build a building that will rise for 20 floors without setback.

It is a request that flies in the face of the intent of the city's zoning laws and challenges the very integrity of the zoning code. It has a kind of Alice in Wonderland logic to it.

This real-estate developer, like every other, knew the city's zoning laws when it bought the property. But this only enhances the irony—for the land at 81st and Lexington presumably was purchased at so high a price that only a large-scale development that violates the zoning code could ever make it profitable. The company was gambling on the fact that the city, which has been lenient toward most new construction lately, would go along with its request to make this sliver both economical and legal.

The City Planning Commission has, however, been less sympathetic to slivers as public concern has grown. Late last month the commission did modify its Madison Avenue Special District to all but ban slivers there, and it has also strengthened height limitations in midblocks to reduce the likelihood of sliver buildings within the Upper East Side and Carnegie Hill historic districts. But the Planning Commission has chosen to attack the problem piecemeal: it has not moved to create blanket legislation to outlaw slivers throughout Manhattan.

And the commission's very localized zoning changes may have come too late to stop the 22-foot-wide, 24-story sliver that has been proposed for 95th and 96th streets, a building that will stick its narrow head 10 floors above the venerable 1920's apartment houses that border it on 96th Street and nearly 20 floors above the townhouses that flank it on 95th Street.

Although this building would not be legal under the commission's new restrictions, the law states that it can go ahead if construction on its foundations has been substantially completed before the zoning laws change. The commission's zoning changes are now before the Board of Estimate, which has not scheduled them for consideration until March—by which time the foundations on East 96th Street, which are now being dug, may well be finished.

—*February 8, 1982*

The City Planning Commission did pass a stronger set of restrictions later in 1982, after this article was published, and the sliver epidemic has been drastically curtailed.

"A Place Only People Who Couldn't Go Anywhere Else Would Want"—The Cedar Riverside Fight

The tall towers of Cedar Riverside stand out boldly against the small houses surrounding them, their sharply detailed concrete forms intended to herald a new age for urban housing. Cedar Riverside, started in 1971, was the first "new town in town" sponsored by the federal government's Department of Housing and Urban Development. Its exposed concrete design, mixed-income population, and multilevel public spaces were going to provide the model, both the federal housing agency and the city of Minneapolis hoped, for similar inner-city renewal developments across the nation.

Now, barely three years after the first 1,299-unit section was completed, Cedar Riverside is broke, its tenants are, by and large, unhappy about living there, and H.U.D. has been enjoined by a landmark suit from putting funds into the project's second stage. The suit may affect the way all future publicly assisted housing is designed.

The lawsuit, decided in U.S. district court last spring, charged that H.U.D., the Minneapolis Housing and Redevelopment Authority, and Cedar Riverside Associates, the project's developer, had inadequately considered alternatives to the project's high-rise high-density design. A coalition of community groups that filed the suit used it as the basis for contending that the government had filed an inadequate environmental impact statement for Cedar Riverside. This legal tactic led the federal court to decide that the community groups were right—that the project's high-rise design was unnecessary and socially destructive.

The lawsuit is unusual, first because it is one of the few cases in which a court has been forced to consider design matters. It is also different from other disputes involving publicly assisted housing, such as that at Forest Hills, Queens, since it was initiated to force higher design standards for low-income groups, not to block them from entering a neighborhood. "We were always supportive of the idea of mixed income, but by creating this design, they made a place that only people who couldn't go elsewhere would want," said John Herman, the lawyer who argued the case against the project.

The lawsuit is also believed to be the first major legal action to emerge from the increasing conviction of sociologists, architects, and planners that high-rise housing is rarely workable for low- and moderate-income families with children. For example, before its financial difficulties in 1974 led it to halt new construction, the New York State Urban Development Corporation had virtually abandoned building high-rise housing for families. Moreover, continuing problems with many older high-rise projects have brought further disrepute to that building form.

Cedar Riverside's future is uncertain: while its rental agents print colorful posters urging potential tenants to "LIVE! in Award-Winning Cedar Riverside" and list the project's many architectural awards, tenant groups meet to grumble about what they consider inadequate play space, dangerous corridors, and poor maintenance. The project is in such a precarious financial state that sources within H.U.D. suggest it may be forced to take over the project in December.

Cedar Riverside was designed with a knowledge of the failures of earlier projects, and that is what makes its own problems all the more disturbing to housing experts. It is the work of Ralph Rapson, a Minneapolis architect whose work has always been marked by a more humanistic approach than that of major commercial design architects. Cedar Riverside was intended to break away from the stereotyped red-brick box into something more serious architecturally, as well as to replace low-income segregation with a tenant population of mixed economic and social backgrounds.

"We wanted the physical expression to show choice and richness," Mr. Rapson said recently, and indeed, the exposed concrete towers, inspired by the Brutalist work of Le Corbusier, are an abstract composition of considerable dignity. They do not enforce the sense of total anonymity that so many housing projects do: There is a lively interplay of color, mass, and texture in the composition. But there is little of the traditional image of the house in these buildings.

The project's appeal, for all its well-meaning attempt to break away from the public-housing mold, remains essentially as formalist architecture. In terms of its social workings, it appears to echo the difficulties faced by its less architecturally distinguished counterparts.

A group of residents interviewed by *The New York Times*, all of them mothers who worked or attended college during the day, said they felt the complex was unsatisfactory as an environment for raising children. Their complaints ranged from sunless play areas designed as abstract sculpture more than as workable recreation places, to what they felt was the impossibility of supervising their children in the high-rise community.

"The play areas are not very safe, but even if they were, you can't let a child go down thirty-nine floors—a motherly instinct makes you want to keep him a lot closer to your sight," said Francine Murphy. Her seven-year-old son, she said, almost never goes out to play. "I feel more comfortable having him play in the old neighborhood across Cedar Avenue than I do right here next to our own building," she said.

Most of the tenants said they found their apartments "fairly nice," in the words of one of them, and Mrs. Murphy said that she knew of a number of single residents who were content.

But there were also complaints among the tenants about noise, about the units' narrow balconies, and about the floor-to-ceiling glass windows, a design element considered a luxury but one that the tenants say requires custom-made curtains, a difficult expense for residents of subsidized housing.

Some tenants say they have thought of moving—but that they stay because rents are low and alternate housing near downtown and the University of Minnesota is scarce.

Don Jacobson, Cedar Riverside's director of planning, pointed to the effort the design made to avoid discriminating between subsidized and unsubsidized sections. This was done, he noted, by using a similar architectural motif and by "the subtle idea of not making our luxury apartment section the tallest tower" but of letting subsidized apartments occupy the highest building. It was a design decision that may have symbolized equality, but it also meant that even more low- and moderate-income families were placed on high floors.

Mr. Jacobson preferred to talk about the praise the project has received from

Cedar Riverside, Minneapolis

the national architectural community—it won a design award from the American Institute of Architects in 1975—than about local reaction. But he said that the project's second stage, which was curtailed as a result of the lawsuit, had "profitable design advantages" over the existing sections, including the restriction of apartment units for larger families to lower floors. Also, he said that he saw many of the complaints about the project as the result of "a period of consumerism—people want us to provide something better at a time when costs are going up and our rents are practically frozen."

Mr. Rapson, the architect, admitted that many aspects of Cedar Riverside's physical form were based "on political and economic considerations rather than design considerations," although the basic idea of towers of mixed height with multi-level plazas and covered walkways carried through to realization. "I conceived of the complex as a kind of megastructure," the architect said, "and I thought that all the activity and people on the plaza would make it self-policing."

The economic considerations underlying Cedar Riverside's final form were crucial, the federal district court found, since the high costs of assembling land had made high density a necessity if the project were to be economically viable.

But the court also agreed with the community groups which brought the suit that Cedar Riverside Associates, the developer, deliberately avoided using subsidies to reduce the net cost of the land so as to make high-rise, high-density construction the only economical possibility and thus protect investors who had joined Cedar Riverside Associates as a tax shelter.

"The high densities and high-rise construction were dictated only by profit-making and, probably, by tax shelter considerations," wrote Edward R. Parker, the special master of federal district court who heard the case. He also found that "the decision to proceed with Cedar Riverside based on the project's environmental impact statement is arbitrary and capricious."

The Department of Housing and Urban Development has appealed the decision. But the Minneapolis Housing and Redevelopment Authority, another defendant, has not joined the appeal—a decision that many observers here feel suggests that the city has given up its support of the project. A city grant to a local community planning group identified with Cedar Riverside's opposition further underscores the city's apparent desire to separate its own philosophy from that of the new town.

"It was a kind of dream of an all-new way of life, for the rejuvenation of the city," said Mr. Rapson, somewhat wistfully, about the project. "I don't advocate high-rise housing for everybody. But to house so many people, what is the alternative?"

—October 8, 1976
Minneapolis

Emery Roth and the Age of Apartment Buildings

The name Emery Roth means glass and steel towers to most New York building buffs, and with good reason: the architectural firm of Emery Roth & Sons has designed more than a hundred Manhattan skyscrapers since World War II. But ironically, the architect whose name is signed to all of these glass and steel buildings never thought much of modern architecture. He believed in masonry buildings covered with Renaissance detailing, and from 1903 through the 1930's he filled New York with apartment buildings and hotels in his favored mode.

Emery Roth himself, the man who started the firm of architects that has so shaped contemporary Manhattan, had as much of an impact on the New York of his day. He left his mark on New York in the form of such major structures as the San Remo and Beresford apartments on Central Park West; the Ritz Tower on Park Avenue; the St. Moritz, Drake, Dorset, and Oliver Cromwell hotels; and the Normandy apartments on Riverside Drive.

Roth's first major building in New York, the Belleclaire Hotel on Broadway at 77th Street, opened seventy-five years ago, and so it is an appropriate time to look back at this architect and the changes both he and his successors have brought to the cityscape. Roth was a Hungarian immigrant with no formal architectural training; he came to the United States in 1886 at age thirteen and became a cabinetmaker's apprentice. He moved to Chicago in 1890 to work as a draftsman in that city's epoch-making building project, the World's Columbian Exposition of 1893.

The exposition was a triumph for the growing movement toward re-use of classical forms in American architecture. Its buildings were grandiose and elegant testa-

Belleclaire Hotel,
Manhattan

211

ments to the Beaux Arts—infuriatingly reactionary to the small modern movement exemplified by such figures as Louis Sullivan and Frank Lloyd Wright, but a portent of a new nobility to the majority of the nation's architects.

"There never was an architectural setting to surpass the chaste beauty and dignity" of the World's Fair, Roth wrote many years later, and it was clear that he had found his style. He moved to New York shortly thereafter, worked as an apprentice to other architects, and then, in a partnership called Stein, Cohen and Roth, designed the Belleclaire.

The Belleclaire is richly ornamented, with a round corner tower and grand ornamental arches. There are hints of Art Nouveau; it is clear that the architect, who was under thirty when the building was designed, was still seeking a style with which he could feel fully comfortable. By the time he designed 417 Park Avenue, the venerable apartment building at 55th Street completed in 1911 which, like the Belleclaire, is still standing, Roth's work had become more chaste and disciplined. The facade of 417 Park is controlled and carefully proportioned, with ornament clearly intended as punctuation on a smooth, solid surface rather than as the definition of that surface.

By the time 417 Park Avenue was under way, Roth was established as one of the city's leading apartment-house architects. Apartment buildings, considered a strange kind of residence for the middle class until just a few years before, were booming by then, and Roth was sewing up more and more of the available work. The firm of Bing & Bing, for years among the city's most distinguished and active builders of apartment houses, gave Roth virtually all its projects to design, and other builders followed suit.

"He became an apartment house architect because he thought that kind of building had a future," said Richard Roth, Sr., Emery's son and one of the partners in the present Emery Roth firm. "He came from the same part of Hungary as Adolph Zukor, who had wanted him to do movie theaters. But Father said no, he didn't think there was going to be any future in the movie business."

Roth was pragmatic—as are his sons, Richard and Julian, and his grandson, Richard, who now run the firm—he prided himself on his ability to work comfortably with builders. He was not an esthete but a practical participant in the building process of his day.

Roth felt strongly, however, about classical details. His best buildings, structures like the Beresford, the San Remo, and the Oliver Cromwell, combine details from various periods of Italian architecture with the overall massing of skyscrapers. Their profiles are landmarks of the West Side skyline. The buildings use architectural precedent interpretatively, not literally—Roth's greatest gift was his ability to adapt Renaissance and classical details to modern building forms. The result was facades and building masses that were elegant compositions, put together as much by a strong intuition as by anything else.

Roth is credited by his sons with having invented the notion of grouping apartment rooms around a central foyer, rather than stringing them out along a long corridor as was done in most early apartment buildings around the turn of the century. Whether Emery Roth was the first to design foyer plans, he was an active and skillful proponent of that idea. His floor plans generally combined efficiency with generously proportioned, well-lighted spaces.

Roth generally worked alone, although he joined forces with Thomas Hastings, surviving partner of Carrere & Hastings, in the mid-1920's to produce the Ritz Tower. "Hastings and Father used to sit at a drawing board and draw profile after profile," said Julian Roth. "They got so excited that they would grab the pencil from each other."

Roth's favorite building, his sons say, was the Oliver Cromwell, the residential hotel of 1928 at 12 West 72nd Street. The Cromwell has a powerful base of rusticated limestone, a strong brick midsection with subtle verticals punctuated by a few broken pediments, and a carefully massed tower section culminating in an elaborate top. There is no precise precedent—how could there be for an Italian Renaissance skyscraper?—but there is a splendid sense of composition and an exuberant sense of urbanity.

The Roth firm took on modernism slowly—the Normandy apartments of 1938 at 140 Riverside Drive have an Art Deco-like base, but the ornamental housing for the water tower lurches back suddenly to the Italian Renaissance. There were a few other such schizophrenic designs from the 1930's, and buildings such as 930 Fifth Avenue and 875 Fifth Avenue of 1940 show a gradual disappearance of the old ornament.

Work slowed down during World War II; by the end of the war, technology had spawned a new era. Emery Roth's sons wanted to strip their designs down and modernize them; Richard Roth, Sr., recalled that the firm was designing the office building at 505 Park Avenue just after the war. "It was to have been classical, but we didn't like it and tried to make it more modern," he said. "Father thought it was terrible."

But craftspeople were becoming harder and harder to find, and glass and steel were becoming easier and easier to build with; time was clearly on the sons' side. Emery Roth died in 1947, and his firm continued into a new age, a time whose buildings might have pleased him for their pragmatism and power, but would have troubled him for their starkness.

—February 16, 1978

Back to Basics—The Levittown House

It is hard not to believe that a certain sense of gloom descended upon every breakfast table in the nation on the morning not long ago when news reports of the annual meeting of the National Association of Home Builders were published. The home builders are as aware of the cost of housing as any of us, and they understand fully how difficult it is to produce new housing at an affordable price.

They had no message of comfort for the average American—their prediction was that the only possible thing for new housing to do is to shrink in size. The big, detached house is increasingly becoming a creature similar to the big automobile—and new houses, therefore, are likely to start looking the way new cars are looking already. As one builder put it, "We'll have to go back to basics, to the kind of house you built in the fifties. They'll be minimum, 1,000 square feet, one bath, and you'll get rid of all the extras."

Well, nothing could be more timely in terms of fashion than going back to the 1950's—it has been chic for some time in certain circles to collect the furniture of that decade—but that is not the kind of 1950's image the builders are talking about. It is not molded-plywood Eames chairs and amoeba-shaped coffee tables and Danish modern "studio couches" that they have in mind. It is something more like Levittown that the current economic winds may be pushing us toward, and that is a world away from the nostalgia that the 1950's have increasingly come to represent.

But is it altogether a bad thing? The standard, developer-built houses of the early 1950's, from the Levittowns of Long Island, New Jersey, and Pennsylvania, to the tract developments of Daly City and the San Fer-

The original Levittown house

215

nando Valley in California, were hardly works of architectural distinction. No one could look at a Levittown Cape Cod and be inspired to wax eloquent about Palladio. But these houses were practical and well designed, and they possessed a degree of common sense that was frequently lacking in their counterparts of the 1960's and 1970's.

Levittown houses were social creations more than architectural ones—they turned the detached, single-family house from a distant dream into a real possibility for thousands of middle-class American families. The houses were down-to-earth and unpretentious; their point was not to stir the imagination, but to provide reasonable and decent housing. The idea of the single-family house was more important than any specific image or style that house could convey; as a result, the early Levittown houses (and many of their counterparts created by other builders around the country) had few if any of the stylistic affectations that were to bloat the suburban house in later years.

Levittown houses were not colonial, and they were not Tudor, and they were not Georgian, and they were not split-level. They were Cape Cod only in shape; underneath the peaked roof was a straightforward, almost modern object—strikingly close, in its own way, to fulfilling the dictum of Le Corbusier that the house become a "machine for living."

The original Levitt house on Long Island was a one-story house with an unfinished attic, advertised as potential expansion space. There was no basement, and the single living floor contained a kitchen, two bedrooms, a single bath, a living room, and a fair amount of closet space. It totaled 720 square feet of living space, not much bigger than a medium-sized Manhattan apartment. It cost $6,990 in 1947.

That version was very basic, to suburban housing what the Model T Ford had been to automobiles. Mass production made the Levitt houses possible as it had made the automobile—the Levitt organization took advantage of economies of scale and a tightly organized system of construction to keep prices down. The early Levitt house, first built at Levittown on Long Island, sold so well that two years later, in 1949, it was refined into a $7,990 version, which added a few amenities that showed true concern for design without losing the basic commitment to economy and simplicity. If the 1947 house was the Model T, the 1949 version was the Model A.

It had a floor plan of considerable intelligence—the kitchen was moved to the front of the house, near the entrance, and the living room was put in the back and given a 16-square-foot picture window looking out to the backyard. What more sensible way to enter the standard American suburban house than through the kitchen area? The kitchen also had one entrance connecting it to the bedroom area, as well as access to the living room, acknowledging in the floor plan what it has always been in actuality—the true center of the house.

A fireplace was added as a divider between the kitchen and the living room, and a rather deft, Danish-modernesque movable storage wall containing a coat closet, bar, and glass storage was hinged to it. As a further space saver, specially manufactured furnaces were hung in a corridor above the washing machines, freeing a considerable amount of floor area.

This house was probably the finest moment for the Levitt organization: it summed up the best impulses of the 1950's as a period of commitment to low-cost, practical housing that would reflect the realities of suburban, middle-class life. It is hard, really, to fault the Levitt house—as an object in and of itself it was exemplary.

The problem was not in the house itself, but in the Levitt organization's insistence upon packing thousands of them, one the same as the next, into relatively tight suburban tracts. The economies of scale that made the house itself so fine made Levittown an urban-planning disaster—a sea of virtually identical cottages, the intelligent planning of the individual house obscured by the banality of their total effect.

As the 1950's wore on, the Levitt organization turned toward slightly more expensive houses, and in a decision that reveals much about the direction in which the culture was going, switched to a more literally colonial design for a new Levittown for New Jersey. As Herbert Gans put it in his perceptive study *The Levittowners:* "Levitt officials chose the pseudo-colonial design for New Jersey, not because of its popularity, but because they felt it would help them attract higher-income purchasers."

That was a crucial moment—suddenly, image had become more important than substance. The houses the Levitt organization built in New Jersey were not without the intelligent planning of the early Long Island houses, but this aspect was clearly secondary. And as it was for Levitt, in those days the nation's most prominent suburban builder, so it became for others as well. By the 1960's, houses had grown bigger and bigger and more and more unwieldy, and the feeling of tight, sensible planning of the early houses was lost.

Disappearing, too, was any real sense of design discipline or commitment to innovation. Style—or some struggling attempt at the evocation of style—had become the major thing, rather as it had in the automobiles of the time, what with their fins and grilles and swooping shapes.

It is hard not to come back again and again to the analogy of the automobile: it is clearly relevant again now, as the builders are telling us. But as the new generation of American automobiles seems to bespeak a common sense that has been missing altogether for years, so, too, may the next generation of houses. There were problems in the developer-built houses of the 1950's, but there were lessons in them, too.

—April 2, 1981

Great Beach Houses Defer
to the Ocean

Humankind has tried to put almost every type of architecture beside the sea, and only a few styles have seemed even remotely at home there. Of course every kind of sublime landscape calls for some restraint—only a fool would design a house for the desert or the mountains without respect for those places—but the ocean seems especially to mock the arrogant architect, to make his or her efforts seem trivial, almost petty.

The greatest beach houses have been those that understood the power of the ocean and deferred to it, not only in the purely physical sense of being certain that the structure would not be swallowed up by the elements but in a stylistic sense as well. The great shingled houses of the late nineteenth and early twentieth centuries come to mind here. They are rambling and generous expanses of space—arrogant, perhaps, in the social sense of the grandiose lifestyle they were designed for, but architecturally the epitome of modesty. For all their grandeur, they are deferential to their surroundings.

The shingled houses of East Hampton and its neighboring villages sit calmly by the sea. They do not attempt to belittle the ocean or to upstage it as do the palaces of Newport, glorious confections designed with deliberate indifference to the landscape they sit beside. How serenely accepting of the ocean is the shingle style, how nervously defiant of it is the marble palazzo!

At first glance nothing could be farther from the grandiose historical piles of Newport than the sleek wood and glass beach houses that cover so much of Long Island's South Shore. But these stylistic differences mask a certain conceptual similarity. For the new generation of houses by the sea, the sharp, angular structures that occupy some of East Hampton and far more of Bridge-

Arrogance by
the sea,
Long Island

hampton, Westhampton, and Quogue seem, like the great houses of Newport, to be trying to defy the ocean. They do not accept it: they challenge it.

Now there is nothing brand new about what we might call the basic Long Island beach-house style—the house of crisp geometries wrapped in vertical cedar siding, with lots of plate-glass windows and usually a roof that cuts into the sky at a sharp angle. That style owes much of its form to Charles Gwathmey and Richard Henderson's house and studio for the painter Robert Gwathmey in Amagansett, completed in 1967.

But where the Gwathmey house was a subtle play of geometries, the knock-offs have generally been no more than cheap theatrics. And by now the style has been reproduced over and over again, cheapened more and more each time, it seems, covering the beaches and even—heaven help us—being used to provide the design for a Burger King in Southampton.

The stretch of the Hamptons known as Dune Road in Westhampton and Quogue has been particularly afflicted lately. There has been construction along this beachfront for some years, but it has increased dramatically in the last year or two, with wild geometries breaking out all over.

There are slanted roofs and sloping roofs and round windows and trapezoidal windows and octagonal towers, sometimes all in the same building. There are houses with roofs that slope all the way into the ground, making the whole structure look like a great shingled bunker, and there are houses that have roofs going in many directions at once.

It is all a cacophony. One senses that the architects responsible here some-how thought that building by the sea freed them from the sort of restraints they are accustomed to operating under elsewhere; perhaps they assumed that the freedom from the social restrictions of city life that people enjoy at the beach should be expressed in architectural form.

That is not how it works. Not to sound stuffy about it, but there is a kind of protocol that all buildings should observe, whatever their functions. And buildings that will be seen in conjunction with other buildings have a special responsibility to observe such protocols, to work as parts of greater wholes. Houses by the sea should not resemble city houses, of course—the expecta-tions, the protocols are completely different—but that is hardly license for architectural anarchy.

There are a couple of exceptions to the mediocre level of quality in the Westhampton-Quogue stretch of the beach. One is a small house by Charles Gwathmey and Robert Siegel that is tight and disciplined, its white tautness a welcome relief from the wildness of its neighbors. Another is a cottage that was completed recently by Robert A. M. Stern, the architect whose efforts at reviving the shingle style have been a significant contribution to current domestic architecture.

Mr. Stern's house shows a respect for the traditions of turn-of-the-century beach architecture, and it seems to sit far more comfortably by the sea than most of its neighbors. But even this house has a self-conscious, mannered quality to it. It is not the arrogance of silly geometries but the more subtle arrogance of an overload of architectural elements crammed into a very modest house, as if to show off its ability at quotation.

But better the pretension of architectural quotation than the pretension of wild exhibitionism. It is hard, really, to know why the wild geometric forms seem as active in the first place. They do not make particular sense as oceanside houses although they are open and airy, which is a start. They seem so anxious, so tense, in spite of the fact that they are intended to evoke relaxation.

It must be a comment on something that we find it so difficult, now, to evoke relaxation in our architecture or that the architecture we create to do that job is, in fact, anxiety-provoking instead. It would be nice to be able to believe that there was some sort of intentional ironic comment being made here, that the architects responsible are telling us that we are not very good at relaxing and that this is what happens when we try. But no: the fact of the matter seems to be that the architects themselves are not very good at relaxing or at expressing it in their work.

The real irony is that at the serene setting of the sea we seem to create forms that are the opposite of serenity—forms that speak of self-consciousness, of anxiety and tension. It was so at Newport, and it is so now in the Hamptons.

—July 9, 1981
East Hampton, L.I.

The Unsung Hero of the Urban Neighborhood

There are a lot of overlooked parts of the American landscape, but none, surely, is more consistently ignored than the wooden frame houses that fill working-class districts of older cities. They are not slums, they are not suburbs, they are not townhouses, they are not part of chic gentrification. They are the sorts of houses the camera pans over in the opening sequences of *All in the Family*—they fill much of Queens and Brooklyn and Staten Island, and much of Jersey City and Paterson and Boston and Baltimore and Pittsburgh.

Most date from the early decades of this century, but some are older, and some, especially on Staten Island, are relatively new. They run the gamut in style, from little bungalows to Cape Cod cottages to two- and three-story wooden-frame houses, sometimes joined in "semi-detached" twos or attached rows of three or more, that have no particularly classifiable architectural style at all. Whatever style these houses may have had at the beginning they often lose as time goes on—for their occupants tend to modify them constantly, altering them to accommodate changing needs and changing styles.

And it is these changes that are the subject of "Transformed Houses," a small but provocative exhibition prepared by the Smithsonian Institution's Traveling Exhibition Service. It will be on view through October 24 at the Parsons School of Design exhibition center, 2 West Thirteenth Street.

"Transformed Houses" takes as its starting point the notion that the American working-class urban house constitutes an unstudied vernacular, and that the transformations that have occurred in this type of house over the years have created an entirely new style in and of itself.

"The thrust of these transformations," the exhibition's

Houses in
transformation

223

text tells us, "has not been to restore the past but, from the user's point of view, to improve upon it—not to remove siding but to install it. The result of this piecemeal renovation over many years has been the emergence of a different, sometimes striking vernacular architecture that has changed the look of America's older neighborhoods."

So what we are looking at, in other words, is the other side of gentrification—the aluminum siding, the asbestos brick, and all the rest that is added to houses by people who do not have the upper-middle-class urge to re-create a past, and who are too close themselves to some of the discomforts of the past to want to bring back its visual appearance. For them, the appearance of newness is crucial.

As a Hoboken homeowner says in a quotation in one of the show's text panels, "Thirty years ago you would have wanted your house to look modern; today the trend is to preserve it. I still think if something is old, you should get rid of it and go toward the future. Time has to go on; we had to modernize our house."

By "modernize," of course, this homeowner did not mean to turn her house into a little corner of the Bauhaus, replete with Breuer chairs and Mies van der Rohe tables. In all likelihood what she really had in mind was a new front of stone veneer, perhaps a metal awning or two, and an interior of wood-grain Formica kitchen counters. Is this exhibition asking us to love such things—trying, in other words, to expand the boundaries of taste?

Well, yes and no. One of the impressive things about it is that it is truly nonjudgmental. It is an honest inquiry into the nature of a major part of the cityscape—far calmer, in fact, than the exhibition organized by the architectural firm of Venturi, Rauch & Scott Brown in Washington some years ago that touched on a similar theme. There is nothing patronizing about this exhibition, and that is a relief.

But does this material justify such attention from a design standpoint? Are all of these houses significant architecturally? The fact of the matter is that the "transformations" they have undergone are rarely interesting, and still more rarely are they esthetic improvements on the originals.

The exhibition includes one pair of turn-of-the-century houses in the Bronx in which the original has a lovely turret, iron railings, and an ornate cornice, while its neighbor has had its turret and architectural ornament removed and is covered in white and pink aluminum siding with a metal canopy over the front door.

One might admire the aspirations of the homeowners who did this alteration—the desire to express themselves, the desire to be up-to-date, the desire to feel that they were improving, and hence also leaving their mark on, their property. But this hardly makes the results themselves worthy of praise; in this case they are, instead, rather poignant—in the name of improvement and self-expression, good architecture has been destroyed.

But this raises another crucial issue, which underlies the entire exhibition. A great many people do not see "old" and "ordinary" architecture as particularly desirable—like the Hoboken homeowner, they often want to change it to express their own needs. Preservation is largely an upper-class movement, in taste and education if not in financial standing.

So there is a real conflict here: is it reasonable to suggest that decent, if undistinguished, houses in working-class neighborhoods be left alone, or should people be permitted to alter them as they please, even if the alterations result in a loss of architectural quality?

The residents of these neighborhoods, obviously, tend to opt for personal expression. They speak in this exhibition through a few quotations scattered through the photographs and maps, and these quotes are often more revealing then the visual material itself.

"The two houses should be identical, otherwise it would be like a man with two different shoes," says a Brooklyn man whose views are clearly in the minority, for most of the pairs of semi-detached houses show that neighbors have rarely consulted one another when doing alterations, with results that seem almost deliberately designed to clash.

These joined houses seem only occasionally to be perceived as a pair. (In an extreme example, half of a double house under a single gable in Pittsburgh was moved away, leaving the remaining house with just half a gable, slicing into the Pittsburgh sky at an odd angle, looking like a Fire Island beach house.)

These changes and alterations are, at bottom, an esthetic based on the use of one material to look like another—aluminum to look like wood, asbestos to look like brick, and so forth. And this is the real problem, the reason these buildings are, ultimately, not very interesting. They are pleasing in their intentions, but when one sees building after building they tend to blur, in the way that popular music and commercial art tend to blur.

Much more important than any point about design, however, is the point the show makes about the future of urban areas in general. These houses in working-class neighborhoods do constitute an important part of our housing stock, and the renovations and transformations done by homeowners on an ad hoc basis are an unheralded effort at urban renewal. They deserve to be praised—not as design but as a kind of salvation.

—October 22, 1981

To Utopia by Bus and Subway

Housing in and around New York City can be described in many ways, but rarely as generous and even more rarely as idealistic. Most housing in the metropolitan area, from single-family houses in the suburbs to apartments in the center of Manhattan, was built for profit, and it tends all too frequently to be mean in its space and conservative in its design. This may be a city of innovative ideas, but one would not know it from the places in which we live because so few of them involve even the slightest degree of experimentation or adventure in design. When it comes to building lots of housing units, we seem like a city and a region of formulas, not of creativity.

But like all simple assumptions about New York, this one is not so true as it seems. While it cannot be denied that the general level of housing design in New York is mediocre, the city and its surrounding region have some of the most important pieces of experimental housing and planning in the world. There were planned suburbs in New York as early as 1891, and in the 1920's so much was happening that this city was a center for utopian planning. And although we tend to think of the 1930's, 1940's, and 1950's as decades in which large-scale housing meant nothing but the banality of identical red-brick towers, the fact is that even during those years there were developments built here that attracted international renown.

The names of many of these places—Sunnyside Gardens, Radburn, Fresh Meadows, Forest Hills Gardens, Prospect Park South—are known to planners and architects, but very rarely to New Yorkers other than those who live in them. They are not at all cut out of the same mold, but tend to look quite different from one another. What makes them special—besides the fact that they

Forest Hills
Gardens

227

almost always have thoughtfully designed, well-laid-out houses or apartments—is a commitment they share to a sense of community. That might mean shared open space in some cases, compatible architecture in others, but in every case it emerged out of a certain idealistic, almost utopian yearning for perfect order. These were places created by architects and developers who truly believed that better housing could create a better society.

That sense still pervades most of these places: they still seem like refuges from the anguish of the city, and in some of them there is almost a feeling that time has stopped.

Prospect Park South

One of the great surprises in the New York cityscape—fifteen blocks of gracious, rambling turn-of-the-century houses on wide, tree-lined streets, just yards from the harsher streets of central Brooklyn—is Prospect Park South. To enter it is to move in one step from urban tensions to an almost rural sense of ease.

This neighborhood was the forerunner of all of New York City's fashionable in-town suburbs, Fieldston and Riverdale in the Bronx, Jamaica Estates in Queens, and innumerable suburban areas around the country. It was laid out in 1889 by Dean Alvord, a developer who envisioned Prospect Park South as a place in which "people of intelligence and good breeding" might find comfortable, esthetically pleasing homes reasonably close to downtown Brooklyn (which was then a separate city) and Manhattan.

Alvord laid out Prospect Park South with wide streets, in some cases with malls down the middle; he put all utility lines into the ground before any houses were built, a dramatic advance for his time, and he created a series of design guidelines to assure that the houses of Prospect Park South were compatible with one another. Property owners were severely limited in where they could put houses on their land; the result of that is an even property line down each street, and to make the streets grander still, Alvord planted great trees not at the edge of the street or just in front of the houses, but at the property line just inside the sidewalk, creating the illusion that the streets were as wide as boulevards.

The result was, and remains, an unusually serene, restful place. Within the gateposts that mark the entrances to the community along its bordering streets—Church Avenue, Beverly Road, and Coney Island Avenue—lie a remarkable number of first-rate houses, most of which remain in superb condition. Among the best are the great stately mansions of Albemarle Road, such as Nos. 1510, 1305, and 1440, which have sumptuous classical colonnades: they could be northern, urban versions of Tara. But there is considerable stylistic variation here. Beside the classicizing Queen Anne mansions there are some lovely eccentricities, such as a vaguely Japanese house at No. 131 Buckingham Road and a lovely Shingle Style house beside it at No. 115, and the house with Ionic columns and a bowed front porch at No. 154 Rugby Road. And Buckingham Road, with a curving central mall, is itself as fine a collection of turn-of-the-century eclectic houses as can be found anywhere in the city.

Forest Hills Gardens

There is frequently some sort of angel behind utopian communities: rare is the case when a profit-minded developer, such as Dean Alvord, creates an ideal project within the confines of the real-estate market. In the case of Forest Hills Gardens there was a philanthropic angel, the Russell Sage Foundation, which purchased a large plot of land in then undeveloped Forest Hills and set out to build what it thought would be housing for the working classes. Grosvenor Atterbury was hired as architect, with Frederick Law Olmsted, Jr., as landscape architect.

The foundation's plan did not quite work, for the reason that it worked too well—Atterbury and Olmsted created a garden suburb of such quality that it quickly developed into one of the city's choicest residential enclaves, which it remains today. Forest Hills Gardens is the epitome of the garden suburb: it is built around a central square, loosely English Tudor in style, that is tied into the Forest Hills station of the Long Island Rail Road. The square is a wonderful example of picturesque American eclecticism—it has brick paving and an arched bridge over one of the streets leading into it, as well as a handsome, rounded-top tower that serves as a symbol of the entire project. It is almost a storybook version of an English village—but good enough so that it never appears precious or cute.

This level of design is carried through the entire project. Although most of the houses are Tudor in style, they all have red-tile roofs, which call to mind Spanish mission architecture; the contradiction does not matter at all, for the overall effect is so handsomely picturesque as to give the entire design coherence. Moreover, the organization is superb—there is an exquisitely landscaped, beautifully scaled central park area, called the Greenway, that leads from the central square through the residential blocks, which themselves curve and wind gracefully. There are also lovely street lamps and signposts that carry a sundial motif throughout the project.

Forest Hills Gardens has been added to gradually over the years, usually with sensitivity. There is a large apartment building at one end of the Greenway that blends 1930's-style casement windows with the red-tile roofs and Tudoresque towers of the original architecture, and it could be a textbook example of how to mix old and new creatively. The houses themselves vary in quality, and most are neither so grand nor so interesting as the best houses of Prospect Park South, but there is a sense of more continued prosperity, of lawns a bit greener and general maintenance a bit crisper.

Sunnyside Gardens

With Sunnyside Gardens, in 1924, entered three of the great names in twentieth-century utopian housing: Clarence Stein, Henry Wright, and Alexander Bing. Stein and Wright were idealistic architect-planners, and Bing was a real-estate man with a passionate interest in improving the lot of housing for the average worker. Together they made a remarkable team: Bing's financial assistance and Stein and Wright's design gifts were to create two of the most important of all the metropolitan area's housing developments, Sunnyside Gardens in Queens and Radburn in New Jersey.

Sunnyside, a 1,200-unit garden-apartment complex, was the group's first effort, constructed between 1924 and 1928 on fifty-six acres of undeveloped land a few blocks north of Queens Boulevard in the Sunnyside section. The complex was intended as an early American test, on a very limited basis, of the garden-city theories of Ebenezer Howard, the English city planner, who had argued in favor of relatively low densities and open space as an alternative to traditional cities.

The Sunnyside plan is simple and direct: it groups apartment units closely together as a means of freeing land for common use. The low-rise buildings themselves are of brick and quite plain; they were constructed on a tight budget, and open space was clearly the priority—Stein and Wright did not want to allow elaborate construction to cut into the outdoor space they could afford to provide.

The buildings line several blocks of Sunnyside, and they turn a somewhat sober face toward the street. Their special quality is all inside, in the private world of the huge, block-through inner courts shared by each group of residents. The courts are mostly large and parklike; residents have small, private yards just behind their houses, but most of the space is given over to a large, central communal area.

There was a covenant to protect the open space for fifty years in the original plans for Sunnyside, and the residents chose not to renew it when it expired in the 1970's. As a result, a couple of the inner courts have been divided into larger and more conventional private yards for the units facing onto them. Most of the central open spaces remain intact, however, although in varying conditions—some are fairly rundown and have received almost no maintenance, while a couple of others look so lush one would think they were tended by full-time gardeners.

For active sports, the planners also provided a park and playing field around the corner from the complex on 39th Street, which remains in fine condition. A caution: the open spaces within each group of Sunnyside Gardens apartments are not public property. It is often possible to walk through on the marked

Sunnyside Gardens

paths, but visitors must obey any requests from residents to remain outside.

Incidentally, there is another Stein project just a block or two away, the Phipps Garden Apartments on 39th Avenue at 50th Street. Phipps, a philanthropic project of another great advocate of improved housing, the steel magnate Henry Phipps, is a more elegant stepchild of Sunnyside. It consists of 4- and 6-story units arranged around a single courtyard, more varied than at Sunnyside, with Art Deco ornamentation in the brickwork. In addition, the project has been wonderfully maintained—it looks as if it might have been finished yesterday.

Radburn

Sunnyside Gardens was an economic success, though its prosperity may well have been as much due to the boom of the 1920's and the resulting need for housing as to any great popular belief in the garden-city theories of Ebenezer Howard. In any case, after Sunnyside's completion, Stein, Wright, and Bing were moved to attempt to put Howard's notions into practice on a larger scale and try their hand at an entire garden city.

Alexander Bing's City Housing Corporation purchased a tract of farmland in 1928 in Fair Lawn, New Jersey, and the team set to work on Radburn, which it envisioned as a town of 25,000 with its own industry. It never quite turned out that way—industry was not growing in the area when planning began, and then the Depression killed all possibility of it—but what was built nonetheless ended as one of the most important suburbs in American planning history.

Only 408 houses had been built at Radburn when the Depression stopped all further growth. But their design and layout makes them special. Stein and Wright wanted Radburn to offer a solution to two problems they saw in conventional suburbs, the poor use of land and the constant and dangerous presence of the automobile.

What they did at Radburn was to group houses tightly around cul-de-sacs, which function as automobile service roads. The service side of each house faces the road, while the living areas face landscaped open space on the other side, which is reserved for pedestrians. Huge, sprawling common lawns sweep through the town, and these great green spaces, plus a couple of bridges and underpasses, make it possible to move on foot from any house to any other without ever crossing an automobile road.

The Radburn houses are small by today's standards. But they are in fine condition, and the well-kept open spaces can only be called luxurious. The "Radburn idea"—the layout that makes Radburn the spiritual father of every cluster-house development in the country—remains convincing. The spirit that created it was far more utopian than that which gives birth to most housing design today, but the fact is that Radburn, unlike most utopian schemes, truly works.

Hillside Homes

Another Stein and Wright project is Hillside Homes, in the North Bronx. It is a bit later than Sunnyside and Radburn, and sadly, it is not in nearly as good condition. One must use some imagination to understand exactly what Stein and Wright had in mind. Once again these are low-rise units, grouped tightly to preserve open space, but there are no great central spaces—the wings of Hillside are set around a myriad of smaller courtyard spaces, some of them paved rather than landscaped. There is a larger central play area, but it, too, lacks the pleasant air of the open spaces at the earlier projects.

Yet this is no place to be dismissed or ignored. Not only are there good apartments inside, but the 1,400-unit complex also contained a nursery school, workshops, and club and community rooms, something of an innovation for the mid-1930's. And there is considerable sophistication to the overall layout. The multiblock site is on a steep hill, and the project steps down in terracelike fashion, its design ever respectful of the topography.

The notion, as in all of Stein's projects, was to create an architecture that would enhance the sense of community. Unfortunately, Stein tended to feel that such a sense was impossible in the existing city, and he turned the project inward, rejecting the traditional street. If Stein had any failing at all, it was his refusal to understand that the average stoop on the average brownstone on the average street can be as important a socializing influence as any open space in any utopian housing.

Parkchester

After World War II, Metropolitan Life built a number of immense housing projects in Manhattan, including Stuyvesant Town, Peter Cooper Village, and Riverton. Parkchester, designed by a board of architects chaired by Richmond H. Shreve, was their predecessor in the East Bronx. It was built between 1938 and 1942, and it is the finest large-scale housing complex in New York by far.

There have been two basic inspirations for many of the housing complexes built in New York: the garden-city notions of Ebenezer Howard, which gave birth to Clarence Stein's projects, and the visions of towers in open space of Le Corbusier from the 1920's, which led to so many banal, red-brick housing projects. Parkchester follows neither model directly and manages, surprisingly, to come much closer to feeling like a traditional city than either model does.

Parkchester is huge—it was built to house 40,000 residents—but it is less intimidating and vastly more alive than such later blockbusters as Co-op City or Starrett City. The project consists of red-brick towers built around open space, but set along an active commercial street. That central street, Metropolitan Avenue, functions like a spine: it brings as much to this complex as Broadway does to the Upper West Side. The towers on Metropolitan Avenue have large, rounded bases, their facades covered with colorful glazed terra-cotta tiles and their insides filled with stores and movie theaters.

In the center of the complex is Metropolitan Oval, a large and well-maintained park with a central fountain, flowers, trees, and benches. The apartment buildings themselves are relieved by facade sculpture that looks somewhat tacked on, but is still friendly in feeling; the whole place stands as a crucial reminder that it is possible to build housing on a mass scale and not lose touch with what we like to call the human values.

Fresh Meadows

What Parkchester was to the Bronx, Fresh Meadows was to Queens. It was the New York Life Insurance Company's turn, and the date of construction, 1949, was a bit later. Different, too, was the mood: if Parkchester can be considered the quintessential *urban* mass-housing complex, Fresh Meadows is the quintessential suburban one. Built on the 166-acre site of the old Fresh Meadows Country Club, this is almost all low-rise; the buildings, designed by Voorhees, Walker, Foley & Smith, sprawl all over the land.

Fresh Meadows was lavishly praised by Lewis Mumford, who saw in it a continuation of the principles of Sunnyside Gardens. But to eyes trained to seek out more traditional, citylike places, it appears far away from its distinguished predecessor. There is a nice mix of row housing, low-rise housing, and a few towers, but the architecture is very dull, more so than at Sunnyside.

What made Fresh Meadows special when it was new was its site planning. There is an enormous amount of landscaped open space, and it is accessible from every one of the apartment units. There are no semiprivate landscaped areas, as at Sunnyside, but there is a range from small, yardlike areas to huge, sprawling parklike ones. Fresh Meadows has its own school, theater, and shopping center; the retail complex was among the first automobile-oriented shopping centers to be built, and this, too, helped earn for the project its place in planning history.

—April 17, 1981

A Major Landmark Battle
for the 1980's

Model of
St. Bartholomew's
tower

Not since the Penn Central railroad tried to put a sky-scraper atop Grand Central Terminal has a land-use issue in midtown Manhattan ignited such passions as the proposal to sell off some of St. Bartholomew's Episcopal Church on Park Avenue for the construction of an office tower. Indeed, if the Grand Central controversy, which spanned the decade from 1968, when the skyscraper was first proposed, to 1978, when the United States Supreme Court put it finally to rest, could be said to have been the major landmarks preservation battle of the 1970's, this one seems to be shaping up to play the same role in the 1980's.

The reason is simple. St. Bartholomew's, the Byzan-tine church built in 1919 to the designs of Bertram Goodhue, sits on the east blockfront of Park Avenue between 50th and 51st streets. It is on the last piece of land on the city's premier commercial boulevard not now occupied by commercial real estate.

The new tower would block the brick office building recently completed just to the east at 560 Lexington Avenue, although it would preserve the small garden on Park Avenue in the southwest corner of the site, which would become an entrance plaza for the new office build-ing.

To get right to the point, this is the wrong building in the wrong place. And there is considerable question as to whether there is such a thing as a right building for this place.

St. Bartholomew's has both immense financial value and huge symbolic importance. To the church and to its designated real-estate developer, the special quality of this piece of property is a chance for unusually great financial gain; to the city's preservation community, it is

237

the only opportunity left to keep some light and open space on Park Avenue.

The project the church has accepted is not likely to quell the controversy. Designed by the architectural firm of Edward Durell Stone Associates, it is a 59-story tower of mirrored glass intended to reflect the domed main building of the church and the masonry walls of surrounding structures such as the Waldorf-Astoria Hotel and the General Electric Building.

The plan calls for a many-sided skyscraper, with setbacks at the top and a sequence of zigzags creating a series of corners along one side. In overall shape, it looks to be very much like the Trump Tower now rising on Fifth Avenue.

The tower will be set in the southeast corner of the St. Bartholomew's property, on the land now occupied by the church's community house, which was added to the church by Goodhue's firm after his death. The house would be demolished, but its facade would be preserved and tacked onto the front of the base of the tower.

Not only does the landmark grouping of St. Bartholomew's Church and its community house have great importance to the city, but this part of New York is also crowded to the point of absurdity by serious overbuilding. These issues make one wonder if any building, no matter how well designed, should be added to Park Avenue.

But this one would be wrong even if Park Avenue were crying out for more skyscrapers. The architects are trying to save St. Bartholomew's with mirrors, and it is a gross and awkward solution. It is an intrusion of glittering glass into a grouping of buildings noted for their masonry quality; it will be belittling not only to the church, but to the graceful and exuberant General Electric Tower behind St. Bartholomew's.

It is a particular slap in the face to the new 560 Lexington Avenue building, whose architects, the Eggers Group, conscientiously worked in brick to blend their building softly into the existing fabric of this crucial midtown block.

If this tower is built, their work will be to naught, as will the careful efforts of Cross & Cross, architects of the General Electric Building, back in 1931 to tie their 51-story tower to the church by virtue of its slender profile and the use of materials identical to those used in St. Bartholomew's.

As the block containing St. Bartholomew's now stands, it offers not only a rare and vital piece of open sky in midtown Manhattan, but also an object lesson in sensitive architectural relationships. The new tower seems to miss these entirely.

It is not for want of trying, however. Both the architect, Peter Capone of the Stone firm, and the church's architectural consultant on the project, Robert Geddes, dean of the Princeton University School of Architecture, have written justifications for this project that use words like "appropriateness" and "harmonious." They point with pride to the manner in which the tower has been set back from Park Avenue, preserving the small garden in the southwest corner of the property, and to the way in which the community house facade has been saved.

There can be no better reminder of how, in matters architectural, one must watch what architects do, not listen to what they say. The words make sense here; the design does not.

To tack the community house facade onto the base of a 59-story glass skyscraper, for example, is not so much sensible as sentimental, a bone thrown to the preservationist impulse. The important thing about the community house as it now stands is its massing, its sculpted shape; to save the facade alone is an empty gesture, and it will only look awkward and foolish as the front door to a high-rent office building.

Similarly, while the architects refer to the shape of the tower as having minimal impact on the surroundings, the fact of the matter is that a light, reflective form that is taller than any nearby skyscraper is almost certain to have a rather jarring impact. The tower's unusual, multifaceted shape pretends to a certain deference to the church, but this is deference of the most simplistic sort. There is nothing subtle to this form at all.

What the tower does have is a rather intricate and ingenious organization, with new facilities for the church's community house neatly tucked into the lower floors and a separate entrance from the office tower. In this sense, it calls to mind the tower Marcel Breuer designed and the Penn Central tried to build atop Grand Central; it, too, was quite skillful in its complex organization.

But as those technical qualities hardly made the Grand Central tower right, so do they not justify the St. Bartholomew's tower. The church and its developer, Howard Ronson, are proposing an awkward intrusion into an already horrendously overbuilt part of New York.

—October 30, 1981

By the spring of 1983, the St. Bartholomew's project had become curiously dormant. It remains officially alive, but the slowdown in the real-estate market and rumored second thoughts on the part of the developer have prevented it— thus far—from coming to life.

Two Landmarks Preservation Debates

I. The Rice Mansion

When the Board of Estimate begins today to debate the matter of the Rice Mansion, the 1901 house at the corner of Riverside Drive and 89th Street, it will bring to a climax a battle that has raged for months between the city's landmarks advocates, members of the surrounding Upper West Side neighborhood, and members of the Jewish community. These groups have been frequent allies in the past, but they have clashed long and hard in this case—perhaps the most agonizing landmark fight in Manhattan in some years.

The issues are esthetic, political, and social. The house—about which more in a moment—is one of the last two freestanding mansions remaining on Riverside Drive, once a street of great houses. It has been occupied for some years by the Yeshiva Chofetz Chaim, a Jewish religious school, which has indicated a need for cash; the school has said it has an offer from a real-estate developer to purchase the property for $2 million, and it would like to sell. Such a sale would mean the replacement of the mansion by a 30-story apartment tower, drastically changing the aura of the neighborhood, now a community of row houses on side streets and 15-story apartment buildings on Riverside Drive.

To prevent this occurrence, the New York City Landmarks Preservation Commission named the house a landmark in February, and now the Board of Estimate, which legally must approve all landmark designations before they become law, is about to decide whether to ratify the designation or to reject it.

The public debate has been unusually long and angry for a landmarks question, and perhaps for the first time in the fifteen-year history of the landmarks commission, religious issues have become part of the argument. Some of the yeshiva's supporters have suggested that since landmarks designation would deprive the school of its chance to earn $2 million from the sale of its property, naming the Rice Mansion a city landmark would amount to a restriction on freedom of religion or, worse still, to discrimination against the Jewish community.

These arguments do not seem to deal with the issue of whether or not the Rice Mansion is of the architectural quality demanded by the city's landmarks preservation ordinances; indeed, they ignore this question. But many of the advocates of landmark designation have appeared no more interested in finding an honest answer to this same question—many of the supporters of designation are neighbors of the mansion who seem concerned only with the future of the views from their apartments, not with the larger issue of what is best for their entire neighborhood.

For when all is said and done, the Rice Mansion *is* of landmark quality. It is a handsome freestanding mansion, mixing the Beaux-Arts and neo-Georgian styles in the eclectic manner of so much of New York's very finest residential architecture from the turn of the century. The architects were Herts & Tallent, a distinguished firm of the period, and the design has one particularly distinctive element, a porte-cochere on the 89th Street side that is scooped into the mass of the house. The building has a vague similarity to the grandiose Andrew Carnegie Mansion, on Fifth Avenue at 91st Street, which has been preserved as the Cooper-Hewitt Museum, but if anything, the somewhat more freewheeling and eccentric Rice Mansion is the better of the two.

Indeed, the Rice Mansion—which was built opposite the Soldiers and Sailors Monument for Isaac L. Rice, who made a fortune in railroads and electric cars—is at least as good a work of architecture as many houses now under landmark protection. It is now in a very different kind of architectural context than the one for which it was intended, however, and that is another part of the debate.

When the Rice Mansion was new, it was surrounded by similar houses, buildings that were its architectural equals. Now, it is nearly alone, hemmed in by apartment houses, and its role as the survivor of Riverside Drive has given it a symbolic importance that even outweighs its architectural significance.

Those opposed to landmark status argue that the mansion is now so far removed from its original context that its good architecture has relatively little meaning, and that since Riverside Drive is now, for better or worse, a street of apartment houses, there is no reason to make the corner of 89th Street any different.

But landmarks advocates point out that the single landmark left as a remnant of an architecturally better age can take on a vital role in a neighborhood, as an anchor to the past, and in this case, as a device to preserve just a bit of open space and small scale.

In the end, the best argument in favor of preservation—aside from the inherent architectural quality of the mansion—is this very issue. As the last mansion, or very nearly the last mansion, on Riverside Drive, the Rice Mansion has a special role to play, and it is much more than the role of a historical remnant. It can stand as a symbol of a city of smaller, more human scale, as a reminder of a city in which open space, light, and public and private amenities were considered necessary parts of urban design, not pointless luxuries.

So the last house becomes, in a sense, more important, not less important—it becomes vital, from an urban-planning point of view, to retain. Of course, it makes sense to ask whether it is fair to ask the yeshiva, a nonprofit organization, to bear the financial weight of saving such a landmark—its resources, after all, are small, and if the house is deemed to have all the more symbolic importance, that would suggest all the more pressure upon the religious school.

But here again, the landmarks ordinance is heedful. The city's landmarks law permits the Yeshiva Chofetz Chaim to sell the house to any other owner who will preserve it, at any price. While it is unlikely that a buyer of the house would be willing to pay the vast sum a real-estate developer would, it is reasonable to ask whether the city must guarantee the owners the highest possible profit from their landmark, or merely a reasonable return. And in any case, should a reasonable return not be possible, the landmarks law permits the yeshiva to claim financial hardship and, after a period of a year, petition the landmarks commission for permission to demolish the building.

—*June 26, 1980*

The Rice Mansion was declared a landmark in 1980, and it remains on Riverside Drive.

II. The Davies Mansion

There is a bright, Yale-blue bumper sticker that is turning up around the university's campus here, and it reads "For God, For Country and For the Davies Mansion." It represents something of a last-ditch effort by a coalition of students, faculty members, and citizens of New Haven to save one of Connecticut's finest houses: the sprawling, French Second Empire mansion built in 1868 for John M. Davies by New Haven's leading nineteenth-century architect, Henry Austin.

The house sits on a high hill atop Prospect Street, one of those great avenues of eclectic residential splendor laid in virtually every American city in the late nineteenth century to bring the newly rich a noble address at the edge of town. It commands a view not only of the Yale campus, to which it is adjacent, but of all New Haven also out to Long Island Sound.

The house is now boarded up, its stucco peeling and its roof leaky. But it is still easy to see what a rich and powerful building this is, sumptuous and self-assured as only the very finest works of its period are. The twenty-three rooms run on and on with a wonderful sense of endless space, of corridors turning back on themselves to make of each passage a sense of new mystery.

Now, the rooms are crumbling, and they are filled with mattresses, chairs, electrical equipment, metal drums, and miscellaneous junk stowed there at random over the last decade. Its paint is peeling and some of the fine architectural detail, like carved banisters and mantelpieces, has been looted.

The house has been empty since 1972, when the Culinary Institute of America, the chefs' school that had occupied it since 1947, moved to Hyde Park, New York. The property was taken over by Yale University, and that, oddly enough, is when its troubles began. For Yale's intent was not so much to use the house as it was to gain access to its 7-acre plot, the largest piece of potentially developable land remaining beside the great downtown campus.

Yale, by its own officials' admission, has let the house run down. "It is fair to say we have not kept the house in great condition," Henry L. Chauncey, Jr., the secretary of the university, said this week. Now, admitting that the Davies Mansion is in dangerous shape, Yale has decided to tear it down.

Demolition is scheduled for the end of this month, with only a couple of possible reprieves: the university may simply change its mind or it may agree to accept one of several proposals received from real-estate developers to restore the mansion and turn it into a paying property. If that happens, Yale would lease the house to a developer who would pay all costs of restoration and presumably allow the university to share in his profits.

Restoration would cost $600,000 to $900,000, depending on whose figures are used and how thorough a job is done. By any standard, it is not a cheap proposition, and this is the problem. Yale says that, given how hard up for funds private universities are these days, it cannot afford to divert funds from

Davies Mansion, New Haven

academic purposes to put this house back in shape.

University officials seem to feel it is beside the point that it was the university's own neglect that contributed largely to the house's condition; they argue that the only thing to do right now—unless one of the developers' proposals, the specific details of which Yale refuses to disclose, should be accepted—is to tear the house down.

The controversy has become quite heated on this campus, which, like most American universities, has been a serene island of academic preoccupation for the last few years. The situation bears little resemblance to student-administration confrontations of years past, for here it is the administration that is arguing for a practical and "real-world" solution. And it is the dissidents, in the name of the Yale Ad Hoc Committee to Save the Davies Mansion, who assert as beleaguered administrations did in times past that tradition is a noble value to which universities should aspire.

To a certain extent, they are right. This is not like most historic preservation stories. This remarkable piece of architecture is not threatened by a large corporation eager to increase its profits by turning its land to the most lucrative purpose. It is threatened by a university, one with a long and distinguished reputation as a center for the study of architecture and as a haven for the humanities in general. Everything about the university's history would suggest that it would see its role as that of custodian of Yale's and New Haven's finest architecture.

Instead, Yale seems to view this house as a burden. Administration officials concede its quality, but complain constantly of the costs of upkeep ($25,000 per year, they say, even boarded up). They cite a wish to avoid federal restrictions as an excuse for not seeking federal restoration grants that could have gone a long way toward restoring the house for the university's own use. There has been no earnest, large-scale effort to seek other preservation funds or take advantage of tax laws that favor restoration by offering substantial deductions as an attraction to potential donors.

When Yale reluctantly agreed to entertain proposals from real-estate developers, it did so under an almost impossible timetable, and did not even produce a set of guidelines so that potential developers would know what the university wanted to happen.

Still, proposals have come in, and a few seem quite serious. One is from the Schiavone Construction Company, which is now turning New Haven's huge old Taft Hotel into apartments; Schiavone wants to turn the Davies Mansion into a restaurant and conference center, which could benefit the university both academically and financially.

The situation has been made more ironic by the presence just a few blocks down Prospect Street of the new campus for the School of Organization and Management, Yale's new business school. Here, the architect Edward Larrabee Barnes has built an entire complex around two fine old mansions (one, coincidentally, designed by Henry Austin, the Davies Mansion architect), and new architecture and old have been integrated superbly. It is hard to imagine old mansions being put to better re-use than has been done here by the very same university that has let the Davies Mansion deteriorate so drastically.

University officials are meeting with potential developers, and the house may yet be saved, even though Yale officials say that as of this week, the March 31 demolition date remains firm. If a developer can convince the university of the value of his proposal, the Davies Mansion will remain.

What is so sad, though, is that so much effort has had to be devoted to persuading a university—a center of cultural artifacts as well as a forum of ideas—of the value of saving a fine piece of historic architecture in its midst.

—March 20, 1980
New Haven

Yale did agree, in the nick of time, to accept proposals for the restoration of the Davies Mansion—and thus this treasure of New Haven is still there.

Davies Mansion, detail

New York City's New Architectural Battleground

Churches may be thought of as sacred and theaters as profane, but the two building types have a lot in common in New York. They are both places in which crowds gather, they both constitute a major share of the city's inventory of architectural treasures, and they are both customarily housed in smaller, freestanding buildings. And that may be their undoing—for in many cases the airspace above a church or a theater has more financial value than the structure itself.

That did not matter terribly much in a day when real-estate values were lower and pressure less. However, now that developers have been building with a frenzy that surpasses even the boom of the 1920's, and have sought to shoehorn skyscrapers into every possible mid-town site, the future of many of the city's churches and theaters has become a serious issue. By now virtually everyone knows that St. Bartholomew's Church on Park Avenue is considering selling off part of its site for a skyscraper; less known is the fact that several smaller, less prominent churches in Manhattan are looking into demolishing their buildings altogether and replacing them with high-rise, income-producing construction.

Theater owners, though generally committed to the preservation of most of the theater district's important theaters—and eager not to see their image tarnished again as it was when they concurred in the demolition of the Helen Hayes and Morosco theaters for the new Portman hotel—two weeks ago managed to force into new midtown zoning regulations a promise that the city would give them some special considerations to make theater preservation more financially attractive. Briefly, the city has agreed to look into some means by which the theater owners might sell off the air rights over their buildings to make nearby skyscrapers still larger.

It is too early to know precisely what the city will come up with in the theater district, but whatever plan is devised, the implications are clear—the clouds are gathering for major battles between the custodians of churches and theaters and the city's landmarks preservation officials. The conflict is most severe right now on the ecclesiastical front, where the St. Bartholomew's controversy is but the tip of a very large iceberg, but things are hardly quiet on Broadway. The Landmarks Preservation Commission has placed virtually all of the theaters in midtown on its calendar for a public hearing on June 14 and 15, the first step toward official designation—and it was only the promise in advance of some sort of city relief that has prevented the wholesale opposition of this act by the theater owners and operators.

What the battle is about is not the propriety of landmarking, which has been upheld all the way to the United States Supreme Court, but the extent to which the city should exercise its landmark-designation powers. Churches, more particularly than theater owners, have been claiming that landmark designation can constitute a severe financial hardship to them; they have been asking why they cannot develop their land as freely as a private real-estate operator might.

Indeed, the church issue has become so bitter that last January the Committee of Religious Leaders of the City of New York issued a forty-page report strenuously denouncing the Landmarks Preservation Commission, claiming that landmarking of church buildings was "a threat to religious freedom" and concluding that "we strongly object to the forced diversion by Government of resources dedicated for religious ministry to serve instead the cause of architectural preservation."

The argument the report offered was similar to that put forth by the leaders of the congregation at St. Bartholomew's—namely, that good architecture is something of a frill, and that a congregation can do more for society with the wealth it will receive from selling its property than it can by maintaining its landmark church. Implicit in this view is the idea that social values and architectural values are inconsistent—that good architecture does not, in and of itself, do any good for society at all.

It is the kind of argument that is unfair on its face, of course—and impossible to answer. Who can demonstrate the value of art against the value of bread, the value of architecture against the value of water? When the argument is cast in this manner, no one would claim that even Chartres is worth preserving if that were to mean that more people would go hungry or unclothed.

But that is not, in the end, what the argument is really about, or should really be about. The reason the city needs St. Bartholomew's Church, or the Mount Neboh Synagogue on West 79th Street, or the Second Church of Christ, Scientist, on Central Park West (the fine neoclassical church by Frederick R.

Comstock that is the latest important building to be threatened), is that these buildings and others provide symbols of continuity and stability in an all-too-rapidly changing place. This is a city of constant upheaval, of unending demolition and reconstruction; one would hope that churches, at least, would choose to tell us that everything does not change, that some things remain the same—and that the values of commerce do not really control every last thing in New York.

The city's churches, like its theaters, do something else, too. Because they are smaller than its skyscrapers—and thus unable to function in New York as the controlling presences on the skyline that churches and civic buildings in smaller towns and villages traditionally are—they bring us a different pleasure, that of intimacy. They are small, and the space above them is open. There is precious little sky available in Manhattan, and there is less and less of it visible every day. One of the greatest gifts the city's churches and theaters convey, then, is the open air above them.

Now, providing sun and sky are gifts to all of us, not just to a church's own membership, just as the pleasure of a handsome and well-proportioned facade is something that is experienced by everyone. The public good a landmark provides is the very basis upon which the landmarks law stands. Given this, then, is it fair that the burdens of maintaining such landmarks fall so completely on their owners? Is it really fair that a small congregation with limited resources be required to keep its building in shape for all of us to enjoy?

That is a valid question, and one that should be kept separate from the issue of whether or not the owners of a landmark church or landmark theater have the right to exploit the value of the land underneath by developing it. The courts have held that the city can, within reason, require proper maintenance of landmarks, and there are legal procedures for relief if the financial burden becomes intolerable. Over the years a few landmarks have been demolished as a result of these provisions.

In the case of churches, of course, burdens have never fallen entirely on the congregations—the exemption from taxes that religious buildings receive has always been a kind of expression of interest in the proper maintenance of that building on the part of society. Indeed, tax exemption is also a means by which religious buildings are by definition removed from the normal pressures of the real-estate market—which in a sense makes the demands of some congregations, that they also have the right to exploit their buildings for the full profit that same real-estate market offers, something of a contradiction.

Common sense and fair play, however, would have it that society has at least some responsibility to help. One possible mechanism is tax relief, though this is of little comfort in the case of religious buildings, which pay no real-estate taxes anyway. More tempting—and certainly more talked about these days—is the possibility of transferring the unused development rights over a church to some other building site, so that the church can still gain its income, but keep its building intact.

It seems, at first glance, like having one's cake and eating it, too. Some form of air-rights transfer is what is being studied for the theater district, of course, but there it will have clearly defined limits—air rights will not be able to be transferred willy-nilly all over the place, but only from specified sites to other specified sites. Creating such a system for religious buildings, which do not group together in a single part of town as do theaters, poses some much more difficult problems.

First, who is to value the air rights? Can they be sold on the open market to the highest bidder? Second, where can the air rights be transferred? The reason St. Bartholomew's is so eager to build its glass tower is because its land on Park Avenue is so valuable—if the city permits those development rights to be transferred elsewhere, it will almost certainly be to a site of lesser value.

Most difficult of all is a third problem—how can the city keep the "market" of air rights from overflowing and govern the fair use of them? If St. Bartholomew's, which is truly considering selling off part of its land for a skyscraper, is permitted to transfer those development rights elsewhere, does not St. Patrick's Cathedral around the corner have the right to demand the same treatment, whether or not it is really considering a similar transaction of its own? And if the city grants every such building these rights, it is conceivable that the market could become so flooded with churches' development rights that their value could be depressed so sharply that they would not provide the religious institutions with the income they needed in the first place. The landmarks commission has estimated that there is nearly 20 million square feet of potential transferable building space over present and potential landmarks in Manhattan—an amount that could flood any market.

Over the theaters, meanwhile, there is between 3.5 million square feet (the landmarks commission's estimate) and 4.5 million square feet (the city planning department's estimate) of transferable air rights. The theaters themselves look right now to be a lot safer than some of the churches; they do, after all, make money, if not quite so much as their owners would like. But there is no full theater that is ever going to turn the kind of profit a 60-story office building does, just as there is no church building that can exploit its land the way a 40-story apartment tower does.

At this point, the fact that we have any theaters and churches at all in certain parts of Manhattan is something of an accident—a piece of luck brought on by the fact that the forces of real-estate development, active as they were in the boom preceding the present one, still tended not to be quite so desperate to fill every inch as they are today. There are, in the end, two ways to view theaters and religious buildings—as underused pieces of land or as precious remnants with a symbolic importance for us all. The way we choose will determine what kind of city we have.

—May 30, 1982

Since this was written, the concern over the future of both churches and theaters has become more marked. A special Theater Advisory Council was set up by the City Planning Commission to advise the city on mechanisms by which theater owners might receive special treatment, and it was expected, at the time of this writing, to propose the city's first widespread system of transferable development rights. If such a system is permitted for landmark theaters, a similar privilege will surely be requested by owners of landmark churches.

The Future of Lever House

Is Lever House worth saving? Nothing could speak more clearly of the passage of time than the mere fact that such a question might have to be asked. Lever House, after all, is a modern building, and a postwar one at that: it is the glass tower on Park Avenue that was designed by Skidmore, Owings & Merrill, and hailed as the vision of a new age when it was completed in 1952. Lever House's thin vertical slab, which appears to float on a horizontal slab that is set on columns in an open plaza, was one of the most powerful images of modernity produced by the 1950's. It was Park Avenue's first glass skyscraper, and only New York's second after the Secretariat Building of the United Nations, and it is no exaggeration to say that it was Lever House, more than any other building, that set midtown Manhattan's postwar redevelopment in a new direction.

Now, however, Lever House is threatened, and for a simple reason: it is not big enough. If there is one element of Lever House's design that is more unusual, in retrospect, than even its green glass "skin," it is that it is significantly smaller than the size building the law permits on its site. The small size is a gift to the public in terms of additional light and air, but it brings no pleasure at all to real-estate developers, who have long realized that the Lever House site between 53rd and 54th streets could hold a much bigger—and thus much more profitable—building.

For years there has been talk of Lever House's replacement by a larger structure, but the Lever Brothers Company—which built the tower thirty years ago as a means of enhancing its corporate identity, but does not own it and simply holds a long-term lease—always spurned such rumors. Indeed, in 1977 the company

Lever House

253

marked the occasion of the building's 25th anniversary with a full-page advertisement in *The New York Times* hailing Lever House as "the first streamlined
office building of gleaming glass and steel with a plaza, a breathing space, so
that in the canyons of the city there would be a place for the sun to shine." The
advertisement went on to declare Lever House "a revolutionary idea in architectural design," and to praise New York City as an ideal corporate locale.

Now, Lever Brothers is not so sure—the company is mulling over a move to
New Jersey, though no decision has yet been made. But a series of other events
have occurred almost simultaneously to thrust the future of this important
building into confusion. In recent days, Metropolitan Life Insurance Company,
which owns the building and leases the land under it, has agreed to sell its
position to Park Tower Realty, a major New York developer. The estate of
Robert W. Goelet, which owns the land underneath the building, has agreed to
sell that, too—but not to Park Tower. The purchaser of the land is a rival
developer, the Fisher Brothers interests, which has announced its intention to
demolish Lever House and erect a 40-story skyscraper on its site. Over the
Fisher Brothers' objections, the Landmarks Preservation Commission has just
declared Lever House an official city landmark, making the demolition of the
building more difficult, but not impossible.

The story does not end there. Indeed, it becomes almost Byzantine. Lever
Brothers' lease on the building has another twenty-eight years to run, making it
an important player in this game—unless, of course, it decides to sell its lease
and move out of town. If Lever Brothers should decide to stay in Lever House,
then Lever House will remain. If Lever Brothers should decide to leave,
however, then all bets are off.

What will happen then? Park Tower, which will now, technically, own the
building, is a developer noted for its commitment to architectural quality, and
its chief executive, George Klein, would like to be known as the man who saved
Lever House. Mr. Klein's preference is to restore the landmark, which is an
expensive undertaking, since even advocates of Lever House's preservation
agree that the glass sheathing has deteriorated badly over the years, and that
the building requires restoration costs numbering in the millions of dollars.

Mr. Klein is not interested in engaging in pure philanthropy, however, and
although he refuses comment, real-estate sources say that his hope has been to
finance the restoration of Lever House by the profits he would earn from
erecting what would, in effect, be a Lever House annex—a large tower just to
the west of Lever House, on a site that Lever Brothers already controls. Now,
one way to make such a tower big enough to throw off the desired profits would
be to transfer Lever House's unused "air rights" to this adjacent property. The
catch is that the air rights would belong not to Park Tower Realty, as owner of
the building, but to Fisher Brothers, as owner of the land—and Fisher Brothers doesn't want to help Park Tower build a tower next door; it wants to tear
Lever House down and build a tower of its own.

At the moment it is a stalemate—two powerful New York developers and a Fortune 500 corporation are locked in a battle on the chessboard that is Manhattan real estate. To make things more complex still, the landmark designation must be ratified by the Board of Estimate within the next three months, and it is virtually certain that Fisher Brothers will mount an aggressive campaign to have the designation overturned. Indeed, that campaign has already begun—the architectural firm of Swanke, Hayden & Connell, which has been hired by Fisher Brothers to design its proposed new tower, has delivered to the commission a "white paper" denouncing Lever House as an undistinguished work of architecture undeserving of preservation.

The notion of a prominent architectural firm delivering a paper intended to undermine the reputation of one of the city's most respected buildings so as to get the right to put its own building on that site is in itself a startling event that sets a deeply disturbing precedent. More troubling still, the report is full of quotations taken out of context—so that criticism by architectural historians and critics of certain aspects of Lever House's design is taken to read like a rejection of the building's overall value.

The report essentially takes Lever House to task for being out of date both technologically and architecturally. In the most literal sense, this is not altogether untrue—the building's glass skin is certainly inferior to the kinds of skyscraper sheathings we can produce today, and it is nothing if not woefully wasteful of energy. But a proper restoration would keep the building's essential appearance while bringing it up to the standards of the 1980's; all that takes is money.

The issue of architectural obsolescence is more complex. Lever House is, indeed, a building of another time—in the very same way that the Dakota apartments, the Woolworth Building, the old McGraw-Hill Building, and Rockefeller Center are buildings of another time. We would not design a building like Lever House today: its unusual shape rejects the even "street wall" of Park Avenue, and while that break with a straight row of limestone-fronted buildings probably seemed liberating, full of fresh air, when it was done in 1952, it is now seen to represent a fundamentally anti-urban attitude. Lever House's plaza is not a particularly welcoming or well-used space, and the overall form of the building is really a pure, abstract object—a most beautiful one, indeed, but a piece of sculpture more than an element that weaves itself well into the complex cityscape.

But none of this denies its status as one of the city's epoch-making works of architecture or its continued value to the public. For if Lever House represented certain ideas which we now find out of date, it represented others that we are desperately in need of today—it stood for a kind of enlightened corporate responsibility that is almost absent in New York City in 1982. The belief of Gordon Bunshaft, the partner of Skidmore, Owings & Merrill in charge of Lever's design, and Charles Luckman, the chief executive who commissioned the building, that every last square foot did not have to be filled, and that a building in a city has a responsibility to the public as well as to its owner, holds an urgent message for us today.

So there can be no doubt about Lever House's value as a landmark—this handsome tower is a crucial example of the yearnings of modernist style at their best. The real question is not whether Lever House should be saved—but who is to pay the price of saving it. In this city in which every inch seems to be translated into dollars, and a thirty-year-old building is denounced as obsolete, we still lack an efficient and fair mechanism for preventing battles like the one now being fought over Lever House from occurring.

—November 21, 1982

Lever House was upheld as an official landmark in March 1983—after a long battle before the Board of Estimate, and after considerable negative public response to the garish design Swanke, Hayden & Connell proposed as a replacement.

The Classical Vision of Mott B. Schmidt

It was 1965 when Mott B. Schmidt's Federal-style addition of a ballroom to Gracie Mansion was completed, an event that was politely ignored in architectural circles. Adding to the old mansion in a period style was hardly the thing to do in those days—architects with any real creativity to them would come up with something modern, or so the common wisdom had it back then. Imitating historical styles was the province of little old ladies, not *real* architects.

Now, of course, real architects seem to like nothing better than imitating history; the acceptance of revivalism in the last few years has been one of the most dramatic switches in taste in this century—comparable, in a sense, to the movement toward modern architecture fifty years ago. We have come not only to see architects like Robert Stern, Robert Venturi, and Charles Moore interpreting historical forms and offering personal variations on older styles, but we also now see architects like Allan Greenberg and John Barrington Bayley producing works in much more literal historical style, as was commonly done all the way through the 1920's.

One offshoot of this reversal of taste has been a dramatic surge of interest in the architects of the twentieth century's first revival period, the years leading up to 1929, when there were literally dozens of designers of talent. Not the least of such figures was Mott Schmidt, an architect who practiced in New York City from the early 1920's, but who did not fade when many of his contemporaries did. Schmidt kept going, producing Georgian and neoclassical houses right through the 1960's in splendid obliviousness to the growing amount of modern architecture around him.

Schmidt was near the end of his career when he

created the annex wing of Gracie Mansion; he was to die in 1977. But for nearly fifty years he had been producing townhouses and country villas in the Georgian and Regency styles in Manhattan, Long Island, Westchester, and around the country. Westchester was his home; he built himself a sprawling brick Georgian house in Bedford that he lived in for decades, until he moved to smaller quarters, also of his own design.

Schmidt's work is the subject of an exhibition through March 2 at the Katonah Gallery, not far from his home turf, entitled "Mott B. Schmidt: An Architectural Portrait—Private Homes in the Classical Tradition." It is the sort of exhibition that would have been considered quite curious, not to say irrelevant, a decade ago, but today this assemblage of Georgian manor houses seems nothing if not *au courant*. It has been attracting architecture buffs from all over the metropolitan area, whose presence in such numbers attests to the renewed respectability of revivalist architecture.

The first point that should be made about Schmidt's work is that it was very, very good. Mott Schmidt was an architect who produced no truly great works of architecture, but an enormous number of very fine ones. His buildings were civilized, in the deepest sense of the word—they were ordered, handsome, knowledgeable, serene places, buildings designed to contain lives that bespoke similar qualities.

Schmidt based his practice in New York City, and Manhattan is dotted with his works. He designed, among other buildings, the townhouses at 1 and 3 Sutton Place, and redesigned the entire block on Sutton between 57th and 58th streets to create a private garden; the Vincent Astor house at 130 East 80th Street and the Clarence Dillon house at 124 East 80th Street, both double-width townhouses; and the handsome, disciplined houses at 43 East 70th Street and 15 East 90th Street.

Each of these buildings is an intelligent, fully thought-out work in itself—for all of their use of Georgian and classical forms, none of them seems designed by rote. Schmidt's gift, which he shared with his best colleagues among the revivalists of his time, was in the ability to take the classical vocabulary and use it to create original, varied compositions. Each facade is a remarkably balanced, even subtle, composition—an assemblage of elements in fine proportion, with strong symbolic content as well. The door was always the centerpiece, its ceremonial role emphasized by a portico or elaborate frame of classical elements; yet the scale was always modest and domestic, no matter how large the structure. Not for Schmidt the overwhelming entrances and ice-cold ballrooms of the great Beaux-Arts mansions!

Indeed, Schmidt's work was, in part, a reaction against Beaux-Arts excesses. The immense, overscaled confections of Fifth Avenue built just before the turn of the century, and for a decade or so after, were considered vulgar by the time Schmidt came into practice in the 1920's, and he sought a more restrained tone, preferring to evoke the modest order of colonial times or of Georgian London rather than the lavishness of eighteenth-century France or Renaissance Italy. The differences between the architecture of Schmidt and of his predecessor revivalists, architects like McKim, Mead & White, Carrere & Hastings, and Warren & Wetmore, are significant, for they remind us that the revivalists were not, in fact, all of a piece, but that different architects at different times had strikingly different values and emphases in their work.

Schmidt's interest really seemed to be in pure composition, for which his gifts were considerable. A facade like that of the Trevor House of 1926, at 15 East 90th Street, is as good an indication as one can ask for: a small house, it is an exquisite, bursting composition, in which a lovely Corinthian portico with a pedimented window behind it makes the whole facade glow, like a tiny red-brick bouquet of flowers. There is no haughtiness here at all, but a self-assured tone, an air of confidence, yet of strength. Schmidt's facades are delicate without ever being prissy.

The exhibition includes a mix of period photographs and new ones, as well as a number of Schmidt's original drawings. Unfortunately, labeling is less than thorough, and oddly, no material at all is included on the superb apartment buildings Schmidt designed, which include 53 East 66th Street, 1088 Park Avenue, and 19 East 72nd Street, the last in association with Rosario Candela.

But happily the exhibition does contain a considerable number of interior photos and floor plans, so that one can study at least a few of these houses in detail. The plans are as tightly, intelligently conceived as the facades—as in the facades, there is no slavish imitation of Georgian precedent, but an easy, knowing re-use of classical forms, adapted to the varying demands of twentieth-century New York.

Schmidt died in 1977, the last survivor of a long line of first-rate eclectic architects from the 1920's. His work lost some of its quality toward the end—the Gracie Mansion annex is excellent, but some of the later country houses seem to lack the crispness of the earlier houses. It may well be that they do not themselves yet have the patina of time; buildings that wish to convince us by use of a historical style that they have a long and venerable history must have at least a little bit of history to achieve credibility, and Schmidt's houses from the 1950's may not yet have enough.

But Georgian villas built in the 1950's were, of course, buildings out of their time, and it may be that this means more. When Schmidt was surrounded by contemporaries doing similar work, it may well have energized his own—which makes one especially curious about what effects this new mood of revivalism now settling upon us will have on the architectural spirit of the 1980's, as architects again talk seriously about picking up on styles of the past.

—February 21, 1980
Katonah, N.Y.

An 1891 "Skyscraper" Reigns in St. Louis

For a long time the residents of this city did not know what to make of the Wainwright Building, a 10-story 1891 "skyscraper" right in the middle of downtown. The Wainwright is the work of Louis Sullivan, Chicago's great nineteenth-century architect, and its design played a crucial role in the development of the modern skyscraper. But to the casual eye it was no skyscraper at all; it was little, squat, and old. No wonder, then, that plans were made in the early 1970's to replace the Wainwright with a parking lot.

The parking lot did not come to be. What happened instead is one of the major events in American historic preservation in the last decade. Last month Sullivan's skyscraper, refurbished and given an addition that stretches it out to fill a city block, was dedicated as the state of Missouri's Wainwright State Office Complex.

Now, instead of an empty spot with cars parked on it, there are offices of the state government, including one for the governor when he is visiting from Jefferson City, the capital, and new quarters for the State Court of Appeals. The building has been cleaned on the outside and renovated on the inside, and it now shines as a jewel in this otherwise drab downtown.

That such a thing would happen at all is significant; St. Louis, like most American cities, is not always quick to recognize its nineteenth-century architectural treasures. But the conversion of the Wainwright is important beyond that. First, since it was done under state sponsorship for state uses, it serves as a reminder that governments can find it in their interest to preserve important parts of older cities. But it is important for a simpler reason: it was done so well.

When the state, under Governor Christopher S.

Wainwright Building with additions, St. Louis

Bond, decided to take over the Wainwright, it gambled and held an architectural competition to find a suitable design. This paid off. The winners were Mitchell/Giurgola Associates of New York and Philadelphia, working in association with Hastings & Chivetta of St. Louis. What they produced was a plan that understands Sullivan's genius but does not kowtow to it; it is respectful, but not slavish.

Adding to Sullivan is a task requiring subtlety. His original building, stubby by today's standards, is extraordinarily graceful. Its facades are the sort of composition from which no part can be removed without destroying the whole. The building sits on a strong stone base and is topped by an elaborate cornice, rich with ornament. The seven floors of the midsection, their windows inset behind strong vertical piers, seem to soar; they express in stone what Sullivan said when he wrote of his desire to make the skyscraper feel "tall, every inch of it tall."

In the early 1890's, as the skyscraper was developing, architects had little sense of how to design one. In most cases they piled floors one atop the other, making buildings that were merely larger versions of the sort they had designed before. It was Sullivan who struggled to express height: the Wainwright is not so much tall as it is an essay about being tall. Its ten stories contain architectural lessons that were to be studied by architects long after.

What Mitchell/Giurgola proposed was not, happily, any sort of skyscraper at all. The architects chose to let Sullivan stand alone. The Wainwright occupies roughly a quarter of a city block, and the architects filled out the rest of the block with a mixture of low buildings of brick, open courtyards, breezeways, and reflecting pools. The brick is orange-red, like Sullivan's original facade, but there is no similarity in style. To have tried to imitate Sullivan's ornament, which can truly be called unique, would have been patronizing.

The Wainwright is thus allowed to stand as a tower, as the beacon of the complex. Sullivan's building looks like a cube from outside, but it is shaped more like a U, with an airshaft in the middle. Mitchell/Giurgola turned the airshaft into interior space, giving it a glass roof and a coat of white paint. The idea of an atrium might seem to bring Sullivan's masterpiece dangerously close to a 1980's cliché, but, save for a rather jarring amount of glass at one end, this has been done well and is not disturbing.

The new wings are laid out so as not to compete with Sullivan's original mass. The wings are set back 40 feet where they meet the Sullivan facade, thus providing both formal entrance courts and architectural deference. On the other sides of the project, where the Mitchell/Giurgola facade is all that one sees, the new building has a simple but subtle facade of brick and slate, with some surprising details, like wooden window frames and slate lined with red-orange mortar.

Those new facades feel flat, almost planar, where Sullivan's sections feel rich and deep, but this, too, is a way of deferring. There is a sense of great mass to

Sullivan's building, a sense of elaborate and complex goings-on that modern architecture can only hint at. By making their sections tauter than Sullivan's, by presenting the new buildings as almost a set of stage flats in downtown, the architects have turned this complex into a lively and significant dialogue between the generations.

What gives that dialogue power is the continuation of the humane quality of the Sullivan building into the Mitchell/Giurgola additions, for all their stylistic differences. That is the ground on which the generations meet: the belief that the design of an urban building must relate to human use and human perception.

Mitchell/Giurgola laid out the Wainwright complex in a way to complement and extend the humane quality of Sullivan's building. The overall layout— courts and breezeways that give the new sections their special character— weaves the complex into the fabric of the city. The Wainwright once stood a trifle aloof in downtown; it now feels connected to its neighbors.

That connection is jeopardized, unfortunately, by a plan to tear down a group of fine buildings beside the Wainwright for an open mall. The buildings are not the Wainwright's equals, but they are excellent, and together they help give St. Louis a sense of density that it so desperately needs.

Like many American downtowns, this one seems to consist of parking lots as much as buildings. The mall, if built, will be a continuation of the mall that fronts on Eero Saarinen's great St. Louis Arch, a few blocks away. It makes sense there, as a means of opening the city to the huge arch, but if extended all the way uptown into the city's commercial district, it will bring only more emptiness into this already too-empty downtown.

—July 6, 1981
St. Louis

The Palace Hotel's Landmark
Opening

The project was first proposed in 1974, and it has been so complex that it has taken six years to get it designed, approved, and constructed. But the Helmsley Palace Hotel on Madison Avenue at 50th Street is now finished and ready to open on Monday—and probably not since the twin-towered Waldorf-Astoria opened on Park Avenue in 1931 has a hotel in New York been as much awaited, and as much debated, as this one.

All the attention is not surprising. The Helmsley Palace is not merely a new hotel, but an old one as well, for it incorporates several sections of one of the very greatest landmarks in all New York, the Villard Houses.

The houses, a U-shaped grouping of brownstones completed during the 1880's to the designs of McKim, Mead & White, are among the earliest pieces of Renaissance-inspired residential architecture in New York. They are urbane and elegant, and they have some interior spaces that can only be called incomparable.

Shooting up behind these venerable nineteenth-century buildings is a 51-story tower designed by the architectural firm of Emery Roth & Sons. Needless to say it is the new section, and not the old mansions, that has been the subject of much argument—the new metal tower joined to the old brownstone houses makes for as dramatic a juxtaposition of new and old as exists anywhere in New York. The new section has been denounced in some circles as a piece of vulgar and disrespectful modern architecture, and praised in others as the ideal way in which to save a landmark.

The truth is somewhere in between. The unpleasant side first: the tower, which is a boring box sheathed in a dark-brown colored metal, is as mediocre a new building on the outside as any Manhattan street has seen in a long

Rendering,
Helmsley Palace,
New York

265

time. Its color was chosen to blend in with the dark brownstone of the Villard Houses, but since the houses were cleaned and came out looking like a sort of warm chocolate mousse, the colors no longer match.

The facade of the tower has absolutely none of the quality of the older building to which it is joined; if the Villard Houses are the very finest work of their time, this is among the most disappointing efforts of ours. There are Holiday Inns with more architectural style, and it is hard to believe that to stay in this cheap-looking box people would be willing to pay between $120 and $170 a night.

And to make the tower possible, the rear of the Villard Houses had to be sliced off, leaving the central section so thin it is more a stage set than a real building. But despite all of this, the place gives every indication, from the standpoint of design at least, of being a wonderful hotel in which to spend time. The extravagant interiors of the south wing of the Villard Houses, the section that was built for Henry Villard, a journalist and railroad magnate, to occupy (he planned to sell the five other houses), have been meticulously restored and respectfully integrated into the overall structure. They are, without a doubt, the finest public rooms of any hotel in New York—there is nothing of better architectural quality even in the Plaza, the hotel that is every architecture buff's traditional favorite.

And much that is within that unpleasant tower structure is far superior to the outside. Best of all are the elevators: imitations of the famous red cabs with domes painted with clouds and sky that are a hallmark of the Helmsley Building at 230 Park Avenue, they are a welcome and whimsical element here.

In addition, the guest rooms are large, well furnished, and comfortable. They are largely the work of Leona B. Helmsley, Mr. Helmsley's wife and the president of his hotels, who has a keen eye for detail. The colors are soft and the furniture is what is euphemistically called traditional—but it has a considerable flair to it, since Mrs. Helmsley understands, even if the architects of her tower did not, that the experience of staying in a hotel is part fantasy.

That fantasy is satisfied best of all, however, in the public rooms in the Villard section. The $20-million restoration was conducted under the guidance of James Rhodes, a restoration architect who worked with Emery Roth & Sons, and the work is superb. The original condition of the rooms has been exhaustively researched, and chandeliers, murals, marble mosaics, and oak paneling have been repaired or made new to match the old.

There are a great number of real treasures here—murals and stained-glass windows by John La Farge, a sculpted wall clock by Augustus Saint-Gaudens and Stanford White, an Italian mosaic vaulted ceiling designed by Maitland Armstrong, and glass panels by Louis Comfort Tiffany.

Much of this was done under White's supervision during an 1886 renovation for Whitelaw Reid, who took over the property after a reversal in his railroad fortunes caused Villard to go bankrupt shortly after the house was completed.

The most famous room is the 30-foot-high, barrel-vaulted Gold Room, home of the La Farge murals, created for the Reids out of what had been Villard's music room. Oddly, it is not the most pleasing room in the group—it is the only room in the restored section that seems almost too ornate, too shiny, and fussy in its extravagance.

The Helmsley Palace will use the room for tea and for cocktails, which will also be served in a far more sedate room architecturally, the former drawing room. This is the finer room—a sumptuous, sprawling space fronting on Madison Avenue with green marble columns and a gold-leafed ceiling.

Still more pleasing is the bar in the former oak-paneled dining room. The intricate oak inlays remain, and a warm and handsome bar has been crafted to match the oak paneling.

But best of all, surely, are the corridors and grand staircase in the Villard wing—they are all lined in marble, and the hall has a vaulted ceiling and an extraordinary Saint-Gaudens–sculpted fireplace, a rich, deep recess full of mystery and drama.

The process of joining these extraordinary rooms to the new sections of the tower is complex, and the architects have done it well. There is an entrance with a grand staircase from the main courtyard on the Madison Avenue side (which has itself been repaved in a dignified pattern of marble and granite), and the connections between old wing and new are, for the most part, clear and logical.

The public rooms in the base of the tower are "decorated" more than designed (they were the work of Tom Lee Ltd.), but they are not too bad as frilly interiors go—testaments to the growing realization of designers that the public is not as satisfied with modern design as the profession might wish.

But that fact gets us to the heart of the problem with this new hotel. If one accepts the premise that fine old rooms, like the ones in the Villard Houses, and rooms that try to capture the spirit of older, more traditional designs, like the rooms in the newly built sections of the hotel, are preferable to a harsher modernity, then why was the tower permitted to be such a blunt and harsh intrusion into the skyline?

None of the values evident in the interior of the Helmsley Palace seem to have come into play in the design of the tower itself. On the outside, this complex merely tries to steal the elegance of the Villard Houses and market it to a willing public. On the inside, it offers something more substantial.

—September 12, 1980

The Sterling Library: A Reassessment

It has an entrance hall like a nave, a circulation desk like an altar, and a reading room like a medieval banquet hall. It is more earnestly Gothic in its decoration than many a cathedral, and for years the Sterling Memorial Library at Yale was denounced by serious students of architecture as a hopeless fraud—what sense, after all, did a twentieth-century library that looked like a fourteenth-century church make?

But a twentieth-century library has been functioning quite well within this mock-medieval shell for half a century now, and earlier this month, as librarians and architecture buffs gathered at New Haven to mark the building's 50th anniversary, the building received nothing but praise. The event was notable for its tone of complete acceptance of the architecture, which even a few years ago was still thought rather foolish, if not downright evil; architectural historians who tolerated it at all tended to smile rather apologetically and talk about how the Sterling Library was pleasantly romantic, but of course not really very good.

Now, no one seems afraid to come right out and say that the building is very good indeed—as good a piece of monumental library design as the twentieth-century has produced. The hero of the 50th anniversary ceremonies on October 10, which included an exhibition tracing the building's history and a dinner given by Yale's president, A. Bartlett Giamatti, was clearly James Gamble Rogers, the library's architect. He was not himself present—he died in 1947—but he was represented by several of his children and eulogized by his grandson, James Gamble Rogers III, a New York architect, who delivered a talk explaining how he, as a young architect trained in a more

Sterling Library,
Yale University

269

modern idiom, had come gradually to respect and learn from his grandfather's eclectic work.

The revisionist view of Sterling Memorial Library parallels a rethinking of American eclectic architecture from the early decades of the twentieth century that has been going on for some time now. Most of the mock-Gothic, mock-Georgian, and mock-classical buildings of those years were dismissed by most historians of modern architecture as nothing more than stage sets; they were called utterly false and unfaithful to their time by some critics, and were even thought immoral by others.

Few buildings were as roundly criticized upon their completion as Sterling. It came rather late in the game as eclectic buildings went; by 1930, the year of its completion, the Chrysler Building was finished and the Empire State Building was rising; in Europe, the great modern houses of Le Corbusier and Mies van der Rohe were already a few years old. It did seem rather strange to design one of the largest libraries in the world to look like a Gothic cathedral, entered through a grand Gothic portal beneath leaded glass leading to a central nave. Strangest of all, perhaps, was the book-storage tower which rose behind the sumptuous entry masses, a 15-story steel-frame skyscraper, a product of the most advanced engineering that was sheathed entirely in stone and Gothic ornament to match the rest of the building.

William Harlan Hale, the writer who was a Yale undergraduate at the time, took particular issue with the design. Following the argument of modernist architects that the building's Gothic facades were a falsehood, he wrote a stinging essay in an undergraduate publication called the "Harkness Hoot" that posed the question, "Is there any honesty in hiding the magnificent function of a tower of books under a cloakage that has no more relation to it than a grain elevator? All this, in a university whose motto is *Lux et Veritas*. There is not one suggestion of *Veritas* in the Sterling Library—and for that matter there is precious little of *Lux*."

James Gamble Rogers, who had designed many of Yale's other Gothic buildings and was, by then, one of the leading eclectic architects in the nation, was no intellectual. He saw architecture not in terms of theory or integrity of structure, but in terms of visual effect. To him, Gothic architecture seemed a comfortable image for a great university, and Rogers's thinking went no deeper; he occupied himself instead with specific issues such as the composition of the exterior masses, the organization of the interior spaces, the design and crafting of the details, and the smooth functioning of the interior.

And in all of these areas, Sterling works superbly. It remains a remarkably easy library to use—all of the main rooms are organized around the long central nave on the street floor, a system that not only makes the various departments easy to find but which, as Yale officials concerned with the conversion of the university's older buldings to meet the needs of the handicapped have found, renders the building unusually accessible to wheelchair users for a structure its age. The layout has also made the building reasonably adaptable to modernization; there are now computers behind windows of delicate Gothic tracery in the cataloging offices, but they do not intrude any more than the telephones and electric lights that were there from the start.

But far more important than this building's functional success is its role as a symbol of changing architectural currents, not only in this university but around the nation. James Gamble Rogers's original notion that the Gothic architecture of Sterling and the other buildings he designed on the Yale campus were by virtue of their medieval associations appropriate to the idea of the academy is not particularly convincing today, but that does not seem to detract in any way from an appreciation of the architectural virtues of the building itself. Sterling is a beautiful, elegant object, almost sensual with its carved stone, leaded glass, rich paneling, and landscaped, cloister-like courtyards.

It works not so much because of any literal associations with the Gothic period, in other words, as because of the sheer pleasure inherent in the materials and details Rogers used. The building is well made on the most basic architectural level—its rooms are gracious and well-proportioned interior spaces, its facades are handsome arrangements of masses. Its scale is always comfortable, never overwhelming. The skill with which these fundamental elements have been crafted seems, today, to override the issue of the rightness or wrongness of reproducing Gothic forms.

The basic notions of the design, incidentally, stem from some sketches of one of Rogers's competitors, Bertram Grosvenor Goodhue—one of the most creative eclectic architects in American history. Goodhue, the architect of St. Bartholomew's and St. Thomas's churches in New York, had been the original architect for Sterling Library; he died unexpectedly in 1924, and the commission was turned over to Rogers, who based his plan for a set of low masses rising before a Gothic "skyscraper" on Goodhue's rough sketches.

The university's administration has never doubted that Sterling Library was something of a treasure, and most renovations over the years have been respectful of the building's architecture. Gothic splendor, even modern, 1930's Gothic splendor, is not easy to maintain, however—the winds and rains and polluted air of New Haven have taken their toll on the delicate stonework, and the building is now fraught with leaks and stone damage. The university's latest estimate for basic needed structure repairs is $4.3 million, more than half the entire cost of construction in 1930.

—*October 22, 1980*
New Haven

The Eldridge Street Synagogue Slips Away

One thinks of ghosts as empty creatures, hollow beings lacking any sort of physical substance as well as life. Architectural ghosts, however, are something different: they still have their physical substance, or at least most of it; yet out of that substance life has been sucked, leaving a physical shell to tell a story.

There is a building on the Lower East Side of Manhattan that is a sort of semi-ghost right now, hovering on the edge of real life. It is a synagogue, one of many in that neighborhood that was once the center of Jewish life in the United States and has now become a quarter shared by Puerto Ricans, Chinese, Italians, and Jews. Many of the synagogues have been abandoned entirely; a few flourish, but this one, Congregation Khal Adas Jeshurun-Anshe Lubz, at 14 Eldridge Street, has fallen into a sort of half-living existence. A tiny congregation struggles to stay together, against not only the demographic odds of the area's declining Jewish population, but also the physical odds of its building's deterioration.

The synagogue, which is also known as the Eldridge Street Synagogue, is one of New York City's finest houses of worship, and it is falling apart. It is clearly of landmark quality, although official landmark designation, while desirable, would do little to solve the building's urgent problems. Its roof leaks terribly, and its foundation underpinnings are weak and need reinforcement if major cracks are not to develop.

The building is of historical as well as architectural importance. According to Professor Gerard Wolfe of New York University, who is preparing a book on the old synagogues of the Lower East Side, Eldridge Street, completed in 1887, was the first synagogue to be erected in the neighborhood by Eastern European Jews, whose immigration in large numbers had begun just a few years before.

The building was designed by Herter Brothers, among the city's most fashionable interior decorating firms of the nineteenth century. Herter Brothers' usual sort of work was along the line of drawing rooms for the Vanderbilts, so Eldridge Street, as both an entire building and a synagogue, was especially unusual.

The facade is a mix of Romanesque, Gothic, and Moorish elements with a huge rose window at its center. There were once finials and a parapet at the top, but aside from their disappearance, the facade is in superb condition—a curious, exotic presence in the midst of the drab shops and tenements that constitute the rest of this block of Eldridge Street.

Now, the synagogue can be entered only through a small side door to the basement level; the main doors have been sealed for years, and the sanctuary, or large hall of worship, has not been used since the early 1930's. The lower level is where the tiny congregation meets for daily worship services, conducted under the light of bare bulbs in a shabby room. Handwritten memorial plaques to deceased members of the congregation, written by Benjamin Markowitz, the volunteer sexton, are set in dime-store frames and line the walls, a far cry from the elaborate bronze plaques in wealthy synagogues uptown.

The abandoned sanctuary is the building's real treasure. The room is immense and opulent, a testament to the congregation's faith in the New World and its continued presence in that part of New York. Elaborate brass chandeliers with Victorian glass shades hang in the midst of the huge, barrel-vaulted space; ornate walnut carving covers the front of the balcony and the ark where Torah scrolls are stored. There are pews, with an unexpected Gothic trefoil motif, and small domes over the balcony areas along the sides of the large room.

Reaching the room, however, is a different kind of architectural experience altogether. When Professor Wolfe, who has been instrumental in helping draw attention to the synagogue's plight, made his first visit, no one had entered the sanctuary in years. He and Mr. Markowitz had to use tools to pry open a sealed door. Now, the passage is unobstructed, but still decrepit—up a crumbling stair from the lower level, through a vestibule of peeling plaster, rusted tin ceiling, and overall decay.

One turns through the vestibule and is thrust suddenly into the sanctuary. The feeling is still very much as Professor Wolfe describes his first visit: "Suddenly the light streamed through the broken stained-glass windows. It was like the twilight zone, like going into the past—dust was over everything, prayer books left strewn around the pews." Everything in the richly furnished room is still there, if broken and slightly damaged in places, and the soft light still flows in through the windows. It is somber and haunting, still grand, and with dust and disarray, the sanctuary is mysterious in a way that it could never have been in its active day.

The congregation so far has managed to stay alive and pay the salary of a part-time rabbi, and maintains a schedule of services. But restoration of the building seems, at this point, a financial impossibility. Right now the Eldridge Street Synagogue stands, its remarkable grandeur ebbing away, a touching reminder of a time when the Lower East Side was a neighborhood of hope.

—*September 15, 1977*

Eldridge Street Synagogue, Lower East Side

What a Law Can Do to Architecture

It was not so very long ago that the Mayflower Hotel on Central Park West at 61st Street was typical of the city's fine apartment buildings of the 1920's. Designed by Emery Roth, one of the city's great apartment-house architects, it was one of those solid brick structures whose boxiness was lightened by an overlay of handsome and graceful stone and terra-cotta ornament. Today, however, the Mayflower is not at all like the buildings that are its peers—it is now a harsh and ponderous box, looking more like a warehouse than a residence. Every piece of ornament, from the cornice at the top to the window pediments toward the bottom, has been stripped, and the result is a building that might better be named the De-flower. The hotel looks as if someone had applied a huge sanding machine to its facades, smoothing over everything and removing any object that dared project beyond the surface.

The effect of this crew-cut architecture is worse than the intentional blankness of many modern buildings because, since the Mayflower's architects intended the building to be decorated, every aspect of its design was created as part of an overall pattern. With the decoration removed, the facade looks desperately naked.

The owners of the Mayflower were not trying to make any sort of esthetic statement with this act of vandalism on their own property. They were merely reacting in a rather extreme fashion to a city ordinance that will have been on the books for three years next month, but which is only now coming to have major effects. Known as Local Law 10, it requires that owners of large buildings make periodic inspections of the conditions of their buildings' facades, and that they be held responsible for any damage or injury caused by elements that fall onto the street or sidewalk.

The law was a logical enough reaction to a tragedy that occurred in 1979 on the Upper West Side of Manhattan, when a Barnard College student was killed by a piece of masonry that fell from an apartment building on Broadway owned by Columbia University. It was unthinkable after this death that the city not take steps to protect pedestrians and make certain that such an accident not happen elsewhere. The expectation was that Local Law 10 would force owners who had been indifferent to the maintenance of their buildings to take better care of them, thus assuring the public's safety.

Unfortunately, the law is turning out to have a rather different effect in some cases, because one of the things that Local Law 10 has done is to give some landlords an excuse to commit the kind of destruction that has already happened at the Mayflower and at several buildings owned by Columbia University, which even before the accident had been shearing off cornices as a way of simplifying maintenance.

The law's requirements are fairly simple. It states that owners of buildings greater than six stories in height must have the buildings' exterior walls inspected every five years by an architect or engineer, and that after filing a report of any unsafe conditions with the Buildings Department, owners "shall immediately commence" repairs.

The law took effect on February 5, 1980, and it required all buildings to have an initial inspection within two years. By last February's deadline, approximately 3,700 of the 8,846 buildings that come under Local Law 10's jurisdiction had yet to be inspected, suggesting that the time limits set by the law were unrealistic. There are, after all, only so many licensed engineers and architects capable of doing this sort of work, even in New York City. And there are also only so many stonemasons capable of doing proper repair and restoration work.

The fear of many of the city's architectural experts is that the combination of time pressure set by the law and financial pressure caused by the high costs of repair work will encourage landlords to follow the example of the Mayflower and certain other buildings, and destroy architecturally significant ornament. It is not altogether implausible, then, that we may end up with a city of naked buildings—a city of once elegant buildings that will face the street with the same plodding awkwardness that the Mayflower now does.

Taking it all off is, after all, the easiest way to comply with the law's requirements, for it not only frees building owners of the costs of repairs, it also frees them from the responsibility for continued inspections. Unfortunately, such actions also change the face of an individual building forever, and the cumulative effect of the removal of ornament on the city at large can be devastating.

Right now there are scaffoldings up all over town, as the facade inspections mandated by Local Law 10 proceed and landlords evaluate whether it will be cheaper to repair or destroy. No doubt more well-to-do owners will make an attempt at keeping their buildings' ornament; many are already at work on such restoration, and owners of landmark buildings, in fact, are legally obligated to do so. But New York is rich in first-rate buildings that have never received official landmark status, and many of these are owned by individuals or institutions of limited means. It is these that are now put in jeopardy.

The fine buildings of the city that are not of individual landmark quality make up the fabric that holds the city together as a visual entity. It is no exaggeration to say that the city cannot afford their loss—that New York will be a different city altogether if the Mayflower experience is repeated up and down Park Avenue, West End Avenue, and Riverside Drive. It is not a matter of sentimentality—it is a matter of preserving the visual texture that makes this harsh city palatable, that gives this rough environment some softness and civility. The cornice of a classical apartment house is not a frivolity—it is a contribution made by that building to a civilized public environment.

There is a particularly cruel irony to this current move to sweep ornament

Mayflower Hotel—Local Law 10's victim

from the city's buildings, for it comes at a time when architectural taste and theory have returned to a respect for ornament and to a desire to re-create it in some modern form. We seem to want ornament now far more than we did in the years of the International Style's triumph, in the days when the stark glass box represented an architectural ideal.

But architects here have known for some years that they can no longer create ornament of the sort that previous generations of architects so richly endowed us with, and this merely underscores the seriousness of the present losses. Although James Marston Fitch, the architectural historian and preservation consultant, has advanced the encouraging possibilities inherent in Fiberglas or aluminum as a means of using modern technology to reproduce old-style craftsmanship, these innovations are far from being economically competitive. It is still a lot cheaper to rip off a classical cornice than to make one.

Local Law 10 also has the effect of putting particular power in the hands of those engineers who conduct inspections of facades, and thus of implicitly encouraging an engineering-oriented, rather than a preservation-oriented, response to problems. There is no provision in the law right now to encourage preservation of ornament, especially where a building's facade is in bad shape, and there is certainly no financial incentive for preservation and restoration. Neither tax abatements, which would be one possible way for the city to offer some financial assistance to owners who chose to restore their building's ornament, nor any other mechanism that would favor preservation are provided for.

So a long-term result of what Local Law 10 may do, unfortunately, may not be to end a tragedy but to compound it—and turn the private loss that has already been suffered in the case of an unnecessary death into a public loss in the form of a diminished city.

—January 18, 1983

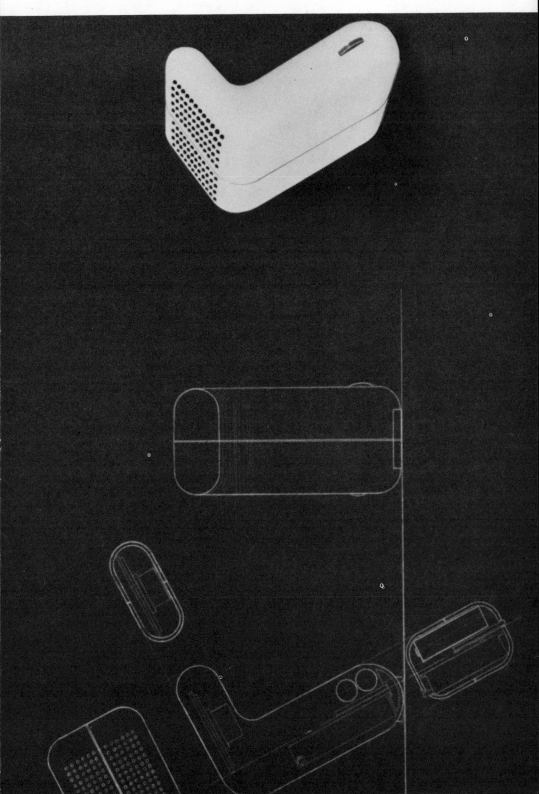

The Design Fallacy

The well-designed object has become a standard of our time—it is no longer surprising to walk into a New York apartment and find sleek Marcel Breuer chairs of cane and tubular steel, elegant tulip-shaped wineglasses, or handsome sofas covered in Haitian cotton. These things, and so many more like them, have gone from being rare, almost exotic objects to being commonplace—objects that by now even have a hint of cliché to them. So-called good design has become so institutionalized that it is now purveyed in medium-priced stores patronized by large numbers of people, places like Conran's, the Pottery Barn, Design Research, and The Workbench.

All well and good—a bit of cliché is a small price to pay for a general rise in the standard of the household object. But if many finely designed objects are becoming trite and commonplace, the far worse danger is a tendency today to value the so-called designed object so much that we often fail to hold it up to rigorous examination. Designers may take issue, but I feel we too often fail to challenge the well-designed object; we let the concept of design seem like a *Good Housekeeping* seal of approval, a sign of legitimacy sufficient in itself.

Although our lives are full of undesigned objects or of objects whose creators were uninterested in design, they are also full of objects that were very much designed but simply do not work very well. The design fallacy is the notion that an object that represents a certain degree of sophistication and strives after a certain esthetic is therefore good and noble. In reality, plenty of those objects are failures. The one that might be said to best represent the design fallacy is an extremely popular consumer object, the Trimline telephone.

The Trimline is a sleek, small telephone, far more

elegant at first glance than anything else the telephone company offers. It is no wonder that many people who pride themselves on the quality of their houses or offices are attracted to the gently curving form, in which mouthpiece, earpiece, and dial are all enclosed in a single piece of plastic.

When the Trimline telephone is placed in its cradle, neither dial nor mouth-piece and earpiece are visible, and all that can be seen is the curving piece of plastic, looking like a tiny modern sculpture with a wire sticking out of it. But none of this makes for a very efficient telephone. The mouthpiece-earpiece, so attractive visually, is difficult to hold; it does not fit the hand comfortably as does the handset of a more conventional telephone. Neither can it be slipped comfortably between the neck and the shoulder to free the user's hands, as can a regular telephone.

And the placement of the dial (or the much-too-tiny buttons, if the model has push-button dialing) makes dialing more difficult than on a regular phone. The Trimline is also far too light, so that desk models may slip off tables during use.

The Trimline was never really necessary, which represents another aspect of the design's fallacy. The conventional telephones available in recent years do a fine job. They are not going to end up in the design collection of the Museum of Modern Art, but no matter: they are decent and efficient and, unless they have been ordered in one of those strange colors like turquoise or pink, are not unattractive. But somehow it was felt that more was needed, and the impulse toward a more handsome object was allowed to get out of hand. We'll show those design buffs, the telephone company seems to have said, let's show 'em how sleek and trendy we can be. And the result was a loss in quality, not a gain.

The Trimline, in the final analysis, is just too self-conscious an object. It tries too hard; and that is the problem with most objects that illustrate the design fallacy. Many household appliances fit into this category—including many made by the West German firm of Braun, for years a leader in the design field. Braun toasters tend to have extremely thin slots for toast, a design feature that makes the appliance far more elegant than any other toaster, but also makes it virtually impossible to toast anything but a thin slice of bread. The designers were trying so hard that they lost touch with the primary goal.

Many well-designed objects do not work that well mechanically, but that, to be fair, is another matter. Complaints about the breakdown rate of Braun appliances or Jaguar automobiles, to name another item on virtually everyone's list of well-designed objects, are legion. But these problems, if they exist, derive from certain internal mechanical deficiencies.

Similarly, many stereo experts rate the equipment made by the Danish firm of Bang & Olafsen, far and away the most beautiful stereo equipment manufac-tured anywhere today, as not equal in quality to competing brands in its very high price range. But if this is so, it is a case of the people in charge of catering to the needs of our eyes doing a better job than the people in charge of catering to the needs of our ears.

Where catering to the needs of the eyes *has* been a cause of the problem is where the design fallacy comes in. The elegant Olivetti portable electric typewriter with a single round typing element is a good example. It is a handsome machine, graceful, almost sensual, in its form. You look at it and you want to touch it, even caress it. But the keyboard is placed at such an angle that it is uncomfortable to type on it for long, and ultimately you want to forget the whole thing and go back to Olivetti's competitor, the less elegant, but far more comfortably solid I.B.M. Selectric.

The world of furniture is full of self-conscious, overdesigned things. But somehow a not-entirely-functional chair is less disturbing than a not-entirely-functional typewriter—we expect a chair to be part function, part esthetics, and if the proportions get a bit out of kilter, and esthetics get the upper hand, it is not as serious.

And we sometimes base our sense of functional success on our esthetic judgments anyway. Philip Johnson, the architect, likes to tell of the reactions of visitors to his Glass House in New Canaan, Connecticut, in 1949, when the Barcelona chairs he had installed there were relatively unfamiliar objects. Guests who liked the chairs visually would exclaim over their beauty, Mr. Johnson reports, and would sit down and say something like, "My, this chair is not only good-looking, it's comfortable, too." But guests who didn't like the way the chairs looked would make a derogatory comment or two and then, upon sitting down, would invariably sneer, "And these chairs aren't even comfortable, either."

No one has come up with a fully satisfactory definition of a well-designed object. Every good definition—indeed, every good object itself—speaks of a combination of beauty and utility. But these terms themselves cannot really be defined, nor can they really be separated, for utility can influence beauty and beauty can affect utility. The proportions are different for each kind of object and for each design itself.

But it should be reasonable to apply a few rules of common sense. A typewriter that is hard to type on, a telephone that is hard to hold, a clock that has no numbers on its face, a pepper grinder that cannot be held easily, a fork that does not have enough tines to permit the easy holding of food, a glass kettle that is hard to hold and does not whistle to signal boiling water—these are all examples of the design fallacy, cases in which the demands of our eyes get the better of common sense.

In the very best objects throughout history, the needs of the eye and the needs of the hand—beauty and utility—have been in subtle balance. And it is in seeking that balance that the essence of good design lies.

—November 16, 1978

What Do You Get When You Buy a Designer Car?

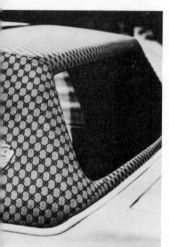

The Gucci Cadillac

The phrase "Gucci Cadillac" has an inherently funny sound—almost like "Welfare Cadillac," the title of a popular song a few years back. There really *is* such a thing as a Gucci Cadillac, but while the song was about those who the songwriter believed could not afford Cadillacs, the Gucci Cadillac is for those who can afford Cadillacs all too well, for this is a special model of a Cadillac Seville, all done up by Gucci, the purveyors of chic leather goods, scarfs, and what-have-you. It is designed to satisfy those customers who might wish to own Cadillac Sevilles but fear that the car is not sufficiently fashionable. Gucci has taken care of that.

Now, Gucci has never been shy about placing its trademark on its goods—its famous interlocking "GG" is often more conspicuous than the object it adorns—and the main difference between the Gucci Seville and all other Sevilles is the fact that the body is virtually dripping with golden G's.

There's a portion of the roof covered in beige and brown vinyl with the Gucci pattern of interlocking G's, not unlike a Gucci handbag or piece of luggage spread out over the roof of a car. (There is, by the way, a set of Gucci luggage that comes with each car.) In case the vinyl top and the luggage do not make the car's Gucci heritage sufficiently clear, the designers have not stopped with this. There is a replication of the interlocking G motif in gold-colored metal as a hood ornament and another instance of the trademark on the side behind the fender, this one topped by a metal buckle that looks something like a bottle opener but is more likely a buckle left over from an overrun of Gucci loafers.

Even all of that may not be enough to proclaim the car's status to the nearsighted, so the word "Gucci" is spelled out in full in gold lettering on the rear of the car, just over red and green stripes similar to the stripes that run across Gucci luggage. The stripes continue all around the car in a smaller version, and there are more interlocking G's on the hubcaps.

It is all, obviously, rather silly, and one of the reasons is that it is all so unnecessary. A Seville is a relatively handsome car—it was a leader in the recent American fad of seeing who could look the most like the Mercedes-Benz, and that is not a bad piece of design to imitate. The "ordinary" Seville has a restrained, taut boxiness to it that is good looking and in no need whatsoever of all this cosmetic treatment.

For a while now there have been three of these cars, one in brown, one in black, and one in white, on display in the public galleria space of the Olympic Tower at 645 Fifth Avenue. There's a certain appropriateness to the setting— the Gucci Seville is clearly a piece of artificial status, without much real quality to back it up (save for the inherent quality of a Cadillac motor car), and the Olympic Tower is its architectural equivalent. It is a building gussied up with fancy tenants and given, by common agreement, an immense amount of status, which the architecture by itself would not have provided.

The Olympic Tower's public galleria, called Olympic Place, is a cold, ill-proportioned room of granite that conveys so little sense of welcome that it was necessary to put a sign on the marquee outside to tell the public it may enter, that public space really *is* within. Since Olympic Place is so unpleasant, it is probably aided by being turned into an automobile showroom; the Cadillacs at least fill up the empty place.

(But the leasing of this space to Gucci does pose a serious question. If the space is to be public—and that is the agreement the Olympic Tower's builders made with the city in exchange for being permitted to erect a larger tower than zoning normally permits—is it then right, boring as the space may be when it is empty, to lease it for such a commercial venture? A cafe or a restaurant, which is sorely needed there, would be one thing; a display of fancied-up Cadillacs is another.)

Gucci is not alone in making its way into the world of luxury automobiles. There are also special editions of the Lincoln Continental Mark V, done by well-known designers or design firms. Most of these cars simply have revived color schemes, however; they are not quite the exhaustive systems of trim that Gucci has so earnestly provided.

The Lincoln Continental Mark V, like the Cadillac Seville, is not a bad-looking car—it is sleeker and more dignified than most American cars, even if it lacks the brilliant, cool restraint of the Lincoln Continental Mark II from the mid-1950's, the truly classic car upon which the current model is based. But these fashion designers appear to have added little to the work of the automotive designers in Detroit.

Bill Blass's Continental, which the advertisements hail as "sleek as a luxury cruiser," is supposed to have a nautical motif; it is really just a blue and white car, with a mock convertible top, all much louder in appearance than the un-Bill Blass-ified Lincoln Continental. Givenchy has done a "crystal blue" Lincoln, Pucci a "medium turquoise" one, and Cartier one in "light champagne," which is actually a rather warm beige and far and away the most tolerable of them all.

Now, neither Gucci, nor Bill Blass, nor Givenchy, nor Pucci, nor Cartier has anything whatsoever to do with the making of cars. Their names and trademarks are distinguished ones, but these associations and their results raise real questions about the nature of trademarks and names in our culture right now. That these odd cars could be produced suggests that we do not relate the names of famous designers to the objects they design, but really to anything they can get their hands on to promote.

For what, after all, can the name Gucci mean in terms of cars? It means a great deal in terms of leather. But when all of the accessories of Gucci's famous leather goods are transferred to a car, the substance behind the status—the reason behind the reputation—disappears. What we are left with is only empty status—sheer promotion, not quality.

It is promotion at a high price. The Gucci Seville lists for $22,900, almost $5,000 above the cost of what we might call the common-folk Seville. It is a great deal to pay for a set of golden G's, even with a set of luggage thrown in.

It is hard to be sure to whom these cars will appeal. But the other day a man was strolling through the Gucci Olympic Tower display carrying a cloth umbrella emblazoned with the trademark of Gucci's French competitor, Louis Vuitton. As he set the umbrella down on the roof of the car, all of the L's and the V's clashed with all of the G's, but he seemed not to notice; it was the presence of these fabled initials, not how they looked, that appeared to count. Perhaps the car was made for him.

—*February 22, 1979*

Commonplace Things of Great Design

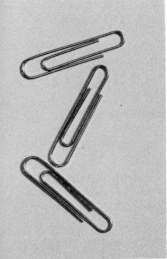

One commonly thinks of professional designers as disdaining the common object—as having the sort of perceptions that lean toward the exotic, the special, the rare, and, all too often, the impractical. The simple, everyday object seems frequently not to be a part of the designer's world at all. Designers, so this piece of the common wisdom tells us, are so preoccupied with visual effect that they ignore objects that were not designed with visual purposes in mind—even if these objects are, underneath their ordinary surfaces, altogether sensible, practical, and handsome.

But a recent and provocative survey suggests that this attitude may not be quite so prevalent as we think. This winter, *Art News* magazine asked a number of prominent members of the design profession to name successful examples of design, and the results showed a surprising amount of respect for the commonplace object.

While a few of the respondents (who included museum curators, executives, and educators as well as practicing designers) cited as their favorites the sort of objects that might be called High Design—things like the Barcelona chair by Mies van der Rohe or the sleek Bang & Olafsen phonograph equipment—a great many of the design professionals admitted that they really like plain and simple things.

Among the most intriguing preferences were the paper clip, the safety pin, the yellow pencil, Levi's blue jeans, the Thermos bottle, and the clay flowerpot. Major brand refrigerators and toasters were also cited as a group, as were certain materials that have become absolutely basic to our physical environment, such as plywood and gypsum board.

It is really a wonderful list. Could there possibly be

anything better than a paper clip to do the job that a paper clip does? The common paper clip is light, inexpensive, strong, easy to use, and quite good-looking. There is a neatness of line to it that could not violate the ethos of any purist. One could not really improve on the paper clip, and the innumerable attempts to try—such as awkward, larger plastic clips in various colors, or paper clips with square instead of rounded ends—only underscore the quality of the real things.

The same could be said of the safety pin. Its job is really quite difficult because it involves a contradiction: a pointed element must be used to anchor two pieces of cloth together simply and unobtrusively, yet that point must be made to disappear so that there is no danger to the wearer. The common safety pin does this neatly and simply, and once again, it is hard to imagine an alternative that would be better to look at.

And while we are on the subject of simple metal objects, there is also the wire coat hanger, which the graphic designer George Tscherny mentioned in the *Art News* survey—once again, something absolutely simple and straightforward and really very handsome. It does not work quite as well as a wooden coat hanger, but its job is not really the same—the wire hanger has a more temporary function, which it fulfills admirably.

It would be a mistake, however, to conclude from these objects that absolute simplicity is the hallmark of all good design. A stripped-down object is not necessarily the best example of design. But it is probably fair to say that a simple object is generally best to perform a simple task.

There are a number of other common objects for which, like these simple metal things, one is hard pressed to suggest improvements. The needle, which no respondent to the survey mentioned, does its job perfectly and is really quite elegant. A needle with a larger eye would be easier to use, of course, but it could not work—given the constraints of the task to be performed, there is no better way to do the needle's work.

The same might be said of those most common of all household objects, eating utensils. How could there be a better way to do what the spoon does? Its shape is comfortable in the mouth, and it is functional for the holding of solid or liquid food. The handle can be varied, of course, although even there dramatic shifts are almost invariably unwise. The best variations on the spoon throughout history have consisted mostly of the invention of decorations for the handle, not of any changes in the basic shape. Moreover, what is remarkable about the conventional spoon or knife or fork is how unself-conscious it appears, even when it is elaborately decorated.

One test of good design—and this is, of course, a subjective test, for there is no way to quantify this sort of thing—is how self-conscious an object is. A well-designed object never appears forced or strained; it does not seem to be trying too hard, no matter how complex it is or how complicated the process of making it was.

Most modern silverware is quite self-conscious: it seems to have the message I Am Designed written all over it. It is not just a question of simplicity, for a good eighteenth-century spoon is surely more ornate than a modern one. But the eighteenth-century spoon has a certain common sense to it—it is a functional end with a decorated handle. The superficially "simpler" twentieth-century spoon that tries to rethink the entire shape of the spoon becomes the self-conscious and overdesigned object.

The idea of a functional end and a decorated handle comes into play in another very common household object as well, the umbrella. Here again, although this time the object at hand is vastly more complicated than the spoon, it is hard to imagine a better way to do the job. The job of the umbrella is complicated, since the object must be capable of being physically transformed from something small and narrow into something big and rounded; given how complex this task really is, the common umbrella is not really all that elaborate at all.

And the umbrella's functional parts are, logically, kept straightforward—there is the handle and the actual plastic or vinyl surface for design expression. Perhaps that is what has kept the umbrella from being too drastically tampered with—designers have been able to change the look of the umbrella totally by using new materials and colors, without ever changing the sensible and basic underlying mechanism.

If that respect for the underlying mechanism—for the parts of any household object that actually do the job at hand—were present every time a device were redesigned, we would probably have a lot fewer foolish and overdesigned objects.

—March 26, 1981

The Grumman Bus

When they first arrived in New York last summer, the city's new Grumman Flxible 870 buses carried messages on their lighted front signboards like "Have a Nice Day." That may have been their first mistake—New Yorkers would probably have taken to these buses better if they had had signs like "Mind Your Own Business" or "Go Away and Take Another Bus."

But the buses have now been in service for several months, long enough to make it possible to judge them as an established part of the city's physical environment. The full complement of 837 buses has not yet arrived, and officials said yesterday that they might cancel the order for the last 200. But the impact of the buses has already been enormous—they have been, collectively, as powerful a symbol of newness in the city as a building like the Citicorp Center skyscraper has been. But while Citicorp Center stays in one place, these buses move all over, and their squarish shapes are beginning to play as much of a part in defining the cityscape of New York as the red double-deckers define London.

It is that sense of newness, the ability of these buses to act as a symbol, that is their most remarkable quality. Although some of their front signs now say things like "Happy Holidays" instead of "Have A Nice Day," and some indicate nothing at all except their route numbers and destinations, there is still a sense that these $106,000 creatures are not quite a natural part of New York. We tend not to believe that things in New York can be so clean and sleek as these vehicles. As Citicorp Center does not seem quite native to this city of brownstones, so the new Grummans seem a bit out of place in the city of graffiti-covered subway cars.

But the Grumman 870's do look wonderful. They have

a cool, refined air to their appearance; their squarish shape comes off as sleek, not awkwardly boxy. Part of the reason is that squarish shapes are more in vogue these days in general—since the Mercedes-Benz became so fashionable an automotive design, the gentle curves of "streamlined" vehicles have come to look old-fashioned, not modern as they once did. But the windows of the Grumman 870's play a part in this handsome appearance, too—they are large and set flush with the side of the bus, more like glass walls than actual windows. So instead of looking like a box with holes punched into its sides, as most buses do, these new ones look as if they have sides of glass.

But if the new buses are an impressive symbol, they do not appear after their initial weeks of use to be as successful as functioning objects. Their record of breakdowns and mechanical problems and their mediocre fuel efficiency have already been reported. Perhaps more important still, the buses leave a lot to be desired in terms of passenger comfort. The interiors, which, like the outside, depart dramatically from the New York City bus standard, have a sleek appearance that is a welcome change from the ramshackle look of most of the older

The Grumman bus

vehicles around town, but this beauty tends to be rather skin deep, and it ignores certain basic passenger needs.

Most of the problems come from an attempt on the part of the designers to alter standard shapes and objects within the bus. The old metal rails that standing passengers traditionally grasp, for example, have been replaced by a rubber rail that is placed quite high in the bus and turned inward, making it impossible to reach for short people and extremely difficult to hold for anyone.

The yellow plastic tape that passengers press to request the driver to stop, which replaces the old pull cord, is hard to find, and hard to reach from some areas of the bus, particularly from the front seats reserved for the elderly and handicapped—presumably those travelers are expected to shout instructions to the driver. Those seats, incidentally, are set quite high over the wheels, and those who are short will find that their feet do not quite reach the floor.

These things are classic examples of the design fallacy—the belief that objects that function well must be redesigned, even at the cost of their success. Metal rails and straps for standing passengers are not elegant and they are not sleek, but they do work, and better than the new rubber rail, a clear case of an object redesigned for no purpose at all other than the designer's desire to see a change.

The windows in the new buses, the large size of which is so welcome, are all made of dark glass, a requirement of the regulations governing federal mass transit subsidies. The dark, sealed glass helps reduce the air-conditioning load, but it makes it difficult for people on the street to tell if an approaching bus is empty or crowded. From within, the dark glass casts a pall on the street, making it always look as if it is about to rain. And there is no back window at all.

On the other hand, the seats in the new buses are set facing forward, a welcome change from the sideways seats in the current city buses manufactured by General Motors. To permit more standing room, there are double seats on one side of the aisle and single seats on the other, a sensible idea that mysteriously has never been tried in the past. And one further positive aspect: the new buses are a lot quieter from within. If they remain in good working order, New Yorkers may become used to quiet transit for the first time ever.

So these Grumman buses are, in the end, a mixed blessing. In reviewing their problems, it must be remembered that they are not the most expensive buses available today—had the Metropolitan Transportation Authority had more funds available, it could have purchased more elaborate vehicles still. And of course it remains to be seen how these buses will fare over the long term. No amount of testing can render the sort of final judgment that a year or more on the streets of New York can do.

—*December 8, 1980*

Cookie Architecture

Sugar Wafer (Nabisco)

There is no attempt to imitate the ancient forms of traditional, individually baked cookies here—this is a modern cookie through and through. Its simple rectangular form, clean and pure, just reeks of mass production and modern technological methods. The two wafers, held together by the sugar-cream filling, appear to float, and the Nabisco trademark, stamped repeatedly across the top, confirms that this is a machine-age object. Clearly the Sugar Wafer is the Mies van der Rohe of cookies.

Fig Newton (Nabisco)

This, too, is a sandwich but different in every way from the Sugar Wafer. Here the imagery is more traditional, more sensual even; a rounded form of cookie dough arcs over the fig concoction inside, and the whole is soft and pliable. Like all good pieces of design, it has an appropriate form for its use, since the insides of Fig Newtons can ooze and would not be held in place by a more rigid form. The thing could have had a somewhat different shape, but the rounded top is a comfortable, familiar image, and it is easy to hold. Not a revolutionary object but an intelligent one.

Milano (Pepperidge Farm)

This long, chocolate-filled cookie summons up contradictory associations. Its rounded ends suggest both the traditional image of stodgy ladyfingers and the curves of Art Deco, while the subtle yet forceful V embossed onto the surface creates an abstract image of force and movement. The V is the kind of ornament that wishes to

Clockwise from top: Sugar Wafer, Oatmeal Peanut Sandwich, Mallomar, Fig Newton, Milano, Lorna Doone.

appear modern without really being modern, which would have meant banning ornament altogether. That romantic symbolism of the modern was an Art Deco characteristic, of course; come to think of it the Milano is rather Art Deco in spirit.

Mallomar (Nabisco)

This marshmallow, chocolate, and cracker combination is the ultimate sensual cookie—indeed, its resemblance to the female breast has been cited so often as to sound rather trite. But the cookie's imagery need not be read so literally—the voluptuousness of the form, which with its nipped waist rather resembles the New Orleans Superdome, is enough. Like all good pieces of design, the form of the cookie is primarily derived from functional needs, but with just enough distinction to make it instantly identifiable. The result is a cultural icon—the cookie equivalent, surely, of the Coke bottle.

Lorna Doone (Nabisco)

Like the Las Vegas casino that is overwhelmed by its sign, image is all in the Lorna Doone. It is a plain, simple cookie (of shortbread, in fact), but a cookie like all other cookies—except for its sign. The Lorna Doone logo, a four-pointed star with the cookie's name and a pair of fleur-de-lis-like decorations, covers the entire surface of the cookie in low relief. Cleverly, the designers of this cookie have placed the logo so that the points of the star align with the corners of the square, forcing one to pivot the cookie 45 degrees, so that its shape appears instead to be a diamond. It is a superb example of the ordinary made extraordinary.

Oatmeal Peanut Sandwich (Sunshine)

If the Sugar Wafer is the Mies van der Rohe of cookies, this is the Robert Venturi—not pretentiously modern but, rather, eager to prove its ordinariness, its lack of real design, and in so zealous a way that it ends up looking far dowdier than a *really* ordinary cookie like your basic gingersnap. The Oatmeal Peanut Sandwich is frumpy, like a plump matron in a flower-print dress, or an old piece of linoleum. But it is frumpy in an intentional way and not by accident—one senses that the designers of this cookie knew the Venturi principle that the average user of architecture (read eater of cookies) is far more comfortable with plain, ordinary forms that do not require him to adjust any of his perceptions radically.

—September, 1977
Originally published in Esquire *magazine.*

WAYS OF SEEING

Why Buildings Grow on Us

If time heals wounds it also heals a great deal of architecture: it is remarkable how much more benign many mediocre buildings seem two, three, or ten years after their completion. For a long time, I thought that nothing could be worse than the "XYZ" buildings on the Avenue of the Americas, the massive Exxon, McGraw-Hill, and Celanese skyscrapers that constitute the western expansion of Rockefeller Center, so named by their planners because of their nearly identical design. The three boxy towers are banal in the extreme, with huge and generally useless plazas dulling the street life in front and straight tops flattening out the skyline up above.

They are not good buildings, and no amount of time is likely to make them so, but nearly a decade of looking at them forces one to admit that they do have a certain presence. They do not bring pleasure, but they no longer bring anger, either. Is this merely because of a numbing of our sensations—do we feel resigned to bad buildings after they have been with us a long time? Or do we feel, as Dr. Johnson consoled Boswell, "How insignificant this will appear a twelve-month hence?"

I think it is neither. Something much more subtle is taking place, and it has to do with the nature of architecture and the role it plays in a city as much as it has to do with perception. A building is only partly finished on the day that it is declared complete; it begins to age only at that moment, and our perceptions only begin to form.

The first time we see a new building, particularly one whose form is striking, can be a time of absorbing its strangeness into our consciousness, and only later, when it is less surprising, do we judge it more fully. And the relationship of an urban building to its surroundings is in a constant state of change; what appears a drastic intru-

299

sion at one point may appear to be the epitome of responsible blending-in at another.

But there is an even more important aspect to all of this, and it has to do with the role of continuity and symbols in a city. One of the greatest benefits of architecture is to provide us with symbols of permanence; we may know that architecture is not really forever, particularly in New York, but it is comforting to feel that it is not there just for the moment, either. Thus, even the mediocre building takes on a certain acceptability over time—not because it is good, but because it becomes part of the established city, part of the world we become used to and expect to see. It becomes a source of stability.

This alone can hardly justify bad architecture, of course. But it does help to explain why many things, small as well as large, seem more tolerable as they age. And it is not the least of the reasons that taste evolves over time; we seem much more accepting of what is not new than we are of what has just been made.

It is no accident that it took more than a generation for Art Deco architecture to be appreciated, and similarly, this is why such 1950's extravaganzas as the Fontainebleau Hotel in Miami Beach seem far less disturbing now than when they were new. It is not perverse taste, it is that they have become a part of the landscape we expect to see, and thus derive a curious kind of comfort from. So, too, with such an oddity as the interior of Dubrow's Cafeteria on Seventh Avenue in the garment district, which has those swirling, amoebalike shapes characteristic of 1950's interiors. I walked past it the other day and was shocked to realize how that room, long an object of derision, is beginning to take on a certain appeal.

—July 30, 1981

Naming What We See

There is a word that has become very much the fashion in talking and writing about architecture lately, and it is "contextual." It is intended as a word of praise—good architecture, it is presumed, is "in context," which is to say it fits in with its surroundings. Bad architecture does not—it violates its surroundings, creating awkward and jarring physical connections to the buildings around it.

The coming of contextualism, as this attitude is called when given its grandest appellation, to the lexicon of architectural criticism is a good thing. The values of contextual architecture are civilized and appropriate ones; it should go without saying that we make better cities when each architect pays attention to what has come before and what sits on either side of whatever he is creating. Frank Lloyd Wright may have been able to get away with the Guggenheim Museum, the contextual argument goes, but for almost everyone else, discretion is the better part of architectural valor.

There is a problem, however, and it has to do with the way any valued concept gets twisted, misunderstood, and, worst of all, exploited. Contextualism has become so much an accepted goal in recent years that nary a building seems to be presented that is not described by its designer as contextual.

We are told, for example, that the Helmsley Palace Hotel, that harsh and dreary tower rising behind the Villard Houses on Madison Avenue, is a suitable backdrop for the Villard neo-Renaissance brownstones; it is nothing of the kind. Architectural Record Books, in a publication titled *Contextual Architecture*, hails I.M. Pei's East Building of the National Gallery in Washington as contextual, since its unusual trapezoidal shape reflects something of the street pattern of Pennsylvania

Avenue. It ignores the fact that this building bears no stylistic relationship whatsoever to John Russell Pope's distinguished National Gallery of 1941, to which it is technically an addition.

The height of it all seems to have come this year, when an office building now rising on Water Street in lower Manhattan, just beside the South Street Seaport Museum, was proclaimed in advertisements as "New York's First Contextual Office Building: Seaport Plaza, a unique and major architectural achievement." The South Street Seaport, of course, is a collection of several blocks' worth of 4- and 5-story, early nineteenth-century commercial buildings that have been preserved and restored as a remnant of what all of lower Manhattan's shorefront was once like.

The notion of an office building "in context" with the Seaport summoned up all sorts of appealing notions—perhaps this was a true low-rise office building of the sort that has been built near the San Francisco waterfront, perhaps it was a building designed to resemble an old factory converted into offices, something

Seaport Plaza— contextual architecture?

that could blend gracefully into the vibrant little group of buildings that constitute the Seaport.

No such luck. The design, by the firm of Swanke, Hayden & Connell, is for a 34-story, million-square-foot tower, with horizontal strip windows on its west facade looking not at all unlike those of a dozen skyscrapers going up elsewhere. Where the building is "contextual," for what that is worth, is on the east side, facing the low buildings of the Seaport, where it abruptly switches to an entirely different facade of individual windows.

Now, there is no question that the east side of this building is a better backdrop for the South Street Seaport than the west side. It is also a more handsome facade on its own terms, and probably should have been continued all the way around the building. But that hardly means that it "echoes the mood of the 19th-century Seaport community," as the advertisements state.

The fact is that the building does nothing of the kind—it is a big, modern office building. There is real reason to question whether any 34-story tower, no matter how thoughtfully designed, can be fully "in context" with a group of small and fairly delicate nineteenth-century buildings. But to claim that this building is contextual architecture is to cheapen that valuable and important concept.

The decision to name this building Seaport Plaza brings up another question of architectural lexicon. Why is it that real-estate developers seem so frightened by normal, old-fashioned street addresses, and so insistent on inventing substitutes that are almost impossible to find? Is there really something so disgraceful about Pine Street that the Chase Manhattan Bank, which started this trend way back in 1961, had to pretend that it did not exist and that its downtown office tower was situated at No. 1 Chase Manhattan Plaza instead?

By now, Chase Manhattan Plaza is sufficiently well known so as not to provoke confusion, and this piece of self-aggrandizement that the bank engaged in is itself as established as any street. But one still finds much confusion when addresses such as 4 New York Plaza, 1 Liberty Plaza, and 1 Astor Plaza are given out. And with good reason—why should anyone remember where such places are? New York Plaza, at the tip of lower Manhattan, is barely a plaza at all; it is simply an invented name, a piece of addressmanship manufactured to take the place, perhaps, of quality architecture, since it is altogether absent there.

There isn't much more connection at Astor Plaza, which sits on the site of the old Astor Hotel at Times Square. As a matter of fact, there is no real plaza at all at Astor Plaza—and there is most definitely no Astor. One can only imagine where it will end—perhaps, some day, should the Landmarks Preservation Commission be lax, with an office building on the site of the Plaza Hotel. That, of course, can only be named 1 Plaza Plaza.

—*October 21, 1982*

Winter Light

There is something about the nature of sunlight in the winter that changes everything. It is intense, crisp and hard, and it offers no tricks, it has no illusions. It affects our moods, and it also affects the way we perceive architecture.

Buildings look different in winter light. After a week in Vermont it is possible to think that the way buildings look in winter light is the way their makers hoped they would look all the time. Buildings leap out at you in the winter. They do not glow, as in some kinds of light; they do not shimmer, as in others. Part of the reason is that there are so few things blocking our view of them—there are no romantic glimpses of a tall, white, country church steeple half hidden through green leaves.

If anything gets in the way of the steeple, it is the cold, spare branches of the tree, which form a rigid pattern of black and white against the building: the sharpness of the light is echoed by the cleanness of the branches. But most of all it is the light itself. This winter sun is a forceful, positive kind of light. This is light that seems almost to be a tangible object. In its crispness and hardness it could have edges, it could be cut—you feel as if you could draw a line where it begins and a line where it ends. It is active where other kinds of light are passive, and it hides nothing. It offers no charity. There are no soft shadows, there is no mist, there is no haze that might smooth rough edges.

Yet, for all its unremitting clarity, this winter light is not cruel. It shows blemishes, but it also raises, ennobles, what it illuminates. At the best moments of the day, the bright light of morning or, better still, the last strong hour of daylight before the afternoon sun begins to set, all buildings, all trees, all structures synthetic and natural seem to stand together as part of the same triumphant landscape. Mediocrity seems to disappear—even an ordinary building takes on a certain nobility when it is seen under this strong, clear light.

Winter light does one particularly important thing to our perceptions of buildings. Since it is so strong and so crisp, it outlines shapes with great clarity, and we feel masses more than we might otherwise do. A Federal house stands with a strength and certitude it never has in the summer. In this sunlight it stands before us with an assurance that calls to mind Louis Sullivan's description of the great Marshall Field Warehouse by Henry Hobson Richardson in Chicago: "Standing there like a man on four legs."

But this is at no loss to details. The house hardly looks like Richardson's powerful Romanesque mass—it merely takes on that building's mood of self-assurance. The house still looks like the gracefully detailed Federal-style house that it is. Indeed, unlike in foggy, softer kinds of light, where all becomes mass and shadow, or pale light, where sometimes an odd detail will show up more clearly than an entire mass or overall shape, in this strong winter sunlight everything is visible, mass and detail, in just the balance the architect intended. The shape is a strong outline and a strong background, the details are clearly etched upon it.

It is not only in the country that this is so, of course. In the city, winter light is also something special. The skyscrapers seem to slice into the sky with an intensity that they do not have in the summer, and their tops gleam. Little buildings, like Edward Hopper's rows of storefronts, become crisp. The shadows in Central Park or on Fifth Avenue are harder and more even. There is a serenity to it all—a sense of solidity, of certainty, as if the whole city in this light were something made of rock.

In the late afternoons in New England when almost every mountain seems a baffle behind which the sun hides, the light begins to change again. There are not the magic colors in the sky of a great summer sunset; rather, there is a soft, slightly golden color that begins to appear. And another crucial thing happens to buildings—we begin to perceive sides of buildings in a way that we did not do earlier in the day when the sun was higher and lighted buildings more evenly. Now, the sun can wash one side of a barn completely and leave another in dark shadow.

It is not only a beautiful image, this blazing light on one side and dark on another—it is an instant lesson about the messages of solar energy, and of orientation of buildings to take advantage of what the sun can offer.

It is, finally, a light of a certain earnestness. Winter light has none of the indulgence of summer sun, none of that sense of plenty, of overabundance. This light is not fat—it is thin and strong and limited, and thus it wastes not a single particle of itself. Willa Cather, in *My Antonia*, said it well: "The pale, cold light of the winter sunset did not beautify—it was like the light of truth itself."

—*January 22, 1981*

Saul Steinberg as Architecture Critic

It is no surprise to learn that Saul Steinberg studied to be an architect. His drawings have always been full of architectural images and ideas; they are often literally *about* architecture and, when they are not, they are about the things that architects must always be conscious of: physical detail, social reality, and style in all its manifestations.

Steinberg's rich, pleasing retrospective, now at the Whitney Museum of American Art, is therefore not only a show of drawings but also a show about architecture. It is no exaggeration to say that the exhibition is one of the best pieces of architectural criticism in years. To start with one obvious but splendid example, it is commonplace these days to complain of the banality of the glass box—but not when it has been done with the grace and deftness of Steinberg's exquisite 1950 drawing, "Graph Paper Building," in which a sheet of graph paper is superimposed on a street of delicate and fanciful little brownstones.

What Steinberg did here was the simplest of all possible gestures: we all think that skyscrapers are as boring as standardized patterns, so the artist merely used that perception, in the form of a rectangle of graph paper, and set it gently into a sketch. The drawing calls to mind Harold Rosenberg's observation that Steinberg, instead of ignoring clichés, "has been inclined to take them literally."

But what makes this drawing so special is not just the use of graph paper, but the juxtaposition of the big, banal box with Steinberg's own lovely landscape of decorated brownstones. The irony of the skyscraper is heightened by the artist's placement of a few television antennas on its roof (how foolish they look) and by the

Saul Steinberg's
Chrysler Building

307

sketched-in canopy out front. The canopy looks oddly out of place, and it reminds us of a crucial problem with the glass box that architects have for too long ignored: in an abstract form, where do you put the door?

It is a devastating critique of the glass box, a reminder of the lack of human values and human scale in so many of our new towers, and an equally urgent plea for something else, for a more comfortable alternative.

Steinberg's love is clearly for the whimsical, the offbeat, and the decorated aspects of the streetscape. Four works of 1951 in the Whitney exhibit demonstrate this with particular Steinbergian wit. In each of the works—"Third Avenue Photo," "Hotel Emperor," "Downtown," and "Two Downtown Buildings"—a photograph of a heavy, ornate piece of furniture is set into a Steinberg-drawn cityscape, then embellished with more details.

It is impossible not to think here of the current debate over the design for the new A.T.&T. headquarters on Madison Avenue, which architects Philip Johnson and John Burgee have defended as a sensible answer to the glass box. Steinberg anticipated all of this twenty-seven years ago with these insertions of furniture into the cityscape.

In part, what Steinberg is doing this time is inverting his graph-paper skyscraper drawing. With the massive pieces of furniture turned into buildings, he shows an alternative, and it is clearly an alternative he prefers. But these drawings are hardly an urban-design proposal; they are more appropriately seen, as is the graph-paper skyscraper, as comments on what the artist recognizes as the difficulty of building properly at large scale.

One route, he tells us, is the banality of the box; the other route also has its pitfall: the result, while delightful, never loses its edge of silliness. And, of course, it is always out of scale, for one of the other things Steinberg is doing is playing with everyday objects, prefiguring what Pop artists were to do in the 1960's by his placement of furniture in the new and curious context of the cityscape.

Steinberg clearly has his likes and dislikes. One of his most polemic pieces of architectural commentary is a drawing that is unfortunately not in the current exhibition; it is of a formal and deliberately sterile classical building with the inscription "National Academy of the Avant-Garde" across its front. Marching in front of the building, in perfect lockstep, are rows of bearded figures.

Steinberg is making a number of comments beyond the obvious point that the avant-garde have a tendency toward conformity. He is also reminding us that the avant-garde can become an academy, as pompous and academic as any other, and he is letting us know how similar the values represented by the sterile and official-looking "Mussolini-Modern" architecture are to certain conformist impulses.

There are similar but more benign observations made in "Monologue" of 1964 and "Bauhaus Dialogue" of 1969, in which Bauhaus and Art Deco details take on new and extraordinary roles. In "Monologue" a woman is speaking, and out of her mouth come not words but a slew of Art Deco details. In "Bauhaus Dialogue" these very details expand into an overpowering and all-encompassing environment in themselves. In "Bauhaus," a print similar to these drawings, there is a wonderful, bizarre structure of sharply intersecting angles that is added to the elements of the drawings. That tortured, angular structure is as devastating a satire of Bauhaus architecture as has ever been conceived. "Bauhaus" is not in the Whitney exhibition, but a number of similarly harsh critiques of modern architecture are.

The more varied, lively, and spontaneous the environment, the gentler Steinberg is to it. There are loving portrayals of streetscapes, both the honkytonk ones of New York City and the quieter ones of small towns. In them the signs grow big and the buildings shrink small. The artist celebrates diversity and vitality—most powerfully, perhaps, in his sketches of such New York street scenes as "Bleecker Street," which suggests a mad, intense city of beautiful strangeness.

Steinberg's ideal New York building is, logically enough, the Chrysler Building. Its splendid crown of stainless-steel arches seems made for Steinberg's pen, and it appears in a number of different drawings: here juxtaposed with the chaotic forms of its skyline neighbors, there portrayed as a series of curves that gradually and subtly metamorphose into the Guggenheim Museum. With the Chrysler Building, Steinberg seems to have gone beyond satire and instead chosen to celebrate—although his celebrations, like those of any great artist, make us see a beloved and familiar thing in altogether new ways.

—May 25, 1978

Frank Lloyd Wright—Twenty Years After His Death

Drafting room,
Taliesin, 1979

I. A Vast Legacy

It is twenty years this week since Frank Lloyd Wright died at ninety-one in an Arizona hospital, and it is no exaggeration to say that the United States has had no architect even roughly comparable to him since. Not Louis Kahn, not Eero Saarinen, not Kevin Roche, not I. M. Pei, not Philip Johnson, nor even all of these men together have had the impact on the art of architecture that Wright did in his extraordinary seventy-two-year career. It began with the shingled Hillside Home School in Spring Green, Wisconsin, of 1887 and extended through more than 400 built buildings, hundreds more unrealized designs, and dozens of books and articles proclaiming that Wright's so-called organic architecture would emerge as the style of the future.

Wright's own style has not ended up as the style of our age, but the influence he holds for architecture two decades after his death is no less sizable for this. Wright remains a perplexing, compelling, nearly superhuman presence to architects and students alike—part deity, part eccentric old man, part brilliant and innovative designer. Today there are students in architectural school who were not even born when Wright died, giving young architects a sense of him as a historical figure—to today's students the man who designed the Guggenheim Museum is as much a part of the past as Stanford White or Louis Sullivan.

Of course, Wright has been part of the past, to some minds, for a long time. His great early work, the prairie houses of the Midwest in which he developed his style of open, flowing space and great horizontal planes and integrated structure of wood, stone, glass, and stucco were mostly built before 1910, and Philip Johnson once insulted Wright by calling him "America's greatest nineteenth-century architect." But Mr. Johnson was then a partisan of the sleek, austere International Style of Mies van der Rohe and Walter Gropius, which Wright abhorred; he was seeing that style as the future, and Wright, for all his continued creativity, looked only like a remnant from the past.

Now, the International Style is in disarray—it is fashionable, but not untrue, to observe that the steel and glass box is no longer the way of building with which our architectural avant-garde feels comfortable. But what is significant here is that Wright's reputation has not suffered much at all in the current antimodernist upheaval. Walter Gropius's star has risen and sunk; Wright's seems to go on above the storm.

One of the reasons that Wright's reputation has not suffered too severely in the current turmoil in architectural thinking is that he spoke a tremendous amount of common sense. He was full of ideas which seemed daring, almost absurd, but which now in retrospect were clearly right. Back in the 1920's, for example, he alone among architects and planners perceived the great effect the automobile would have on the American landscape. He foresaw "the great highway becoming, and rapidly, the horizontal line of a new freedom extending from ocean to ocean," as he wrote in his autobiography of 1932. Wright wrote approvingly of the trend toward decentralization, which hardly endears him to today's center–city-minded planners—but if his calls toward suburban planning had been realized, the chaotic sprawl of the American landscape might today have some rational order to it.

Wright also foresaw the trend toward mixed-use skyscrapers. His 1929 plan for a combined apartment and office tower for St. Mark's-in-the-Bouwerie in New York, which was never built, or his realized Price Tower in Bartlesville, Oklahoma, of 1955, prefigure such current works as Olympic Tower and the Galleria in New York, but with far more grace and style.

And at the other end of the economic spectrum, Wright was obsessed with the problem of the affordable house for the middle-class American. It may be that no other prominent architect has ever designed as many prototypes of inexpensive houses that could be mass-produced; unlike most current high stylists, who ignore the boredom of suburban tract houses and design expensive custom residences in the hope of establishing a distance between themselves and mass culture, Wright tried hard to close the gap between the architectural profession and the general public.

In his modest houses or his grand ones, Wright emphasized appropriate materials, which might well be considered to prefigure both the growing preoccupation today with energy-saving design and the surge of interest in regional architecture. Wright, unlike the architects of the International Style, would not build the same house in Massachusetts that he would build in California; he was concerned about local traditions, regional climates, and so forth. It is perhaps no accident that at Taliesin, Wright's Scottsdale, Arizona, home and studio that continues to function, many of the younger architects have begun doing solar designs as a logical step from Wright's work.

As Wright recedes more into the past, he becomes, if anything, even more the only true hero-figure American architecture has ever produced. Scholarship on Wright is increasing dramatically—Adolf Placzek, the head of the Avery Architectural Library at Columbia University, noted in an introduction to a new bibliography of Wright by Robert L. Sweeney that nearly a third of the 2,095 articles and books listed had appeared since Wright's death.

In Oak Park, Illinois, Thomas Heinz, a Wright scholar, has been publishing a bimonthly brochure called the *Frank Lloyd Wright Newsletter* for the last year, and it is chock-full not only of scholarly insights but of news of Wright buildings under restoration, advice to owners of Wright buildings on their care, and reviews of Wright exhibitions. What had been expected to be the major exhibit since the architect's death, a retrospective at the National Gallery organized by Edgar Kaufmann, Jr., has now been canceled, but the number of smaller museum shows is clearly growing.

Wright talked of creating a new style, an architecture that he claimed would spring from respect for the land and a frank, straightforward, and compassionate use of materials. His "organic" architecture did, in his early years, lead to enough imitators so that something called the Prairie School of Wright and his followers could be said to have existed in the Midwest. But for the most part, Wright worked alone, and his buildings fit into no standard categories. His approach never took over the world, but that is not because it was invalid as architecture—it is because it was so remarkable, so personal, as architecture that it could not really be called a "style" at all, for it could never be imitated or copied.

Wright's major buildings, structures like the Unity Temple in Oak Park of 1906, the Robie House in Chicago of 1907, Fallingwater in Bear Run, Pennsylvania, of 1935, and the Guggenheim Museum of 1959, are works of great individual genius; they are expressions of materials and moldings of space that transcend any idea of style. Like the work of every great artist of any age, Wright's buildings do not fit into our present notions of the dimensions of art; they form new ones, and they open new ways of seeing that had never been imagined before. They are not forms to be copied, but messages of the meaning of certain architectural verities in this complex time.

—*April 15, 1979*

II. An Active Ghost at Taliesin West

The thirty-five architects who work at Taliesin West, the desert home and studio of the late Frank Lloyd Wright, labor in a 96-foot-long drafting room that is dominated by a 5-foot-high photograph of Wright. They send their drawings for approval to Wright's eighty-year-old widow, Olgivanna, although she is not an architect, and they pursue a daily routine that they hope is identical to the one followed when Wright was alive.

Wright died at ninety-one on April 9, 1959, but his architectural practice goes on. The twenty years since the death of the man who is generally acknowledged to have been twentieth-century America's greatest architect have barely been noticed at Taliesin, where middle-aged architects, young student apprentices, members of Wright's family, and assorted associates continue to live in the commune-like surroundings Wright created. They jealously guard not only Wright's reputation, but even his actual drawings and papers— so much so that they have been accused of restricting scholarly access—while they produce new architecture that for the most part is directly imitative of Wright's own.

The Frank Lloyd Wright Foundation–Taliesin Associated Architects, as the practice is known, is perhaps the strangest architectural firm in the United States, for it is entirely dominated by a man who is dead. William Wesley Peters, a longtime Wright associate and once the architect's son-in-law, is the nominal head, but he and most of his colleagues see themselves merely as the conveyors of Wright's word. They speak constantly of him, always as "Mr. Wright," and they defer entirely to the wishes of Mrs. Wright, who lives in the house the couple shared for two decades.

There is an eerie feeling to Taliesin West now, although the place is far from quiet—the practice is booming with clients wanting Wrightesque buildings, and the fellowship program under which students once paid for the privilege of working in Wright's presence now has twenty-six students willing to pay $3,000 a year just to be where the master once worked. The eeriness comes from a sense that everything that happens at Taliesin exists only to keep the flames of Wright's career burning.

Although some of the younger architects are doing innovative work in such areas as solar energy, most of the buildings that Taliesin Associated Architects design look like the work Wright himself produced in his last years, when he leaned toward flamboyant, almost futuristic structures. A lot of the buildings are circular; some of them, like a palace for the sister of the shah of Iran (which has now been taken over by Iran's revolutionary government), look almost like flying saucers.

The firm has also produced a Lutheran church in Paradise Valley, Arizona, that has the craggy, angular look of Wright's famous synagogue in Elkins Park, Pennsylvania, and a community theater in San Jose, California, that closely resembles Wright's own Grady Gammage Auditorium in Tempe, Arizona.

In recent years, Taliesin has departed from its communal approach only to allow individual architects of the firm the right to be credited along with the Frank Lloyd Wright Foundation, and it has been possible to see some personal variations—Mr. Peters's work seems most directly derivative of Wright's circular motifs, for example, while the work of architects like Charles Montooth harks back to the architecture of horizontal planes of Wright's middle years.

For all of Wright's importance, very little of Taliesin's work in the twenty years since the master's death has found its way into the ledgers of architectural history. Indeed, virtually none of it has even been favorably reviewed by critics. Typical, if harsh, are the comments of Robert Twombly, a Wright biographer, who has written that the firm "has absorbed little more than the superficialities of Wright's teachings."

Such comments seem not to bother Taliesin's architects at all; they are convinced, in Mr. Peters's words, "that Frank Lloyd Wright continues and is a living entity," and that the architects of Taliesin have been chosen to carry on Wright's principles to posterity. "Only an organization of total life involvement like Taliesin could do such a thing," Mr. Peters said. "The work that has gone out from here ranks as high as or higher than anything that's being done in the world."

The rituals of Taliesin—the name comes from the Welsh words for "shinning brow"—have changed little since Wright's death. Student apprentices, all selected by Mrs. Wright, take turns working in the kitchen, the drafting room, or on Taliesin's 700 acres at the foot of the MacDowell Mountains. The mood is cheerful, earnest, and welcoming toward visitors. The women live in quarters in the main complex of buildings, while the men live in tents in the desert, although they have a locker room in which to hang the tuxedos that are required for the formal Saturday evening musicales. Everyone except Mrs. Wright eats communally, with different architects and students taking turns waiting on the ornate table set for her and her guests.

Mrs. Wright, a native of Yugoslavia, is slim and intense, with a soft voice that remains strongly accented despite her fifty-five years in this country. She entertains students and visitors frequently, and when the conversation drifts, she turns it firmly back toward the subject of her husband. At one dinner she exhibited great interest in the career of one 18-year-old apprentice who had just arrived from Ohio, and she beamed when he told her he had chosen to come to Taliesin instead of going to Ohio State.

"We like to get them young—that way we don't have to scrape much crust off them," Mrs. Wright said.

No one at Taliesin will say how many apprentices depart, but it is common knowledge that few stay the eight years that Wright suggested when he set up his own architectural academy in the 1930's. Of the twenty-six apprentices now at Taliesin, twelve are new this year, suggesting a considerable turnover. The students come from around the world, and they share a certainty that Wright was a master—but they often do not know much about his work or even about their own objectives in architectural design. When asked to explain why they are there, they often reply in vague terms about "wanting to better mankind," as one apprentice, Jim Fabbri, said. Another, Ralph Williamsen, when asked by a visitor to talk about design, said, "I don't know what I could say that would be of any value."

Wright built Taliesin originally as a winter home, and it was a structure of redwood beams, stone walls, and canvas roofs. It had the air of a desert camp or an oasis, and its form stood boldly in the desert landscape. It grew over the years, but its character became more permanent only after the architect's death, when the Taliesin successors rebuilt the structure, replacing wood beams with steel, canvas with Plexiglas, and some wooden details with painted polystyrene. The result is a set of buildings that looks roughly as it did originally, but it has lost the casual, camplike air it once had and become more rigid and institutional instead. "It's always hard to know what to do in such a case," said Mr. Montooth. "We felt we had to do something to protect these buildings, to make them permanent."

What has happened to Taliesin the buildings is essentially what has happened to Taliesin the institution—it has turned into something far more rigid and permanent than it was ever intended to be. Taliesin is now, in effect, in the business of promoting the name Frank Lloyd Wright. The group gives tours, it sells Wright's name in terms of its use of it on new designs, and it even sells rights to examine Wright's drawings.

The Wright archives are closely controlled by Taliesin; the architect's drawings and letters, far from being in a museum or library, as are most architects' archives, are in a warehouse in Phoenix. The Taliesin archivist, Bruce Brooks Pfeiffer, will not disclose the location of the warehouse; what he does instead is permit selected scholars to come to Taliesin and review drawings he has culled from storage.

Taliesin charges a fee of $75 an hour for use of Frank Lloyd Wright materials. It requires that permission be granted for any reproduction of a Wright drawing, and it will not lend originals at all, even to museums. And Mr. Pfeiffer forbids access of any sort to Wright's letters, but says he plans some day to publish an edited version of them in a book.

"They are all terribly protective of the man, wanting the world to hear only the authorized version all the way through," Frederick Gutheim, a well-known Wright scholar, said of Taliesin today. Mr. Gutheim recalled a visit that Bruno Zevi, the Italian architect and Wright follower, had made to Wright's other home in Wisconsin a few months after Wright's death. "Zevi told the apprentices that they should turn Wright's picture to the wall and never mention his name again and start doing it on their own," Mr. Gutheim said. "That good advice has not been followed."

—April 16, 1979
Scottsdale, Ariz.

Michael Graves

If Philip Johnson stands as a kind of godfather to postmodernism, Michael Graves has now become, in the public eye at least, its very embodiment. It is a role that many critics and historians had expected would be filled by Robert Venturi, the senior designer of the Philadelphia firm of Venturi, Rauch & Scott Brown. Venturi is the author of the book *Complexity and Contradiction in Architecture,* the treatise against the austerity and purism of orthodox modern architecture that, since its publication in 1966, has surely done more than any other single work to set architecture in its current, postmodern direction. Venturi's buildings, however, are an unusual mix of the highly studied and the self-consciously plain, and they do not always have an easy appeal to the untrained eye. He may be his generation's most gifted architect—he is fifty-seven, nearly a decade older than Graves—but he does not seem destined to be this era's most popular one.

Robert Stern, a talented postmodernist who has been highly influenced by Venturi, has turned more and more toward a kind of literal historicism in recent years. He has rejected modernism by designing buildings that look more and more like the actual buildings of the past, making him commercially successful but less naturally a symbol of a new age. Although Philip Johnson has designed numerous buildings that, like A.T.&T., have seemed to summarize the concerns of the moment, his age—seventy-six—has disqualified him from assuming such a role himself.

It has thus fallen to Michael Graves to become the figure around which the public's interest in postmodernism has coalesced. Graves's work is ideally suited to such a position. It is lively, genuinely fresh, and committed

Drawing for the
entrance to the
Humana Building,
Louisville,
by Michael Graves

both to seriousness of purpose and to ease of communication. Graves is perhaps the only architect practicing today who has managed to devise an essentially new style—to create buildings that really do not look like anyone else's and seem to speak in a new voice.

It is no small irony that an architect who designs in a more original language than almost any of his colleagues would become a central figure in a movement based, as postmodernism is, on a certain degree of return to the past. However, Graves's freshness of style is different altogether from the determined antihistoricism of modern architecture. He does not reject the past at all, but chooses to mold and interpret it into a shape that is very much his own. He relies on classicism, not to reproduce it literally but to turn its forms into abstract representations.

The essence of Graves's original style is not really classicism at all, but cubism, the modernist style out of which Graves's murals and drawings have emerged. Although he claims to have put aside modernism for classicism, he has not really abandoned his cubist instinct at all. What he has in fact done is assemble abstract versions of classical elements in what amount to cubist collages.

This style does not vary from one application to another—Graves is consistent, perhaps to a fault. His collages—which might contain a piece of molding, a hint of curtain, a slice of painted sky, all against an exquisite muddy rose background—are not so different from his buildings, except in size. So, too, his teapots, his fabrics, his chairs, which all have similar lines and similar colors.

Graves's fundamental instincts are pictorial; he is not primarily a maker of space. There is more power and tension to the spaces of Richard Meier or of the firm of Gwathmey Siegel & Associates, to name two of Graves's colleagues among the "Five." What drama Graves's rooms have comes more from the processional sequence from one of them to another than from each room's intrinsic quality. At any single point, most Graves rooms, whether round, square, or oblong, are serene and ordered, set pieces of decoration defined by color and detail more than by a dynamic sense.

But the Gravesian mix of cubism and classicism is not an easy synthesis to achieve, and it requires considerable discipline—as any look at the legion of weak imitations of Graves's work on student drafting boards these days will reveal. The failure of most architects, students, and young practioners alike to successfully copy Graves is a testament to his gifts, and in a sense it is welcome, since his work is not, in the end, best thought of as a universal style. The quality of Graves's own architecture should hardly be taken as a prescription for Gravesian buildings everywhere.

Most truly original designers have defied easy imitation, and Graves is no exception. His work has an unexpected sternness that separates it from the more self-indulgent work that follows in its wake.

Perhaps the great appeal of Graves's work lies in his melding together of modernism and classicism. We are at a moment when we have come to reject the sleek austerity of modernism, a style that never served very well as anything but a symbol of corporate anonymity. We want architecture to serve as a symbol, to stand for cultural values and civic grandeur, but we tend to remain fairly uncomfortable with modernism's obvious opposite, the literal re-use of historical style. If we seek a hero, we want one who seems to bring us something we have not seen before.

Graves has managed to do this. His work offers an appealing alternative to what is increasingly seen as a choice between the coldness of modernism and the discomfort of literal revivalism. His brand of architecture is new, yet strives to create the effect of the architecture of the past. It is a way to be at once new and old—to have it all.

The real question now is where Graves will go from here—where this personal style will take him. What Graves has not yet managed to do is create an architecture that seems to address all aspects of building—the social, tech-nological, and esthetic—with equal commitment. His is still an architecture of composition, an architecture that takes as its primary mission the making of a beautiful object.

In this sense Graves, for all his originality, is very much part of the current generation of architects. He shares their reaction against the failed social promises of modernism, as well as their intent to reaffirm the rightness of facades and decoration and their fondness for the manipulation of form for purely visual appeal. In Graves's work, all of this is good enough to transcend mere reaction—the color, energy, and mix of classical and modern sources create objects that are truly seductive. But how much more the Gravesian style will be able to do remains to be seen.

—October 10, 1982

Venturi: In Love with the Art of Building

It is common to hear Robert Venturi, the senior design partner of the Philadelphia architecture firm of Venturi, Rauch & Scott Brown, discussed as an admirable theorist whose theories are more persuasive than his buildings. Mr. Venturi's 1966 book, *Complexity and Contradiction in Architecture*, which did more than any other single work to create the current movement away from the simple austerity of modern architecture, is surely better known than any of the architect's buildings. Even his later writings, like *Learning from Las Vegas*, written with Denise Scott Brown and Steven Izenour, while less *de rigueur* in every architect's bookshelf, still are at least as talked about as most of his structures.

There is no great mystery as to why this happened. The buildings of Venturi, Rauch & Scott Brown are neither as easy nor as precise as the theories—they are highly studied, academic designs, sometimes intentionally quirky and almost never honing any narrow stylistic line. There is no real Venturi "style" at all—there is no easily identifiable trademark, as there is in the work of, say, Michael Graves, to name but one architect who has ridden to considerable popular acclaim on the basis of the same rejection of modernism that Mr. Venturi, in effect, bequeathed to the current generation of architects.

But if Venturi, Rauch & Scott Brown buildings are not easily labeled, and do not respond naturally to a certain popular impulse, they are no less important for this. Indeed, one of the pleasantest aspects of "Buildings and Drawings," the exhibition of the firm's work at the Max Protetch Gallery, is the extent to which it reminds us how wrong the common perception is—how much Robert Venturi is an architect first and a theorist second. For all the importance of *Complexity and Contradiction in Architecture*, a book that deserves every bit of its status as a contemporary classic, Mr. Venturi is an architect who communicates most naturally not through the written word, but through the drawn line.

The exhibition is large, but it is not a true retrospective; it includes only the firm's work from the mid-1970's onward, and not all of that. Moreover, what we are shown is only drawings. There are no photographs and no models, and no word as to which of the buildings we see in drawn form were actually built and which were not, making this not the place for a basic education in the work of Venturi, Rauch & Scott Brown.

These shortcomings aside, this is an important exhibition, a welcome assertion of the abilities of Mr. Venturi as a pure designer and as a maker of architectural drawings. Most of the drawings are from his own hand, as are most of the firm's designs for individual buildings (partner Denise Scott Brown is in charge of the firm's work in planning and urban design). The installation, which was designed by the Venturi, Rauch & Scott Brown office, is characteristic of the firm's work—it is at once simple and fanciful, combining allusions to classicism and plain, almost banal, decoration. The walls are a rich medium gray, and stenciled faintly all over them are flower petals, recalling the huge flowers that decorate the facade of the Venturi, Rauch & Scott Brown store for the Best Products Company. A red line runs around the gallery just above eye level, with large and precisely wrought drawings below and casual sketches on yellow tracing paper in Mr. Venturi's light, almost prancing style running above, like the frieze on a classical building.

The large drawings below the red line are in the fine-lined, almost cartoon-like style for which the firm is known; they are gentle, amiable pictures, the best of them looking like frames for an animation film. (Indeed, in the colored drawing for the Brant-Johnston House, a skiing lodge in Vail, one almost expects the tiny figures to begin to move and the animated cartoon to keep rolling.) Mr. Venturi's sketching style is different—it is deft and easy, and like the brief drawings of so many gifted architects, it gives us the illusion that we are seeing a completed work in only a few quick and tentative lines.

What is most impressive from all of these drawings is how thoroughly buildings emerge here as objects of friendliness, even of love. It is odd, perhaps, to speak of architecture in such emotional terms, particularly of an architecture that has had so powerful an impact on theory as that of Venturi, Rauch & Scott Brown. But one cannot emerge from the Max Protetch Gallery without a clear sense that Robert Venturi and his colleagues are architects who love the art of building above all, and who communicate this love more clearly than any of their contemporaries.

For these buildings, quirky or even willfully eccentric as they may be, are invariably amiable and not a little playful. Many of Venturi, Rauch & Scott Brown's buildings, such as Mr. Venturi's celebrated house for his mother in

Chestnut Hill, Pennsylvania, of 1962, or his Tucker House of 1975, are basic, primal houses, houses that are almost—but not quite—what a child might draw. At their best they merge a kind of childlike delight with an adult's ironic sensibility, bringing to architecture an attitude not altogether different from that which Lewis Carroll brought to literature.

Not that Robert Venturi is a *naif*; quite the opposite. This is a knowing and

Sketches by Robert Venturi

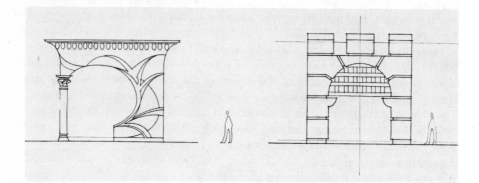

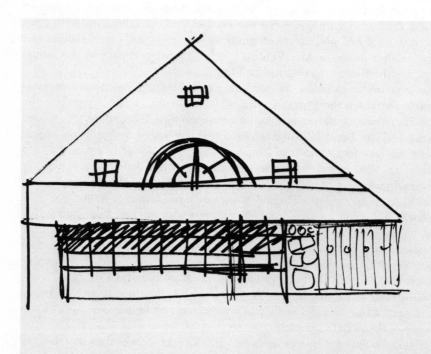

highly studied architecture; for all its benign qualities, it could not be less innocent. Indeed, in Mr. Venturi's insistent refusal to be bound by a particular style he is perhaps indicating his greatest worldliness—to him there are no simple rights and wrongs, no absolute ways in which buildings ought to be or ought not to be. Unlike so many of the so-called postmodernists who follow in his wake, Mr. Venturi eschews the literal historicism that has recently become so fashionable. There are no precise replications of Georgian mansions here, no latter-day shingle style cottages. There are buildings that rely heavily on these and other architectural traditions, but the Venturi version is always slightly "off"—not wrong, just twisted slightly in its mix of elements and proportions in a way that convinces us, as the best mannerist architecture has done since Michelangelo and Giulio Romano, that for all its oddity, it could have been no other way.

Mr. Venturi's design for a branch bank for County Federal in Stratford, Connecticut, for example, is a kind of Palladian pavilion, blown up to bank scale, all of its elements slightly off in proportion in such a way as to give this little classical object civic grandeur. His Hubbard House, for Nantucket, merges elements from Nantucket town's Federal traditions with his genuine eclectic sensibility into a lively but coherent composition. His addition to the Allen Art Museum at Oberlin College adds what is essentially a decorated modernist box to Cass Gilbert's original Renaissance palazzo, a gesture that in other hands would represent defiance, but in Mr. Venturi's manages to communicate respect.

The Oberlin building is represented by a thorough set of drawings and sketches that help trace the design process through several versions. It is unfortunate that no photograph of the completed building was included here, merely as a kind of visual footnote, since the casual visitor to the Protetch exhibition is not likely to know which version was in fact built. Similarly, the concentration on displaying material that stands on its own as a kind of architectural art led to the inclusion of only a single and partial view of Venturi, Rauch & Scott Brown's distinguished Western Plaza for Pennsylvania Avenue in Washington, with not a hint of what the entire design looks like.

Similarly misleading are the collages for an urban-design project the firm did for Hennepin Avenue in Minneapolis, that city's tawdry downtown artery, in which the avenue is portrayed as plain to the point of primness, and Venturi, Rauch & Scott Brown's new signs and lights as the only real life on the street. These are drawings that make the city look too pat, too pretty, too ordered, which is ironic, given how important Robert Venturi and Denise Scott Brown's theorizing has been in convincing us that neither buildings nor cities should be perceived as neat and ordered places.

—September 19, 1982

Diversity and New Directions

Careers in architecture begin slowly and advance more slowly still. The reason is simple. Rare is the client who is willing to entrust to a thirty-year-old the responsibility for a $10-million or a $5-million or even a $1-million piece of construction, which is more or less what anything bigger than a house costs these days. As a result, major projects are almost always created by architects who are at or beyond middle age, and smaller, less visible jobs are what is left to their younger colleagues.

One would think, therefore, that young architects are positively bursting with ideas, full of fresh thinking that can find no ample outlet. But ideas and influence in architecture travel a strange and slow path. This is not an art in which fresh ideas are incubated solely by ambitious young designers, frustrated at their inability to take notions from paper to the realm of real building. Ideas move, more often, in the other direction, from successful practitioners down to their newer colleagues.

A visitor to an East Coast architecture school these days might think that Michael Graves was Michelangelo and Charles Gwathmey and Robert Siegel were Stanford White and Charles McKim, so prevalent are student imitations of their work. But our time is not without its cadre of influential younger practitioners, architects who have managed to speak with an original voice and to stand out from the crowd. There are, at this point, a dozen or more architects under the age of forty whose work shows the promise of becoming what Mr. Graves, Mr. Gwathmey, and such other architects as Robert Venturi, Frank Gehry, Charles Moore, and Stanley Tigerman are now: not corporate powers, but influential design presences.

It is unfair to group these younger architects into a

school; it is still more unfair to attempt to infer from their work the directions in which architecture appears to be going. There is too much diversity now, too much flailing about in different directions. But if one thing can be said, it is that the latest group of architects seems to be merging a respect for classicism with an impulse toward abstraction. They are not rejecting modern architecture altogether, but are seeing the classicizing impulse within it. They seem, in other words, to reject Mies van der Rohe's austerity but to rejoice in the love of classicism that lay underneath it, and they are seeking to express that in ways that are very much their own.

There are other generalizations that can be made. There are differences between the East and West coasts. There always have been, and in the last decade they seem to have become more, not less, marked. The most promising young architects in Los Angeles—Robert Mangurian and Craig Hodgetts of Works; Thom Mayne and Michael Rotondi of Morphosis; Eric Moss and Frederick Fisher—all owe a debt to the seemingly slapdash, casual work of Frank Gehry. Like his, their work is brash and startling at first glance, though it turns out to be highly studied, and their houses are objects more than they are buildings set into urban contexts.

The architects on the East Coast—Tod Williams; Michael Rubin and Henry Smith-Miller; Roger Ferri; George Ranalli; Jon Michael Schwarting; the Miami group Arquitectonica; Paul Segal; and Susana Torre, to name a few—are more ordered, more suave, and often more self-conscious. Their buildings tend to use historical elements more literally than do those of their West Coast counterparts; in this case the younger easterners are closer to the postmodernists of the generation ahead than are the westerners.

Some East Coast architects, most notably the whimsically titled Friday Architects of Philadelphia and the East Coast-influenced Taft Architects of Houston, have made a point of emphasizing elements from vernacular, or everyday, architecture as well. But they rarely inject historical forms with the zeal of, say, a Robert Stern or a Michael Graves. And as they look back into history with a distance that their elders do not have, they often find modernism to be the most entrancing historical style of all.

Tod Williams, Paul Segal, and the partnership of Michael Rubin and Henry Smith-Miller, for example, all make modernist elements quite central to most of their work. But they do so with none of the ideological insistence of their elders; their work is more relaxed, more picturesque, and above all more eclectic.

In a large duplex apartment in Manhattan, for example, Mr. Rubin and Mr. Smith-Miller integrated antiques into a modernist space that had been designed more by instinct than according to any rigid theories. Tod Williams's work, though it, too, bears many of the hallmarks of modernism, has none of the austerity one usually associates with, say, the architecture of the International Style. Where that is cool, his work is warm, almost sensual.

There is a crisp, direct kind of power to the modernist imagery of Arquitectonica, a group of Miami-based architects who have had the unusual luck of being able to design a number of projects at large scale. Their buildings are sharp, colorful images, something like modern architecture as a designer of sets for television programs might envision it, but with an overlay of discipline and intelligence that makes this work something other than the Buck Rogers fantasizing of so many large-scale urban projects. The firm's major completed house, the Spear House in Miami, is as lyrical in its use of color as any house of the 1970's.

There is a commitment on the part of all of the architects of this group, easterners and westerners alike, to a view of architecture as a set of basic elements, to a quest for the clear expression of an essential idea. In this sense they all owe a debt to Louis Kahn, as far from Kahn as their work is in outward appearance. They want very much to express, in an almost metaphysical way, the "houseness" of a house, and the ways they do this range from the playful and absolutely self-assured studios by Morphosis in Venice, California, to the rather more self-conscious condominiums by George Ranalli in Newport, Rhode Island, which include mock facades set within two-story living rooms.

In neither case is there literal historicism, the precise copying of forms from the architectural styles of the past. But in both instances the architects have attempted to evoke a basic, almost primal, image of the house. In Morphosis's case it is the childlike, though hardly innocent, elements of small scale, bright colors, and exaggerated details; for George Ranalli, it is the urban and cultivated exercise of a facade within a room, a deliberate play on the notions of interior and exterior.

Now, the idea of expressing the basic image of the house as a child might draw it is not one that originated with this generation; it is something Robert Venturi did almost twenty years ago in his celebrated house in Chestnut Hill, Pennsylvania, and Charles Moore did in his houses of the 1960's in Orinda, California, and in New Haven. In each, the architects were motivated by an anger at the extent to which the orthodox modern architects of the International Style had rejected this basic image that we all carry around in our heads and replaced it with something they found to be cold and boxy.

But as they tried so hard to restore the image of the traditional house to our architectural culture, they did so in a way that was often as radical, and as much a polemic, as the International Style works they were rejecting. Their houses thus existed to prove a point as much as to be easy, relaxing, and beautiful, and here is where they differ from the houses of the current generation.

For the generation now in middle age, modernism remained the potent force, the force some chose to react against and others to reinterpret and extend in new directions. In each case, though, modernism was a constant presence, an ideological force that had to be contended with.

For the new generation of architects, ideology—and modernism—have far less meaning. They are concerned with ideas, and with theory, but they seem less inclined to fight, and less inclined to believe that there is a right way and a wrong way in which to make architecture. The best of them tend to be relatively unconcerned about rules and "style" per se and much more concerned about such fundamentals as form, proportion, clarity, and common sense.

This is not to say that they are merely pragmatic; far from it. Such architects as Roger Ferri, whose work attempts to merge nature into the urban fabric; or Susana Torre, who has subtly woven the transparency and openness of the modernist esthetic into a more traditional background, or Steven Holl, who gives his simple, primal forms considerable subtlety, are dealing in the realm of ideas as much as have any architects of any generation.

But they do not deal in formulas, and this is the crucial difference. They do not search for systems that can be used to make building after building according to predetermined theory; their instinct is fundamentally pluralist, and they seem to approach each problem with an expectation that it will yield a different solution. For them the meeting of practical needs and the service of serious ideas need not, in the end, be incompatible.

—September 16, 1982

For permission to reproduce the illustrations that appear on the following pages, the author gratefully acknowledges:

Page 7, Joe Pineiro; pages 12, 28, Edward Hausner/*The New York Times;* page 41, Marilyn K. Yee/*The New York Times;* pages 47, 55, Peter B. Kaplan; page 58, Bill Raftery/*The New York Times;* pages 63, 65, Micha Bar-Am/*The New York Times;* page 68, George Tames/*The New York Times;* page 72, Mickey Pfleger/*The New York Times;* page 77, Steve Rosenthal, Benjamin Thompson & Associates, Inc.; page 80, *The New York Times;* page 82, Wendy Watriss/*The New York Times;* page 86, Colin Poole, Camera Press Ltd.; page 91, D. Gorton/*The New York Times;* page 94, Brian Payne/*The New York Times;* page 96, Carl Iwasaki/*The New York Times;* page 100, John Portman; page 102, The Rainier National Bank; page 104, Transamerica Corporation; pages 107, 110, Johnson/Burgee Architects; page 112, Sara Krulwich/*The New York Times;* pages 119, 121, 126, D. Gorton/*The New York Times;* page 129, Nathaniel Lieberman; page 131, D. Gorton/*The New York Times;* page 135, Jerry Lodigruss/*The New York Times;* page 140, Doug Wilson/*The New York Times;* page 142, D. Gorton/*The New York Times;* page 146, Ezra Stoller, Esto; page 150, Jack Manning/*The New York Times;* page 156, Fred R. Conrad and Keith Meyers/*The New York Times;* pages 160, 163, Proto Acme Photo; page 167, Wendy Watriss/*The New York Times;* page 168, *The New York Times;* page 178, Sara Krulwich/*The New York Times;* page 182, David Strick/*The New York Times;* page 187, *The New York Times;* page 190, Fred R. Conrad/*The New York Times;* page 192, Cathedral of St. John the Divine; page 197, William E. Sauro/*The New York Times;* page 203, Stan Ries Photography; page 208, Gary Settle/*The New York Times;* page 210, Jack Manning/*The New York Times;* page 214, *The New York Times;* page 218, Roger Thurber/*The New York Times;* page 222, Camillio Vergara/*The New York Times;* page 226, Paul Hosefros/*The New York Times;* page 231, Robert Walker/*The New York Times;* page 235, David W. Dunlap; page 237, Jack Horner; pages 244, 246, Joseph Kugielsky/ *The New York Times;* page 252, Keith Meyers/*The New York Times;* page 260, Sadin/Karant Photography, Inc.; page 268, J.D. Levine/Yale University; page 274, Star Black/*The New York Times;* page 277, Jack Manning/*The New York Times;* page 279, William Lansing Plumb; page 284, *The New York Times;* page 287, Marjorie Anderson; page 291, Metropolitan Transportation Authority; page 294, Marjorie Anderson; page 297, Max Protetch Gallery; page 302, *The New York Times;* page 306, Saul Steinberg; page 310, Tom Story/*The New York Times;* page 316, Proto Acme Photo; page 322, Robert Venturi.

Index